D0115849

COLETTE

A Study of the Short Fiction

A Selection of Titles from Twayne's Studies in Short Fiction Series

Twayne publishes studies of all major short-story writers worldwide. For a complete list, contact the Publisher directly.

Twayne's Studies in Short Fiction

Gordon Weaver, General Editor
Oklahoma State University

Colette
Photo by Gisele Freund. Reprinted by permission of Photo Researchers, Inc.
New York.

COLETTE

A Study of the Short Fiction

Dana Strand
Carleton College

TWAYNE PUBLISHERS
An Imprint of Simon & Schuster Macmillan
New York

Prentice Hall International
London   Mexico City   New Delhi   Singapore   Sydney   Toronto

HOUSTON PUBLIC LIBRARY

. R01023 17296

HUMCA

Twayne's Studies in Short Fiction Series, No. 59

Copyright © 1995 by Twayne Publishers

All rights reserved. No part of this book may be reproduced or transmitted in any form or by any means, electronic or mechanical, including photocopying, recording, or by any information storage and retrieval system, without permission in writing from the Publisher.

Twayne Publishers
An Imprint of Simon & Schuster Macmillan
866 Third Avenue
New York, N.Y. 10022

Library of Congress Cataloging-in-Publication Data

Strand, Dana.
    Colette : a study of the short fiction / Dana Strand.
        p.   cm. — (Twayne's studies in short fiction ; no. 59)
    Includes bibliographical references and index.
    ISBN 0-8057-4500-9
    1. Colette, 1873–1954—Criticism and interpretation.   2. Short
story.   I. Title.   II. Series.
    PQ2605.O28Z8345   1995
    843'.912—dc20   94-36702
                                                                     CIP

The paper used in this publication meets the minimum requirements of American National Standard for Information Sciences—Permanence of Paper for Printed Library Materials. ANSI Z3948–1984.∞™

10 9 8 7 6 5 4 3 2 1

Printed in the United States of America

for my parents

Contents

Preface

During her lifetime, Colette's rather unconventional, and at times controversial, lifestyle guaranteed a place for both the woman and her writing in the public eye. Since much of her work was cloaked in the trappings of autobiography, many readers were drawn to what seemed to them the confessional nature of her writing. As a result of this perhaps understandable conflation of life and literature, the seriousness of her work in the eyes of the generally conservative French critical establishment was compromised by its very popularity. Considered a consummate stylist, who shunned metaphysical concerns in order to let her writing flow "naturally" from a place beyond intellect, she was both praised for her intuitive talent and relegated to a position decidedly outside the literary mainstream of her time.

Over the past 20 years, the increasing urgency of the debate over the specificity of women's writing has been accompanied by a full-scale reevaluation of Colette's work. In fact, it would be fair to say that Colette has recently been "in the air," not only in France, where her works have always enjoyed the endorsement of significant portions of the reading public, but also in the United States. The signs of a marked upsurge in both critical and popular interest in this prolific writer are everywhere: at academic conferences, where papers devoted to her works regularly appear on programs; at bookstores and libraries, where newly published scholarly books and articles on Colette's writing can be found next to audio tapes of her novels; and even at newsstands, where a recent issue of an American home decorating magazine featured romanticized views of her childhood garden in Burgundy.

What accounts for the reappraisal of a writer who, despite having attracted a faithful reading public, was seldom accorded a place among the "great" French authors of her time? Some of the credit for this revival of critical interest can be attributed to the general interrogation of the French literary canon, undertaken over the past 20 years with perhaps greater vigor in the United States than in France. Colette scholarship has also benefited from the insights of feminist critical theory, which have laid to rest some of the myths surrounding her life and work, while highlighting the fundamentally important issues her work raises at the volatile intersections of gender, genre, writing, and identity.

Although critics have in recent years brought new analytical tools to bear on many of Colette's best-known novels, such as *Break of Day*, *Chéri*, and *The Vagabond*, her short stories have as yet attracted relatively little attention. While both Elaine Marks and Joan Hinde Stewart devote a chapter to her short fiction in their excellent full-length studies of Colette's writing,[1] and while several articles about one or another story have appeared since the 1970s, no one has undertaken a detailed study of her short stories. While critics have often recognized the literary merits of her short fiction, they have at the same time been struck, and perhaps intimidated, by its dazzling heterogeneity. In collecting her short stories for an English translation, Robert Phelps identified four overlapping categories: *chroniques*, including personal reportage and individual portraits, autobiographical sketches, lyrical meditations, and short stories proper. He was quick to add, however, that these categories "tend to metamorphose into one another," when, for example, an unexpected digression interrupts a story line with a poetic reflection on nature or a childhood reminiscence.[2] Critical analysis of these diverse texts is thus continually complicated by the blurring of generic distinctions.

Part 1 of this study, based on a selection of stories representative of all four of Phelps's categories, is intended as a critical introduction to Colette's short fiction. Bearing in mind the renewed critical interest in her work, I have tried to remain attuned to the chorus of at times dissonant voices that establish a backdrop for my own readings of the stories I have chosen. For, if Colette has been discovered by feminist readers and critics, they have not all come to the same conclusions about her work. While the French writer Hélène Cixous, in her provocative essay, "The Laugh of the Medusa," included Colette in a list of three French authors who had successfully "inscribed femininity" in their writing (the other two were Marguerite Duras and Jean Genet),[3] Duras herself dismissed Colette as a woman who wrote " 'feminine literature' as men wanted it."[4] The contradiction that surfaces when these two statements are juxtaposed is an outgrowth of what has emerged, in recent years, as a confrontation between feminist analysis and theories of the postmodern. The question can be stated simply. Is Colette writing as a woman, expressing in uniquely feminine terms her singularly female experience, or is she rather writing "as a woman," realizing, either consciously or unconsciously, the culturally constructed fiction of the position allotted to her in phallocentric discourse?

The question arises out of a contrast between two notions of identity, one based on the assumption of an underlying, essential female nature and the other positing an elusive subjectivity, with no prediscursive shape, but rather fabricated through socially and culturally determined mechanisms. The general outlines of the debate within Colette criticism can be drawn by comparing the position of Nancy K. Miller, who has written extensively on Colette's works, with that of Lynne Huffer, whose recently published book, *Another Colette*, represents a departure from the approach adopted by Miller. Recognizing the pitfalls of essentialism, Miller nevertheless argues in favor of considering Colette's work from a feminist perspective that acknowledges the role experience plays in shaping women's writing:

> Arguably, Colette's texts self-consciously describe a female nature, they in fact constitute a discourse *on women*, a kind of *Second Sex* in fiction, an 'écriture féminine' avant la lettre. . . . But if her works are studded with details of a female materialism, they are not necessarily the stuff of female essentialism, if by this one means the kind of fatalism, the always already of female history, that delimits an unchanging map or biological tracking of possibility and impossibility. Rather, the oeuvre in its variety—fiction, memoirs, journalism theater, correspondence—constructs a record of *experience* that in its concern for the idiosyncratic calls into question the clichés of sexual difference, and by the same token, the truth of gender.[5]

Miller's decision to read for the "female signature" in Colette's writing is fundamentally a political move, with which she claims to resist the destabilization of the feminist position by deconstructive critics, without falling into the trap of biological determinism.

The drawbacks of Miller's approach are brought into focus by Huffer, whose 1992 study constitutes the first sustained attempt to problematize the issue of gender in Colette's work using postmodern, deconstructive methods. Emphasizing the extent to which representation in discourse produces gender, Huffer cautions that Miller's insistence upon signature encourages a referential reading of Colette that is at odds with the goal of the writer's central project: the construction of the self-in-writing. Huffer sums up the contradictory nature of her own stance before this difficult question in the following way. "As a feminist, I acknowledge Colette's maternally vested authority to speak as a daughter; self-critically (still, as a feminist), however, I recognize the need to question the linked concepts of authority and gender underlying that postulation and, thus, to subvert my own strategic acknowledgement. To put it baldly, this analysis affirms the importance of clearing away a space of intellectual legitimacy for Colette and, at the same time, recognizes the famous 'death of the author,' no matter what the gender of the author might be."[6] Having called attention to the contradictions inherent in her approach, Huffer goes on to highlight the textuality of the works she discusses, stating boldly that "ultimately, Colette is no more than the particular narrative that constructs her." She then explains that the "illusory subject" thus produced is "not only contradictory and incomplete, but also infinite and multiple."[7]

Although Miller and Huffer differ on just how illusory the subject is, according to the relative weight they grant the referential in Colette's work, they appear to arrive at a similar conclusion: that her writing systematically dismantles oppositional "truths," commonly expressed in the "clichés" of gender and sexuality. While I am responsive to Huffer's concerns and find her analyses convincing, my own readings tend to accept the legitimacy of Miller's search for Colette's elusive signature, although I fully recognize that any trace of a gendered inscription is at all times haunted by the specter of forgery. My position has been determined, at least in part, by my conviction that the struggle to secure a place for the voice of the woman writer, however muted or distorted that voice might be, has been too hard fought to abandon it in response to the demonization of essentialism that has characterized recent critical debate on the issue of gender. I therefore accept the difficulty, if not the impossibility, of fixing with any degree of certainty female subjectivity and its aesthetic representation, while still clinging to Miller's notion of lived experience as a legitimate measure of a woman's writing.

Part 2 brings together the various statements Colette made about the process of writing throughout her long career, in an attempt to give the reader an idea of her approach to story writing. Despite Colette's public pose as a writer singularly unconcerned with reflecting on her own creative process, informative insights into her attitude towards her craft can be gleaned from her letters, memoirs, and autobiographical fiction. Part 3 includes a sampling of critical articles on Colette's stories, constituting an overview of scholarly perspectives on her short fiction. Excerpts from the first full-length study published in English, Elaine

Marks's *Colette* (1960), reflect the biocritical approach that had dominated Colette scholarship until fairly recently. Drawing the mainstay of their arguments from feminist critical theory, the articles by Donna Norrell, Mari McCarty, and Jacob Stockinger are representative of the direction of Colette criticism in the 1980s. Finally, the excerpts from Lynne Huffer's book place her analysis at the crossroads of feminist analysis and deconstructive reading practice.

For many reasons (such as her allusive, elliptical style, her vast knowledge of technical botanical and zoological terms, and her syntactic inventiveness), Colette is very difficult to translate. Wherever possible, I have quoted from easily available, published translations of Colette's stories, principally *The Collected Stories of Colette*, edited by Robert Phelps, but have occasionally modified translations slightly in order to give a better sense of the original French. I must nevertheless acknowledge that translations, however carefully crafted, only approximate the efforts of a writer whose unwavering concern for the materiality of language was primordial.

Notes

1. Elaine Marks, *Colette* (New Brunswick: Rutgers University Press, 1960) and Joan Hinde Stewart, *Colette* (Boston: Twayne Publishers, 1983).
2. *The Collected Stories of Colette*, ed. Robert Phelps (New York: Farrar, Straus, and Giroux, 1983), xv.
3. In *New French Feminisms*, eds. Elaine Marks and Isabelle de Courtivron (New York: Schocken, 1981), 249.
4. In *New French Feminisms*, 175.
5. Nancy K. Miller, *Subject to Change: Reading Feminist Writing* (New York: Columbia University Press, 1988), 240.
6. Lynne Huffer, *Another Colette* (Ann Arbor: University of Michigan Press, 1992), 11.
7. Huffer, 128.

Acknowledgments

I am grateful for permission to quote from the following:
  Reprinted by permission of Farrar, Straus & Giroux, Inc.
  Excerpts from *Break of Day* by Colette and translated by Roger
Senhouse. Copyright © 1961, 1963 and renewed © 1989 by Martin
Secker and Warburg Ltd.
  Excerpts from *Cheri and The Last of Cheri* by Colette and translated
by Roger Senhouse. Copyright © 1951 and copyright renewed © 1979
by Farrar, Straus & Young now Farrar, Straus & Giroux, Inc.
  Excerpts from *The Collected Stories of Colette* translated by Matthew
Ward, Antonia White, Anne-Marie Callimachi, and others. Translation
copyright © 1957, 1966, 1983 by Farrar, Straus & Giroux and translation
copyright © 1958 by Martin Secker and Warburg Ltd.
  Excerpts from *Earthly Paradise* by Colette edited by Robert Phelps
and translated by Herma Briffault, Derek Coltman, and others. Copy-
right © 1966 by Farrar, Straus & Giroux, Inc.
  Excerpts from *Gigi, Julie de Carneilhan and Chance Acquaintances* by
Colette and translated by Patrick Leigh Fermor. Copyright © 1952
and copyright renewed © 1980 by Farrar, Straus & Young now Farrar,
Straus & Giroux, Inc.
  Excerpts from *Letters from Colette* selected and translated by Robert
Phelps. Translation copyright © 1980 by Farrar, Straus & Giroux, Inc.
  Excerpts from *My Apprenticeships* by Colette and translated by Helen
Beauclerk. Copyright © 1957 by Martin Secker & Warburg, Ltd.
  Excerpts from *My Mother's House and Sido* by Colette and translated
by Una Vicenzo Troubridge and Enid McLeod. Copyright © 1953 by
Farrar, Straus & Young and copyright renewed © 1981 by Farrar, Straus
& Giroux, Inc.
  Excerpts from *The Tender Shoot* by Colette and translated by Antonia
White. Copyright © 1958 and copyright renewed © 1986 by Martin
Secker & Warburg Ltd.
  Excerpts from *The Vagabond* by Colette and translated by Enid
McLeod. Copyright © 1955 by Farrar, Straus & Young and copyright
renewed © 1982 by Farrar, Straus & Giroux, Inc.

Colette by Elaine Marks. Copyright © 1960 by Rutgers, The State University. Reproduced by permission of Rutgers University Press, 151–58; 180–84.

Colette: The Woman the Writer, eds. Mari McCarty and Erica Eisinger. University Park and London: Pennsylvania State University Press, 1981, 54–65, copyright © 1981 by the Pennsylvania State University. Reproduced by the permission of the publisher.

Women's Studies 8 (1981): 359–66; 367–74. Copyright © Gordon and Breach Science Publishers, Inc. Reproduced by permission of the publisher.

Another Colette: The Question of Gendered Writing by Lynne Huffer. Copyright © 1992 by The University of Michigan Press, 26–29; 107–115. Reproduced by permission of the publisher.

I have been fortunate to have benefited from the advice and support of colleagues, friends, and family in the preparation of this study. I would like to acknowledge the generosity of Anne Ulmer, Scott Carpenter, and Cathy Yandell for their careful reading and helpful suggestions. Gordon Weaver, field editor of *Twayne Studies in Short Fiction*, read the manuscript with great care, offering invaluable guidance for revision. The in-house editor Melissa Solomon's thoughtful and insightful comments also provided me with useful direction. I would like to express my gratitude to Dean Elizabeth McKinsey and Carleton College for awarding me a timely grant that allowed me to complete the manuscript. Finally, I thank my family, Stephen, Mieke, and Erika for their encouragement and unfailing good humor.

Part 1

THE SHORT FICTION

Introduction

Several years ago, when a colleague asked me to suggest short fiction written by Colette that might be suitable for a class she was preparing to teach on the French short story, I had to confess that I knew very little about Colette's stories. While my initial interest in her work had been fueled by my undergraduate students' enthusiasm for her novels, I had at that point read none of her shorter fiction. I nevertheless promised my colleague to do some exploring. It didn't take me long at all to discover, as a few literary critics before me had already done, that Colette's short fiction could arguably be considered among her best work.

From as early as 1908, with the appearance of *The Tendrils of the Vine*, to the years just preceding her death in 1954, Colette's predilection for the short narrative form resulted in the publication of numerous short stories, as well as several book-length collections of loosely associated, often autobiographical pieces, two to three pages long, which defy strict generic categorization. These texts are a rich source for deepening our understanding of her distinctive literary art. They explore a terrain in many ways familiar to readers of her novels, while introducing alternative narrative strategies for developing themes found in the longer texts. Both the overtly autobiographical and predominantly fictional works are dominated by the unique vision of the omnipresent narrator, usually identified as "Colette," whose judgments and reactions continually color our reception of the texts.

In fact, after reading and rereading Colette's short fiction, and, perhaps more significantly, studying it against the backdrop of the literary scene in which she figured at the turn of the century, I am inclined to agree with critic Jacob Stockinger, for whom Colette "must clearly rank among the masters of the short story in this century."[1] At the same time, I caution against a too literal interpretation of his observation. For when Colette's stories are read beside others written in France by male authors at the end of the nineteenth and during the first half of the twentieth century, something curiously unsettling about them appears. Close readings, most particularly of stories written toward the end of Colette's literary career, in the thirties and forties, will reveal an organizational design characterized by digression and meandering narrative lines, frequent shifts in focus between narrator and story, and a general defiance of readers' expectations.[2]

In "Green Sealing Wax," for example, a deliciously humorous autobiographical tale of crime in the provinces, the narrative begins with an anecdote about Colette's mother's instinctive protectiveness of her daughter's virtue and innocence as she enters adolescence. It goes on to sketch a portrait of her father, plagued by a lifelong, unrealized ambition to write, and then suggests a tenuous link between the two story lines as mother and daughter join forces against the covetousness of Captain Colette, who jealously begrudges his child's access to his splendid collection of writing instruments. Only then does the presumably central story line take over, the account of the village widow who poisons her husband and forges his will in her favor, using a telltale stick of gold-flecked green wax (purloined from the young Colette's carefully guarded supply) to seal the will and, as things turn out, her fate as well. The reader, who tries to sift through what may at first appear to be layers of autobiographical substrata in order to arrive at the core of the story, is continually thwarted by the narrator's elusive positioning. In the end, the text clearly refuses to conform to the basic rules for a "well-made" short story, which stress a rather strict linearity and causal temporal structure.

Colette's treatment of certain common literary themes also requires a reorientation of readers' expectations, as she calls into question the conventional wisdom of patriarchal society that constructs, among other things, stringent moral codes, rigid categories of sexuality, and narrowly defined gender roles. For example, in "The Patriarch," an instance of incest, almost reluctantly deplored by "Sido," the narrator Colette's mother, ultimately serves as a vehicle to explore the true consequences of illegitimate sexual relations for women, considered in a context far-removed from more widely accepted moral judgments. In "Rainy Moon" and "Chance Acquaintances," the metaphorical possibilities of needlework finally suggest a revision of conventional attitudes towards this "passive, feminine" activity. As the ensuing analysis of representative works seeks to demonstrate, rather than "mastering" the short story by respecting previously established notions of its underlying practices, Colette's work continually challenged these conventions, thus expanding the limits of the genre with exciting new perspectives and possibilities.

Any number of critics and writers have attempted to identify the distinguishing features of this admittedly elusive form, usually drawing evidence for their conclusions from stories they have read or written. In discussing the difficulties inherent in defining any literary form, Mary Louise Pratt cautions that "genres are not essences. They are human institutions, historical through and through."[3] Arguing that the "significance of generic categories . . . resides in their cognitive and cultural value, and the purpose of genre is to lay out the implicit knowledge of the users of genre,"[4] Pratt reasons that any given definition is likely to reflect the underlying ideological stance of both the stories serving as models and the critic who has judged them exemplary. A brief review of selected definitions of the short story may therefore shed light on the ideological gap separating Colette's approach to the short story from that of her male counterparts. Such a summary may also help explain why the mainstream of critical theory on the short story, which is as much a reflection of the prevailing views of patriarchal society as the literature it claims to explicate, does not adequately account for Colette's short fiction.

According to Edgar Allen Poe, a highly self-conscious narrative form is the most essential characteristic distinguishing a short story from a story that just happens to be short. Stressing the importance of the overt control of the writer over the structure and direction of the narrative, Poe emphasized the teleological force of the short story: "In the whole composition there should be no word written of which the tendency, direct or indirect, is not to the one preestablished design."[5]

In his description of how a short story should function, H. G. Wells echoed Poe's insistence on singleness of purpose, illustrating the techniques he endorsed with a revealing passage that can easily be read as an extended metaphor for male sexual experience: "The short story, in order to produce its one single vivid effect, must seize the attention at the outset and never relaxing, gather it together more and more until the climax is reached. It must explode and finish before interruption occurs or fatigue sets in."[6] The composite definition that emerges from the above summary, foregrounding the writer's authoritarian control over his text and the inexorable forward temporal "thrust" of the narrative describes a model for short fiction that diverges significantly from the short story as Colette practiced it in her mature years, in which linearity and economy give way to circularity and calculated digression.

If we consider the short story as a narrative act, during which someone tells someone else that something happened,[7] the role that the story's performative function plays in determining its shape and texture becomes apparent. Many critics, speculating on the genre's origins, have identified the majority of situations giving rise to the telling of stories as firmly grounded in traditionally masculine experience. Consider, for example, the following assessment by Somerset Maugham: "It is natural for men to tell tales and I suppose the short story was created in the night of time when the hunter, to beguile the leisure of his fellows when they had eaten and drunk their fill, narrated by the cavern fire some fantastic incident he had heard of."[8] The assumption here is that, because it evolved from the oral folk tradition, the short story has emphasized action and adventure, whether fantastic or not (at least in those stories that delimited the genre until the end of the nineteenth century) in response to the storyteller's need to capture and maintain the interest of his listeners. According to this argument, the theme of male initiation, for example, serves as a particularly appropriate subject matter for stories, since for men coming-of-age provides more recountable events than it does for women.

If the above definitions, based on a limited vision of "normal" discursive practice, appear irrelevant to Colette's stories, in which adventure and action are largely supplanted by what Elaine Marks refers to as the subtle, "revealing detail,"[9] a more recently articulated explanation of the genre may better account for her work. Several contemporary critics have noted the preoccupation of some short story writers with what they call the frontier experience, defining frontier simply as "the part of one country that borders on another."[10] Chronicling the passage of individuals through "threshold periods," these stories are played out in boundary areas that often expose characters to the dangers and adventures usually associated with the traditional short story, but also to the disappointment and disillusionment that seem inevitably to result from the contact of a detached, if not alienated, protagonist with the modern world. The Irish short story writer, Frank O'Connor, sees this frontier experience as particularly relevant to the lives of what he calls "submerged population groups," whose marginalized existence furnishes, in his estimation, the most appropriate subject matter for short fiction.[11]

Although Colette's short stories are a diverse lot, offering the reader a great degree of stylistic, structural, and thematic variety, their central characters are often representative of the individuals O'Connor describes, sharing the common experience of exploring, occupying, or traversing an unchartered boundary region. She skillfully exploits this fertile terrain, marking the dividing line between culturally defined sexual identities, past and present versions of the self, or mothers and daughters (to mention but a few of the border territories featured in Colette's stories) in order to evoke the treacherous yet often exciting consequences of flirting with forbidden frontiers. Frequently, her explorations, undertaken from an unstable but dynamic third position, serve to dismantle socially constructed categories, infusing these static oppositions with a richly suggestive ambiguity.

In the discussion that follows, Colette's stories have been organized according to the "frontier" that is their central focus, although in many cases the intricate narratives are difficult to place within a single category. For example, "Bella-Vista," a story that exemplifies the complexity of Colette's art as a storyteller, examines the interrelationship between desire and knowledge, and the confusion of appearances and reality, all the while raising the controversial issue of sexual roles as masquerade. If grouping the stories according to thematic focus may at times appear arbitrary, due to their narrative complexity, such an arrangement has the advantage of permitting a fuller appreciation of both the inventiveness and the coherence underlying Colette's literary art than a strictly chronological approach would allow.

In fact, although a chronological reading of Colette's stories reveals an increased reliance on the autobiographical first-person narrator, there is little indication of a shift in perspective or narrative interest that would reflect her changing personal circumstances over time. Noting that none of Colette's fiction published during the 1940s makes any reference to the war or the Occupation, Elaine Marks remarks that "Colette was continuing to build her own particular world, whose roots remained in the early years of the century."[12] Throughout her career, she seemed to return repeatedly to that world for literary themes that (as her numerous biographers would no doubt readily acknowledge) find their source, if not their exact reflection, in her childhood and early adult years. Her short fiction offers a glimpse of the innocence, purity, and autonomy Colette claims to have savored in her own youth, her symbiotic relationship with nature and with a maternal figure often indistinguishable from nature, the loss of innocence accompanying her first, devastating disappointment in love, and the relentless challenge to conventional moral beliefs launched by the independent mother and later seconded by her equally free-spirited daughter.

The colorful details of Colette's life have been well documented,

although each of her numerous biographers has no doubt been challenged by the formidable task of chronicling the writer's personal story.
Familiarity with Colette's work leads to the conclusion that the minor
discrepancies among the five or six biographies written about her are
due less to the inattentiveness of their authors than to the transformative power of Colette's literary art when unleashed up on the heady
stuff of memories. For example, Michèle Sarde, in her fine biography
entitled *Colette, Free and Fettered*, evokes the idyllic circumstances of
Colette's childhood, the warmth of the household dominated by what
she labels maternal "power," and the pastoral beauty of life in the
provinces.[13] In the most recently published biography of the author,
the journalist Herbert Lottman debunks the almost clichéd image of
a childhood paradise and, supporting his arguments with "factual"
evidence, asserts that Colette's home town "was and is not a congenial
place," that the family home has a "featureless facade,"[14] and that her
parents, through adulterous neglect if not direct action (though he does
not rule out the latter possibility), probably bore responsibility for the
death of her mother's first husband.[15]

Thus calling into question the accuracy of Colette's memory, Lottman casts doubt upon the veracity of her autobiographical writings.
Nevertheless, throughout his lengthy book, he continually draws upon
a variety of Colette's works, quoting them without hesitation as reliable
biographical documents. Lottman is not alone. Many others have been
lured by the seductive aura of nostalgia that surrounds her writing into
blurring the distinction between the actual woman Colette and the
literary persona, between the details of a probably less than perfect
childhood and the idealized past she evokes in much of her work.
Given the explicit goal of biography to represent a life as accurately as
possible, the pitfalls are daunting. Fortunately, the literary critic, whose
principal objective in examining biography is to discover the ways in
which the writer's life informs the text, need not be as wary of these
dangers. In briefly outlining some biographical details, I will therefore
be less concerned with a precise rendering of Colette's life and more
interested in reconstructing the past Colette herself reinvented and
reworked throughout her long and productive career, as it furnished
the raw material for her fertile imagination.

Colette's mother, Adèle-Eugénie-Sidonie Landoy, who would become a pivotal figure in her daughter's life and letters, was born in
Paris in 1835, but spent her early childhood years on a farm near the
village of Saint-Sauveur, in Burgundy, following the death of her

mother. At the age of eight, she returned to Paris to live with her father and older siblings and then, eight years later, moved in with her brothers, who were established journalists in Brussels. On a return visit to Saint-Sauveur several year later, she met a local landowner, Jules Robineau-Duclos, whom she married through an arrangement agreed upon by the two families. By all accounts, Robineau, whose bouts of drunken rowdiness had, among his compatriots, earned him the nickname of "The Savage," was not a good match. A few months after the wedding, he tried to attack his wife, but she fought back, landing a blow with a lampstand that left him scarred for life. There were two offspring of this unhappy union, Colette's half sister, the moody, mysterious Juliette, and her half brother, Achille, who serves as a character in "The Patriarch," a story in which Colette claims to recount his disquieting experiences as a country doctor.

Within a year of Robineau's death in 1875, Sido married the local tax collector, Jules-Joseph Colette, who was rumored to be Achille's father. Jules Colette, born in Toulon in 1829, attended Saint-Cyr, the French military academy and upon completion of his studies was commissioned in the army. Wounded in the Crimean War, he was promoted to captain and posted to Algeria. During Napoleon III's Italian campaign, he was wounded again and ultimately underwent the amputation of a leg. His military career over, he was assigned by the government to a minor functionary post in rural Burgundy. In his daughter's memoirs, Captain Colette is recalled as a kind, though ineffectual man, whose efforts to be a writer, a politician, even a successful manager of the family finances all ended in failure. Despite his devotion to his wife, his place within the tight domestic circle was nevertheless compromised by what Sido considered to be his tenuous connection to the family. Once, according to Colette's account, when he innocently questioned his wife's judgment, she bluntly retorted, "What have you to do with me? You aren't even a relation!"[16]

Soon after the Colettes married they had a son, Léopold, and then five years later, in 1873, a daughter, was born and christened Sidonie-Gabrielle. Growing up among the deep forests and teeming ponds of Burgundy, the young "Minet-Chéri" as she was called, learned through her mother's example to have an almost mystical reverence for nature. Despite the modest circumstances of her family, she claims to have enjoyed unusual independence for a girl brought up in the French provinces during the latter half of the nineteenth century. Sustained by loving parents and her father's well-stocked library (her favorite author was Balzac), she led what she recognized later to have been a charmed existence: "No railway in my parts, no electricity, no nearby college or large town. In my own family, no money, but books. No gifts, but tenderness. No comfort, but freedom."[17]

As a result of Captain Colette's mishandling of his wife's comfortable inheritance from her first husband, the family fell on hard times and eventually was forced to move from the house in Saint-Sauveur to an even more modest home in the nearby town of Châtillon-Coligny, where Achille was practicing medicine. It was there Colette met Henri Gauthier-Villars, an experienced man 14 years her senior, the son of a family friend. Willy, as he was known in Parisian social circles, had already established a reputation as a music and literary critic, deriving much of his secondhand expertise, it was thought at the time, from the knowledge and talent of others.[18] In fact, the liberal borrowing of ideas and the co-opting of talent became a practice that Willy perfected throughout his later career as a literary entrepreneur who managed a "stable" of hack writers and with whom he "collaborated" to produce popular consumer novels.

By all accounts, Willy was a singularly unattractive man, yet the nineteen-year-old Colette fell in love with him, with the promise he held out to her of a glamorous life in the capital, and with the exciting possibility of sexual discovery (Richardson, 8).[19] They married in Châtillon in 1893 and moved to Paris. Once installed in her husband's dreary apartment on the Left Bank, she soon discovered that behind the façade of an urbane sophisticate lay a vulgar and self-indulgent philanderer. If all of Colette's writing, including her short stories, bears evidence of her almost instinctual impulse to return to a reassuring if irretrievable past, then her work also carries the indelible mark of her first shattering disillusionment in love. Several of the stories in the collection entitled *The Other Woman* deal directly with the themes of disappointment and infidelity in marriage and still others explore the seemingly inevitable link between suffering and heterosexual love.

In *My Apprenticeships*, Colette's memoirs recounting the early years of her first marriage, she gives a vivid account of how she came to writing.[20] It seems that Willy, who despite his relative success at orchestrating and marketing the books produced by his "novel writing factory,"[21] decided in 1895 that the couple's "funds were low." In the hopes of earning a little extra cash, he ordered his wife to record her memories of her days as a pupil at the local communal school in Saint-Sauveur. She dutifully complied, filling the pages of school notebooks with her small, even handwriting. Initially rejecting this first draft of *Claudine at School* as worthless, Willy later reconsidered and, after minor editing, submitted the manuscript to his publisher. The book appeared in 1900, with Willy's name alone on the title page. At her husband's insistence, Colette wrote three more books in the series, *Claudine in Paris*, *Claudine Married*, and *Claudine and Annie*, all of which enjoyed enormous popular success. After their marriage broke up several years later, Willy sold the rights to these four books, thus preventing Colette from receiving any income from them.

By 1905, the marriage had disintegrated. When the couple separated, Colette, who had reaped none of the credit for the Claudine series, was just beginning to establish a name for herself as a writer. In order to earn a living during the years following the separation, and no doubt to satisfy her own desire to perform as well, she became a dancer and a mime in the Parisian music halls. In 1906, Colette took refuge with the ex-Marquise de Belbeuf, or Missy, a prominent figure on the Parisian social scene, who gave her both financial and emotional support for the next five years. Meanwhile, amid the scandals of a homosexual liaison and seminude stage appearances, she continued to write, publishing several novels and collections of short vignettes that straddle the line between fiction and memoir. Two of these works, *The Tendrils of the Vine* (1908) and *Music Hall Sidelights* (1913)—the latter drawing heavily upon her experiences as a theatrical performer—include several stories that provide highly instructive examples of Colette's sure control of the short literary form.

A number of the pieces in these early collections were first published in the Parisian newspaper *Le Matin*, edited by Henry de Jouvenel, who in 1912 became Colette's second husband. During the 12 years of their marriage, Colette continued to contribute stories, novel installments, and articles to *Le Matin* as well as to other newspapers and literary journals, so that by the time *The Other Woman* was published in 1924, Colette had firmly established her reputation as a novelist, critic, and essayist. Although the range of topics and situations covered by the three- to four-page stories in *The Other Woman* is quite broad, they share a technical and stylistic brilliance that is underscored by their brevity. Written 10 to 20 years prior to the majority of the longer *nouvelles* Colette produced towards the end of her life, these stories offer early evidence of her consummate skills as a storyteller.

Following her marriage to her third husband, Maurice Goudeket, in 1935, Colette's literary output began to be dominated by works of short fiction. In his memoirs covering the years from their marriage to Colette's death, Goudeket claims she made a conscious choice to move away from the novel, turning to the short story not as a result of diminishing creative powers, but rather because it afforded her the opportunity to pare down her writing.[22] With their stylistic precision, their formal complexity, and their curious blending of autobiography and fiction, these stories are among the most fascinating works produced by Colette over her long and prolific career.

During the war years, Colette wrote numerous articles, eventually included in the collection entitled *Looking Backwards*, in which she chronicled the daily experiences of living under foreign occupation. In 1940, she and Maurice, who was Jewish, fled Paris, staying for a time with her daughter in her daughter's home in the Corrèze. The following year, Goudeket was arrested by the Germans and detained for several months. During this period, Colette also published some of her most interesting stories, included in the collections entitled *Bella-Vista*, *Chance Acquaintances*, and *The Kepi*. Plagued by painful and debilitating arthritis towards the end of her life, Colette was eventually confined to her apartment overlooking the gardens of the Palais Royal in Paris. She nevertheless continued to write, completing a number of volumes of reminiscences before her death on August 3, 1954.

Perhaps the most striking aspect of Colette's short fiction is its total disregard for the sanctity of commonly accepted distinctions between literary genres. The blurring of generic divisions is particularly apparent in the longer stories published in the 1930s and 1940s, in which Colette deftly weaves details from her own life into the fabric of her fictional tales. Adopting the conventional techniques of the *nouvelle*,[23] a literary form that does not coincide exactly with the short story, in these works Colette frequently plays the role of both detached observer and reluctant participant in the events she relates. The author thus relies upon the aesthetic distance inherent in the form to set up a continual shift in focus between the narrator and the narrated. In this way, a fictionalized stand-in for the writer assumes the role of reader of / in the text. Textual data (events, characters, received ideas concerning gender definitions) are thus continually filtered through the optic of the narrator, whose idiosyncratic interpretations of the stories encourages a repositioning of the conventional reader.

Although at the end of the nineteenth and beginning of the twentieth century in France there was no shortage of literary movements whose doctrines a novice writer might consider adopting, Colette avoided identification with the dominant literary schools of her time, preferring to go about writing with all the steadfast diligence and practicality of the "porcelain repairer" to whom she likened herself (MA, 71). As a result, it is difficult, if not impossible, to locate her comfortably within the mainstream of short story writers who were either her contemporaries or immediate predecessors. While her stories bear some similarity to the works of Maupassant in the frequent use of framing devices, or to those of Mérimée in which the narrator's storytelling role is foregrounded, and while she borrows many of her characters and plot lines from the stockpile developed in the popular literature of the Belle Époque, her short fiction always manages to deviate substantially from other models.

The stories' resistance to easy categorization places them, as literary products, in a no-man's-land that bears a resemblance to the terrain each so boldly explores. Carrying the stamp of her distinct voice and presence, graced by the lyric poet's sure sense of style, these works affirm Colette's innovative contributions as an accomplished writer of short stories.

Mothers and Daughters

Infused with vivid reminiscences of Sido, the almost mythical mother figure whose portrait evolves in several volumes of memoirs as well as fiction, Colette's entire opus serves as testimony to the prevailing influence of the maternal image in her writing. Portrayed alternatively as a "beneficent goddess," or a "primal source,"[24] Sido was above all a model whose literary presence her daughter carefully molded over the years. As Mari McCarty warns, "we cannot take Sido to mean Colette's flesh and blood mother, but rather Colette's idea and reconstruction of her mother in the text. After creating herself, Colette created her own mentor."[25] Although in Colette's earliest works, maternal figures were curiously absent, as her writing became more blatantly autobiographical she began to reserve a growing place for the literalized "Sido." Yet, because in these later stories the narrative voice gathers strength and confidence from the mother image it evokes, what Robert Phelps calls the "savory and magnetic presence"[26] of the narrator is brought into clearer focus as her poeticized model takes form.

An early story that appeared in the collection *The Other Woman*, entitled "Secrets," serves as a useful introduction to the complex boundary that both separates and unites the mother / daughter pair in Colette's short fiction. The story is told from the perspective of Madame Grey, the 50-year-old mother of the young Claudie, who is on the verge of announcing her engagement to André Donat, with whom she is clearly infatuated. Observing her daughter as she dances at a social gathering, Madame Grey finds that her resemblance to the girl she herself was at the same age is disarming. Struck by Claudie's loveliness, she is nevertheless still able to maintain a distanced view, feeling what the narrator identifies as "expert tenderness for her daughter, a tenderness incapable of blindness, the sort of critical devotion that ties the trainer to the champion" (CS, 291). Throughout Colette's writing, oxymorons such as "expert tenderness" and "critical devotion" serve to underscore the lucidity that so often accompanies the deep emotional attachment of the female characters in her fictional universe.

In this instance, rather than preventing the mother from assessing her daughter's situation objectively, her devotion to her daughter demands the tough stance of the trainer whose goal is to prepare his fighter for the difficult battles that inevitably lie ahead. The image, borrowed from an exclusively male domain, dispels any notion of the conventional weak and sentimental woman whose judgment is likely to be compromised by her maternal feelings.

Madame Grey draws upon her personal experience in envisioning the battles her daughter will no doubt face. As she watches her future son-in-law, she notices signs of the disappointment that awaits Claudie. For example, she sees in André's insistence upon order, on "arranging his books according to the color of their spines" (CS, 292), the same obsession with precision her own husband revealed to her with alarming candor early in their marriage. Recalling her horror when her spouse declared his inability to sleep if the fringes on the towels hanging from the rack were not lined up with each other and her revulsion at his habit of running his thumbnail over his lip, she decides not to tell Claudie about her disillusionment in marriage, but instead to keep secrets about "the mold that grows on married life, the refuse a man's character leaves behind at the border between childishness and dementia . . ." (CS, 293). Resigned to her daughter's fate and her own, as if they were one, she keeps her silence, sits down beside her husband, "and her hand, that of a good wife, admonished, with a meaningful squeeze, the unconscious hand which had been running back and forth, back and forth over his lip . . ." (CS, 293).

Madame Grey's negative view of the relations between the sexes finds its reflection in other stories of this and subsequent collections eventually establishing a recurrent pattern that, through the force of repetition, takes on the guise of the universal. Yet, her closely guarded secrets do not constitute the sign of solidarity between women, which is viewed in other texts as the product of shared experiences. Registering exclusively the reactions of the mother, who recasts her daughter's experiences as a dim reflection of her own, the narrative presents Madame Grey's reticence as a manifestation of the older woman's subordination of the younger through the withholding of knowledge, which ultimately serves to erect a barrier between the two. Colored by the mother's cynicism towards love and marriage, the daughter's life is all but assimilated into her mother's past. Convinced Claudie's fate can and will be no different from her own, Madame Grey resigns herself anew to humiliation and disappointment, as if to insure that, when the time comes, she will be able to pass the standard of submission on to her offspring.

In the mother-daughter relationships that characterize the majority of Colette's stories, shared and sometimes secret knowledge (often reinforced by anticipation of the young girl's inevitable loss of autonomy upon passing into adulthood) is depicted as a source of renewable strength for the daughter. The mother comes to represent a refuge, providing support and sustenance to the child, particularly in moments of temporary retreat from the male-dominated world. The first short stories in which this important relationship begins to emerge clearly are those that appear in *My Mother's House*, published in 1922.

A loosely organized collection of vignettes based primarily on childhood reminiscences, this work inaugurates the literary image of "Sido," while clearly establishing the authoritative presence of the narrative voice that links present to past as well as mother to daughter. In one of these stories, "The Abduction," Colette sets out a fundamental pattern for the mother-daughter relationship that will reappear with variations throughout her work. The anecdote recounts Sido's instinctively protective response when the nine-year-old Minet-Chéri moves into the room recently vacated by her older sister, who has married. Because the room is far-removed from her own, Sido is apprehensive, fearing the kidnapping of her only remaining daughter. The child, on the other hand, is excited by the prospect of the move, her curiosity aroused no doubt by an engraving hanging in the hallway of her parents' home: "It represented a post-chaise, harnessed to two queer horses with necks like fabulous beasts'. In front of the gaping coach door a young man, dressed in taffeta, was carrying on one arm with the greatest of ease a fainting young woman. Her little mouth forming an O, and the ruffled petticoats framing her charming legs, strove to express extreme terror. The Abduction! My innocent imagination was pleasantly stirred by the word and the picture."[27]

Even a casual acquaintance with Western mythology will suggest the conventional connotations attached to the word "abduction": adventure and romance, yes, but also the threat of violence and sexual violation dreaded by the fiercely protective mother. And yet the child is blind to the darker side of the concept, so captivated is she by her own innocent vision of the image and the word, which both lay claim to her youthful imagination. In fact, her intuition is born out. One windy night, two strong arms lift her from her bed and, cradled in what she cannot know to be their maternal embrace, she is spirited away.

The next morning, she awakens in the safety of her former room and, recalling her dream of a dashing figure in taffeta, calls out, "Mama, come quick! I've been abducted!" (MH, 43). She has learned from this experience that "abduction" signifies an exciting adventure, free from danger, bathed in maternal warmth and tenderness. The word and the image coincide, if only within the enclosed female space of the childhood haven, a domain ordered by a lexicon that blithely ignores the signifying system of the world beyond.

The power that mother and daughter derive from their complicity in this adventure is undermined by the distance separating the narrator, the mature Colette, from the events she is relating, a distance succinctly conveyed by the use of the adjective "innocent" to describe the child's fantasies. The gap between the two irreconcilable moments in time corresponds to the space separating the conventional meaning of the word "abduction" from the one the child, with the help of her mother, claims as her own. Laced with gentle humor, the story locates its narrative interest in the ironic play between the lost world of childhood, in which a titillating abduction is transformed into a mother's embrace, and the very real world of threatening dangers that the imposing presence of the narrator never allows the reader to forget. The tone of knowing indulgence that the narrator adopts as she relates this tale is essential to the overall effect of the story, for the reader can only perceive this unresolved narrative tension when constantly reminded of the inescapable force of the signifying system that is being challenged from within.

A similar complicity and strong sense of continuity between mother and daughter pervade the later story, "Green Sealing Wax," set in the village in which Colette grew up.[28] The autobiographical axis of the narrative is established in the introductory paragraphs, when the young Colette, caught up in the turbulence of adolescence, responds alternatively to the lure of two opposing vices. The first of these she characterizes as her "craze to be glamorous" (CS, 391), literally her "crisis of flirtatiousness," initiating her inevitable passage into womanhood. While Colette seems oblivious to the dangers of crossing this frontier, her mother is only too aware of the threat that coming-of-age poses to the female child. When she finds her daughter at play under the designing gaze of an older man, Sido observes that the girl seems prettier than she was at home: "That is how girls blossom in the warmth of a man's desire, whether they are fifteen or thirty" (CS, 387). Sido speedily whisks her child out of danger's way.

Colette's growing awareness of her own sexuality is counterbalanced by an intense fascination with writing tools. Attracted to the jealously guarded supply of pens, paper, letter openers, and the like, which her father has amassed in the vain hope of literary creation, the child finally yields to temptation and steals from her father's worktable "a little mahogany set square that smelled like a cigar box, then a white metal ruler." Upon discovering his daughter's transgression, Colette's father severely reprimands her for trespassing into the patriarchal domain. "I received full in my face the glare of a small, blazing gray eye, the eye of a rival" (CS, 388).

Although Sido does not fully grasp the attraction that desk paraphernalia hold for her daughter, she actively encourages Colette's acquisitiveness as a welcome alternative to the competing seductions of adolescence with their attendant dangers. As a final diversionary gesture, she takes a stick of green sealing wax flecked with gold from her husband's desk and gives it to the grateful Colette. When the child asks if her father, her "rival," has willingly given up the wax or if her mother has stolen it, the latter replies enigmatically, "Let's say your father's lending it to you and leave it at that" (CS, 390). Through this act of complicity, Sido reaffirms the dual relationship between mother and child that so marks what Freud calls the pre-Oedipal period of the early childhood years, while at the same time fostering in her daughter "ambitious wishes," expressed by the narrator as "the glory . . . of a mental power" (CS, 389).[29] By actively encouraging Colette's retreat to the library, safely nestled within the maternal space, Sido intervenes to arrest or at least forestall Colette's passage to womanhood along the prescribed pathway, while at the same time indirectly supporting her daughter's ambitious drives.

Into this highly personal narrative of the family triangle, Colette inserts the shocking tale in which a former postal worker, Mme Hervouët, coldheartedly poisons her husband and forges a will in her favor. Following M. Hervouët's unexpected demise, his niece, claiming to have seen a will sealed with green, gold-flecked sealing wax at her uncle's home some time before his death, contests the widow's assertion that her husband died intestate. About this time, a visibly distraught Mme Hervouët pays a visit to the Colette home, seeks out the wide-eyed Minet-Chéri in her library lair, and sends the girl off for a few moments in search of her mother. All the threads of the narrative are woven together in the final scene. Having produced at the last minute a second, blatantly contrived false will, bearing the stamp of the telltale green wax, the widow is confronted with her duplicity and flies into a delirious frenzy. Confessing to the double crime of murder and forgery, she is carried off to an asylum. Soon after, caught up in the spirit of confession, Colette reveals to her mother that her stick of green wax disappeared on the very day of Mme Hervouët's visit.

At first glance, the only link between the inquisitive, well-adjusted adolescent girl and the passionate, unbalanced murderess seems to be the sealing wax, a symbol of access to almost mystical cerebral powers for the former, an agent of treachery and deceit for the latter. Yet, on closer examination, it becomes clear that both characters are transgressors against accepted social codes, the one institutionalized by the legal system, the other reified by strictly defined gender roles. The reaction of Sido and Colette to Mme Hervouët's crime underscores their unconscious recognition of shared experience. When they take up the widow's defense, the frustrated Captain Colette exclaims, "There you go, the two of you! Already siding with the bull against the bullfighter!" to which Sido pointedly replies, "Exactly! Bullfighters are usually men with large buttocks and that's enough to put me against them!" (CS, 394). Sido thus establishes, in no uncertain terms, the need for female solidarity as a defense against "fat landowners" like M. Hervouët, calling into question the legitimacy of their claim to privilege, which is derived primarily from the wealth to which their gender has given them access.

When the facts are finally revealed, Sido revises but does not reverse her opinion of the crime and its perpetrator, reproaching the widow only for her failure to recognize her own limitations: "Poisoning poor old Hervouët with extremely bitter herbal concoctions, right, that wasn't difficult. Inept murderer, stupid victim, it's tit for tat. But to try and imitate a handwriting without having the slightest gift for forgery, to trust to a special, rare kind of sealing wax, what petty ruses, great heavens, what fatuous conceit" (CS, 398).

I will postpone considering the implications of the ethical values Sido proposes in "Green Sealing Wax" as a counter to the moral code that prevails in patriarchal society until my discussion of Colette's treatment of the boundary between acceptable social behavior and that judged "deviant" by community standards. Here I would like to stress the importance of Colette's emphasis on the maternal source of the tale. Locating the origins of the story in matrilinear lore, the narrator admits that what little order she has captured in its retelling she owes to Sido, "thanks to the the extraordinary 'presence' I still have of the

19

sound of her voice" (CS, 396). Imbued with the presence of Sido's wise, authoritative voice, the narrative itself stands as palpable proof of the salutary consequences of female-generated discourse.

Colette's account of her own coming-of-age, intricately interwoven with her initial flirtation with writing, is thus played out against a backdrop that affirms her storytelling skills as a maternal legacy, suggesting her natural right to the pen. Yet, in order to fully understand the magic wrought through the literary transformation of both mother and daughter, we must remember that, although Sido's aura may pervade the text, both her voice and her presence have been passed through the same kaleidoscopic lense of memory and imagination at work in "The Abduction." Claude Pichois notes that, driven by the need both to tell a story and to achieve autonomy, Colette eventually replaces Sidonie, her real mother, with a character who becomes her own reflection.[30] As the invented "Sido" is gradually transformed into a theme to be renewed, enriched, and exploited, the mother-daughter boundary becomes increasingly blurred. By recasting her mother in her own image, Colette quietly assimilates Sido's narrative authority into her own, all the while preserving the illusion of stereoptic vision that contributes so effectively to the success of the stories written about her childhood.

In "The Abduction," mother and daughter occupy a protective maternal space so firmly delineated as to create an almost closed border, setting them off from the world beyond. Mari McCarty sees the pattern of conscious marginality as fundamental to Colette's work, in which female space becomes a locus of empowerment for those who take refuge there.[31] This theme is further developed in the framed story, "The Tender Shoot," originally included in *The Kepi*, published in 1943. Unlike the two stories mentioned above, this one is not directly narrated by Colette, although her subtle presence in the guise of the person to whom the story is told is central to the narrative's design.

The story begins when Colette receives a visit from an old friend, Albin Chaveriat, whom she describes as a white-haired 70-year-old with the reputation of an aging roué. Having loosened Chaveriat's inhibitions and his tongue with a fine dinner and brandy, Colette persuades him to reveal the circumstances that led him to renounce his passion for young girls.[32] He explains that, 20 years earlier, he came across a "well-rounded" 15-year-old peasant girl, Louisette, while taking a walk on his friend's estate in Franche-Comté. Her ripe, frank sensuality aroused his desire enough that he returned several times to see her.

Chevariat notes that, although she eagerly accepted physical intimacy with him, she nevertheless took great precautions to prevent her mother from finding out about their trysts. In fact, as he recalls, he found it curious that she insisted upon keeping him at a safe distance, never letting him proceed beyond the crumbling wall that separated the dilapidated "château" in which she lived alone with her mother from his friend's property on the other side. One evening, he continues, when a sudden cloudburst sent the two lovers scurrying for shelter, Louisette led Albin across the forbidden threshold of her home, where they waited for the storm to abate. Suddenly, the girl's mother appeared and, discovering her daughter nestled in the arms of a man, surveyed the scene with "a wide, magnificent gaze . . . that was not upturned in anguish but that imperiously insisted on seeing everything, knowing everything" (CS, 442). Abruptly switching allegiances, Louisette turned the full force of her adolescent rage on Chaveriat, finally joining forces with her mother to hurl stones at his retreating head. Albin admits that, upon his return to his friend's home, he was struck down with a bout of fever probably brought on, at least in part, by emotional stress. He ends his story with a reference to its salutary consequences, for after being nursed back to health by his agreeable host, he left Franche-Comté, cured forever of "all the Louisettes in this world" (CS, 447).

This brief plot summary does not take into account the nuances introduced by the circumstances of narration. While we are kept aware of the narrator's presence by asides, direct remarks to his listener, and minor digressions (often referring to events that preceded or followed those being related), he never asserts the same authority over his story as does the "Colette" narrator in the other stories discussed thus far. Because his audience is an old friend, an experienced woman who knows him perhaps too well, he feels obliged to monitor her responses to what he is saying. At times, he self-consciously interrupts himself in order to offer a defense in response to a raised eyebrow or slight frown that he takes as a sign of his listener's disapproval. So, for example, when he is explaining his fascination with young maidens, he asks the rhetorical question, "What is there in a young girl that is so ripe and ready and eager to be exploited except her sensuality?" Then, no doubt sensing Colette is on the verge of objecting, he quickly interjects, "No, don't let's argue about that, I know you don't agree with me" (CS, 424).

At other times, he will interpret events in such a way as to cast himself in the best possible light, or, under the direst of circumstances, simply to save face. When Louisette and her mother chase him from their domain by stoning him as he hurries down the steep path, he finally turns on his attackers, seized by "a good honest rage, the rage of an injured man," and advances towards them. As he explains, "No doubt they too suddenly recovered their reason and remembered that they were females, and I was a male, for after hesitating, they fled and disappeared into the neglected garden behind some pyramid fruit trees and a feathery clump of asparagus" (CS, 446). The ferocity with which the mother and daughter pursue Albin and the terror that their relentless attack arouses in him are at odds with his self-serving analysis of their retreat, which conveniently ignores the fact that they have accomplished their goal and so can triumphantly return to their own domain, having expelled the interloper from their garden. Colette's silent interventions (through facial expressions and gestures), often in response to Albin's all-too-obvious editing of the facts he presents, constantly undermine what Mari McCarty refers to as the narrator's "patriarchal assumptions,"[33] providing a textual reflection of the physical challenge to male dominion launched by the mother-daughter pair.

There are, in fact, two superimposed readings of this story. The first, perhaps a bit too overtly orchestrated by the narrator, terminates with the moral that Albin articulates: young peasant girls can be hazardous to the health and well-being of a would-be Don Juan. The second, pieced together by the reader from intermittent unmediated access to certain passages of the text in which the voice of Albin is temporarily muted, as well as from the addressee's silent commentary, conveys a vastly different message: young peasant girls, whose closeness to nature makes their innocent sensuality a weapon rather than a weakness, can escape male domination and sexual exploitation through a fortifying alliance with a powerful mother.

The relationship between Louisette and her mother bears further consideration, since the principal surprise in the story results from Louisette's swift betrayal of Albin when confronted with a choice between her "lover" and her mother. The narrator does supply a number of hints suggesting that Louisette's attachment to her mother is decidedly different from that of the typical young girls he has encountered in his previous escapades. Despite her obvious poverty, she refuses the bead necklace he buys to replace the string of wild berries hanging around her neck, protesting, "I can't take it because of Mamma. Whatever would Mamma say if she saw me with a necklace" (CS, 428). When he continues to press her into accepting the gift, asking, "Are you so very frightened of your mother?" her reply is revealing, "No. I'm afraid she'll think badly of me" (CS, 429).

In refusing the necklace, Louisette makes no reference to community standards determining the code of behavior for a 15-year-old girl, nor does she cite the threat of parental punishment, that might deter other adolescents from yielding to temptation. Instead, she bases her decision on the personal relationship she has with her mother, grounded in mutual respect and esteem. The mother's scathing exchange with Chaveriat, when she confronts him in her cottage, is further indication that her moral judgments, like those of Sido in "Green Sealing Wax," do not necessarily reflect those of the larger society. Perfectly lucid and remarkably free from the anguish the narrator expects to see in a mother who fears her daughter's honor has been compromised, she berates Louisette, not simply for becoming sexually involved, but for forming a liaison with a man old enough to be her father. Exhorting Louisette to take a close look at Albin, she screams at her, "Do you see what he's got on his temples? White hairs, Louise, white hairs, just like me! And those wrinkles he's got under his eyes! All over him, wherever you look, he's got the stamp of ancience, my girl, yes, ancience" (CS, 445). No mention here of moral virtue, of preserving girlhood innocence, but an uncomplicated appeal to common sense and practicality, summed up in the mother's brutally frank reproach, "That man who would have been 50 years older than his child, suppose you had been pregnant by him, Louise!"

At the story's end, as Louisette and her mother unite to drive out the intruder threatening the tranquillity of their realm, the boundary between the two, at least in Albin's mind, has been all but effaced. When the narrator is confronted by their combined fury, in the blinding light of an unshaded lamp, he is struck by their resemblance: "Their two heads, close together and so terribly alike, stared me out of countenance" (CS, 445). And again, as they join together to protect their own borders, he describes them as if they were moving in unison: "Two heads, close side by side, followed my movement; they must be starting off again in pursuit of me. I was only too right; the two heads reappeared farther on, waiting for me. White hairs and gold hairs fluttered in the air like poplar seeds" (CS, 446).

All three of these stories, despite their great diversity, trace a similar gesture on the part of the mother figure. Sido's "abduction" of her daughter to the safety of the maternal inner sanctuary, her "surgical intervention" (CS, 388) to save Colette from a brush with burgeoning adolescence in the opening pages of "Green Sealing Wax," and the mother's fierce protection of the sanctity of the domain she shares with her daughter in "The Tender Shoot," represent attempts, futile though they may ultimately be, to stave off their children's inevitable passage to womanhood by creating a temporary haven from patriarchal space. In each case, strengthening the mother-daughter bond emphasizes the continuity between the two while at the same time widening the gap between women and the male-dominated world from which they take refuge.

Woman to Woman

The alliances between mothers and daughters, which serve as focal points for the stories analyzed above, are representative of the solidarity that distinguishes most relations among women in Colette's short fiction. Whether drawn from the unconventional world of the music hall performers or from the Parisian bourgeoisie, her female characters, faced with the physical or emotional suffering that they often view as their lot, find solace and comfort in the companionship of other women. Although the space to which these women are relegated is clearly marginal, they often succeed in occupying the place of the Other with a sense of dignity reinforced by mutual respect and the reassuring knowledge of common experience.

In "The Workroom," a short vignette included in the collection *Music Hall Sidelights*, Colette evokes the oppressive lives of five chorus girls who share a small, cramped, and airless dressing room during the long hours of the nightly performances. The descriptions of the women underscore their poverty while at the same time drawing attention to their exploitation by the insensitive "management" upon which their livelihood depends. For example, little Garcin, who is "as thin as a starved cat," is forced to wear a costume with "two openwork metal discs stuck over her nonexistent breasts. The rough edges of her pearl-encrusted ornaments, the coarsely punched copper pendants, the clinking chain armor she wears scratch and mark her lean and apparently insensitive bare skin without her even noticing" (CS, 118, translation modified). This passage presents the disconcerting image of a very young woman (described a bit later in the story as having "asexual graces") whose body, encased in a decorative metal cage, is reduced to nothing more than an object of male sexual desire.

Summarizing the drudgery of the women's routine existences, the narrator observes that they are not rivals, since none has an enviable advantage over the others, but "they are not friends either, yet from being thus thrown together, crowded and almost choked to death in their cribbed cabin, they have developed a sort of animal satisfaction, the cheerlessness of creatures in captivity" (CS, 117). The relentless pessimism of this scene is almost imperceptibly broken by little Garcin, who, left alone in the dressing room while the others are off performing, takes out of her "sordid handbag" a thimble, a pair of scissors, and a piece of needlework, and quietly but persistently begins to sew. When the others return for the daily intermission, each quickly sheds her theatrical costume, dons a stained cotton kimono, and sets to her sewing. For a brief moment, the squalid dressing room is transformed into a tableau depicting a workroom where the chorus girls allow themselves the "candid illusion of being cloistered young women who sew. . . . In spite of their gaping robes, of their high-pitched knees, of the insolent rouge still blossoming on their cheeks, they have the chaste attitude and bent backs of sedate seamstresses" (CS, 119).

Colette's choice of words draws the reader's attention to the jarring contrast between the two worlds momentarily fused in this brief interlude. In the French version, the adjective "candid" is rendered by the expression "en toute candeur" (in all candor), which, because it is set off by commas, preserves the heavy weight of reality amidst the fragile atmosphere of illusion. Although the cheerlessness of the situation is never completely dispelled from the passage, the final paragraph manages to evoke the inherent dignity of these uncultivated young women as they share a stolen half-hour during which they can play at bourgeois respectability.

"Gribiche," published in 1937 in the volume entitled *Bella-Vista*, provides Colette with the opportunity once again to explore the female-centered setting of the music hall, in which "one sex practically eclipsed the other, dominating it, not only by numbers, but by its own particular smell and magnetic atmosphere" (CS, 208). Colette's assumption of the dual role of narrator and character, who actively participates in the events related in the story, actually serves to emphasize the marginality of the central character, the young chorus girl Gribiche, by underscoring the distance between them. At the same time, the choice of a narrator who is both female and a coworker of the story's pitiable heroine gives the narrative a foothold within the closed circle of poor and disadvantaged women whose experiences it chronicles.

The story begins with an introduction to the suffocating and oppressive atmosphere of the women's quarters in the basement of the theater, with its "rows of identical cells" (CS, 205). The narrator's descriptions of the various denizens inhabiting the theater's subterranean depths, subtly blending respect and mocking humor, suggest her own ambivalence about this world of "monsters and marvels" that she entered following the failure of her first marriage. Although she is somewhat perplexed by what she calls the "latent hysteria" of this "crowd of women," she decides to accept it uncritically, at this moment preferring alignment with other women (even women from a world so alien to her own) to the pain she knows can be inflicted upon her by "one single man." After several paragraphs documenting the harassment that the women performers routinely encounter from representatives of the Establishment (fire inspectors, employers, and the like), Gribiche's horrifying story unfolds.

One evening, the bustling atmosphere backstage is interrupted by Gribiche's screams, as she tumbles headlong down a flight of stairs. When her coworkers arrive to survey the scene, they exchange knowing glances over the bloodstains left at regular intervals on the floor of the passageway through which she has been taken from the building. The inexperienced Colette soon learns what her more savvy counterparts suspected all along: Gribiche has suffered a miscarriage. The narrator is so haunted by the young woman's plight that she takes up a collection for her among the music hall workers. She is persuaded, against her better judgment, to accompany two of the chorus girls when they deliver the money to Gribiche at her home, an eerily large, yet sparsely furnished room, which the girl rents with her mother. Colette and her friends are made very uneasy by the rough treatment that the disagreeable mother, Ma Saure, gives Gribiche, and by the young girl's obviously weakened condition. They finally flee in terror when the frightened girl begins to bleed heavily. From hints deriving from their conversation with Gribiche and Ma Saure, they deduce that the girl's fall actually *followed* her miscarriage, which was brought on by her mother's crude concoctions. The next evening, Colette sees one of her coworkers whispering to a second, who, clutching her hand to her mouth, makes the sign of the cross. In the name of discretion, Colette surrounds Gribiche's memory with "the emblems of silence," allowing her sad fate to remain unspoken.

Throughout the exposition of the story, the narrator dwells upon the extent to which her undeniably bourgeois background sets her off from the others, who openly ridicule her naïveté. For example, she notes that Carmen, one of the performers, turned "severe and suspicious whenever I gave some proof of inexperience which reminded her that I was an outsider and a novice" (CS, 213). The link between her role as an outsider and her bourgeois origins establishes the theme of the boundary separating social and economic classes. This minor theme should nevertheless not be overlooked in assessing this story, for it appears in several other stories as well.

Here, the issue of abortion brings into focus the very real discrepancies between the experiences and opportunities of poor working-class and middle- or upper-class women. Historical data suggest that at the beginning of the twentieth century, when "Gribiche" is set, upper-class French and even British women routinely had abortions in Parisian hospitals, although the procedure was officially illegal in France.[34] Working-class women, who lacked the resources to pay the doctors' fees, had to resort to medically unsound treatment, the gruesome consequences of which are graphically illustrated in this story by the fatal effects of Ma Saure's harmful potions. The narrator's perplexed response to the blasé attitude displayed by two of the chorus girls when discussing Gribiche's predicament underscores their extreme isolation from the larger society: "Neither of them showed any surprise. I saw that they were, both of them, thoroughly aware of and inured to such things. They could contemplate impartially certain risks and certain secret dealings of which I knew nothing. There was a type of criminality which they passively and discreetly acknowledged when confronted with the danger of having a child. They talked of the monstrous in a perfectly matter-of-fact way" (CS, 228).

While the social and economic barriers between the narrator and the "authentic" music hall women are apparent, the common ground between them becomes clearer by the story's end. Oddly, the first suggestion of shared experience comes from Ma Saure, who, philosophizing about the inevitability of abortion, observes, "After all, it's nature. A woman, or rather a child, lets a man talk her into it. You can't throw stones at her, can you?" (CS, 222). Following Gribiche's frightful death, Colette has a nightmare revealing that, at least on a subconscious level, she is aware that no woman is immune to the danger Ma Saure describes. "I dreamed of anguished anxieties which had not hitherto fallen to my lot. My dream took place under the plant of ill-fame, wormwood. Unfolding its hairy, symbolic leaves one by one, the terrible age-old inducer of abortions grew in my nightmare to monstrous size, like the seed controlled by the fakir's will" (CS, 230).

Her nightmare portends the story's denouement, for the next evening Colette observes the whispered exchange between the two women that indirectly signals Gribiche's death. The meaning of the ominous silence that follows is instantly communicated to the women backstage, who understand very well that Gribiche's tragic end could easily be their own. In this moment of horror, laden with all-too-rational fear, the sign of the cross (which the narrator notes is a common gesture in the music hall world) can be read not only as her coworkers' joint prayer for the dead woman's soul, but also as their unspoken plea that they be spared her fate.

When compared with the protective, yet expanding space enjoyed by the mothers and daughters of the stories considered earlier, the women's quarters in the theater are a physical reflection of the legal, social, and economic oppression that constrained the working-class women Colette champions here. Even the cavernous room Gribiche and her mother share seems to enclose a stultifying space that serves to stifle and constrict rather than nurture. The respite afforded the theatrical performers by the meager comfort they find in their temporary woman-centered refuge is noticeably less empowering than the young girls' retreat to the maternal domain. The essential difference between the two experiences is that, having crossed the frontier into adulthood, having left behind them (or in some cases, never having known) the potent, invigorating force of the mother-daughter bond, the women in the music hall pieces are barred entry into the charmed, pre-Oedipal world that dominates the childhood stories. Because they are forced to confront the harsh reality that lies beyond the enclosed maternal haven, they must be content with only the momentary moral support they receive from fellow sufferers.

A far less cynical view of female solidarity emerges from a reading of "The Portrait," included in *The Other Woman*. Lily and Alice, two women in their mid-forties who summer together in a villa by the sea, enjoy a friendship strengthened by a common past: "the same handsome man, famous long before he grew old, had rejected them both" (CS, 282). Although they are very different (Lily, blond and plump, comports herself "like a girl from the Folies"; Alice, dark and slim, is much more subdued), they "share equal disappointments" which they commemorate with a photographic portrait of "the ingrate" that hangs in state on the drawing room wall. Having resigned themselves to growing old, they are watched over by the youthful portrait that for both of them recalls such vivid memories of bygone passions.

Then, one summer, upon their return to the villa, Lily makes a startling discovery: "The exceptionally humid weather . . . had, in ten months in the darkness of the closed villa, worked an intelligent disaster, an act of destruction in which chance had armed itself with an almost miraculous malevolence. Mold growing on the great man's Roman chin had drawn the whitish beard of an unkempt old man, the paper had blistered, puffing the cheeks up into two lymphatic pouches. A few grains of black charcoal, slipping down from the hair across the entire portrait, loaded the conqueror's face with wrinkles and years . . ." (CS, 283).

For a brief moment, they are appalled by the transformation, but their recovery is swift and as miraculous as the "intelligent disaster" that occasions it. In their exchange of glances following the discovery, Lily finds Alice's elegant figure unexpectedly "young-looking" and Alice, in turn, admires with envy her companion's peachlike complexion. During lunch, their animated discussion turns to dresses, diets . . . and other men, an indication of what the narrator terms their "feverish desire to escape." The story ends when Lily, reinforced by her newly found freedom and a few glasses of wine, disdainfully dismisses the portrait and the "great man" it represented with the words, "Poor old thing!"

This humorous tale of women's liberation raises a serious question, which Simone de Beauvoir explores in existentialist terms in *The Second Sex*.[35] Beauvoir speculates that women, who have historically represented an oppressed group, have accordingly always been obliged to accept a fixed definition of themselves that has been imposed upon them by the dominant group. Prevented from laying claim to the status of subject, women are compelled to assume the role of the Other, and so cannot transcend the preordained identity ascribed to them in accordance with the rigid gender definitions of patriarchal society. Colette's very short story (little more than three pages in length) illustrates uncannily well the constraints faced by women who rely on men for their sense of self. During the time the portrait stares down on Lily and Alice, they are transfixed by its incessant gaze,[36] resigned to the asexual existence to which "the ingrate's" rejection condemns them. As soon as the remarkable changes in the portrait take place, they are released from the limitations of "advanced age" that its presence had imposed on them, and they can once again begin to assume the role of desiring women.

The problem, of course, is that the desiring woman in Colette's work is almost always simultaneously a desired woman, who sooner or later, begins to mold herself to the wishes, real or imagined, of a man. The story, "Mirror Games," from the same collection as "The Portrait," describes the lamentable effects of male desire on two women who vie for the attentions of the same man. The narrator records her minute and insightful observations of the women, a blond and a brunette, who mirror one another's gestures, expressions, and actions in the hopes of pleasing the imperious male. As he turns towards one, the other attempts a grotesquely exaggerated imitation of her rival's mannerisms in an effort to win him over. This ritualistic miming exposes their identity as little more than a series of masks worn in order to mold themselves into the object of male desire.

While rivalry between the two women in this story creates pitiful caricatures of them both, more commonly in Colette's fiction women in love with the same man eventually succeed in forming friendships from which they derive increased self-respect and a greater sense of dignity. In a novel entitled *The Other One*,[37] for example, the wife of a philanderer forms an alliance with his secretary, with whom he is having an affair. As the friendship between the women deepens, the husband gradually fades into the background, eclipsed by the bond formed between his mistress and his wife. Here, as in "The Portrait," Colette seems to be suggesting rivalry between women supplies "fuel for the fire of . . . friendship" (CS, 282), engendering mutual respect and true affection.

Colette's interest in alliances between women extends beyond same-sex friendships to include several stories that explore relationships between lesbians. In fact, lesbianism surfaces at the very beginning of her literary career, in her first novel, *Claudine at School*, which depicts the rivalry between the provincial schoolgirl, Claudine, and her headmistress, Mlle Sergent, for the affections of the latter's assistant, Mlle Aimée. In a sequel, *Claudine Married*, the adult Claudine compromises her marriage when she falls in love with the beautiful Rézi, an older woman who is a friend of her husband, Renaud. Despite the candid description of lesbian relations in these initial novels, in later works the frank representation of homosexual love usually gives way to oblique references, intimations of sexual ambiguities that are never made explicit. Interpreting Colette's treatment of lesbianism in her work is a complex undertaking for several reasons. Given the voyeuristic possibilities that lesbian sexual images offered male readers, nineteenth- and early twentieth-century French society was more tolerant of representations of female rather than male homosexuality, and writers from Balzac to Baudelaire freely depicted erotic scenes of lesbian lovers. As the product of collaboration with her first husband, Willy, whose concern for the financial success of her publications led him to insist that she "spice up" her stories with lesbian affairs, Colette's early novels reflect his commercial interest in appealing to the preferences of the reading public.[38]

In evaluating the relative silence that increasingly surrounded an important aspect of Colette's personal experience, from her own long-lasting relationship with Missy to her friendships with noted lesbians of her time (e.g. the writers Renée Vivien and Natalie Clifford-Barney), it is difficult to determine whether her reticence resulted from the social pressure to avoid scandal or from the more fundamental problem of representing the unrepresentable. As Stephen Heath points out, in a critique of Lacan's theory of sexual difference, "the stable relation of a subject in constructed meaning, a specific subject-construction, is the effect of representation, and an ideological effect: any social formation depends for its existence not simply on the economic and political instances but also on a reasoning of the individual as subject, reproduced in images, identities of meaning, finding his or her delegation there."[39] While Heath is primarily concerned here with the problem of representing women through a system of signification that defines them as lack, his argument is equally applicable to images of homosexuality that would necessarily have to find expression through the existing "regulatory fictions"[40] of sex and gender. In light of this quotation, then, we might suppose that Colette, constrained by existing cultural modes of representation for female homosexuality, grounded as they were in voyeuristic and fetishistic practices, resorted to allusive strategies that allowed her to inscribe lesbian desire *covertly* in her later writing.

Several stories present homosexuality as little more than a mirroring of culturally accepted models of heterosexual relations. Colette's "friend Valentine" appears in a short piece from *Paysages et Portraits*[41] (Landscapes and Portraits) entitled "The Sémiramis Bar," passing judgment on the unconventional lifestyle of the bar's gay and lesbian clientele. As she gently ridicules her friend for warning her not to frequent this place with "a bad reputation," the narrator (Colette) evokes the spirit of comradery that reigns in the bar, presided over by the "warrior queen," Sémiramis, a "crassly maternal woman" who "speaks a colorful language to her crowd of long-haired young lads and short-haired girls" (CS, 53). Valentine's fears of what others will think and say are dismissed by Colette, who finds a poetic beauty in the simple men and women she observes at the bar, such as the young girls who "dance for pleasure between the cabbage soup and the beef stew": "I see only the graceful bodies united, sculptured beneath thin dresses by the wind of the waltz, two long adolescent bodies, skinny with narrow feet in fragile slippers that have come without a carriage through the snow and the mud . . . They waltz like the habitués of cheap dance halls, lewdly, sensuously, with that delicious inclination of a tall sail of a yacht . . . I can't help it! I really find that prettier than any ballet . . ." (CS, 55).

By juxtaposing the image of the sexually suggestive *and* aesthetically pleasing intertwined bodies of two young women with that of a ship's sail, Colette invests the seductively erotic feminine with the metaphorical weight of a symbol drawn from stereotypically male experience, evoking adventure, freedom and, above all, uncircumscribed space. Since, as Lynne Huffer convincingly argues, Colette often invokes the metaphor of sailing not only to represent the myth of "gendered destinies" but also to express shifts and displacements in identity, this passage might be read as a validation of the liberating effects of breaking gender barriers.[42] Despite their modest means, these adolescent girls are, in the narrator's eyes, more attractive than ballet dancers, who cannot rival the lesbian couple's natural, poetic grace.

In the final passage of the story, Colette emphasizes the bar's respectability by linking it to the innocence of her childhood. She tells Valentine that Sémiramis, aware of her (Colette's) provincial taste, sometimes gives her a gift of "old wrinkled apples with that musky smell of the cellar where I used to line them up as a child . . ." (CS, 55). Sémiramis, the decadent "Queen of Babylon" (as Valentine calls her), instantly becomes a dispenser of the tastes and smells of Colette's charmed childhood. By the time the wily Colette has finished her defense of the bar and its unconventional owner, Valentine's moral outrage has been mockingly discredited.

"Gitanette," from *Music Hall Sidelights*, is, in many respects, typical of the accounts of failed love affairs that abound in both Colette's short stories and novels, with the exception that, in this story, the "eternal" triangle is made up of three women. Enjoying a leisurely Saturday night dinner at the Sémiramis bar, Colette is approached by a former acquaintance from her days in the music hall, a young woman named Gitanette, who, dressed in drag, would regularly perform "Cosmopolitan Dances" with her girlfriend, Rita. With a little encouragement from the sympathetic narrator, Gitanette pours out her tale of woe. Her years of unqualified devotion to her lover were rewarded with betrayal, for the unfaithful Rita left her for Lucie Desrosiers, another music hall artiste. Reliving the awful moment of discovery, she relates,

"Lo and behold, before my very eyes, that great Desrosiers gets out of the cab, her hair disheveled, her dress all undone, and waving goodbye to Rita, to my Rita, who is still sitting inside the taxi! I was that taken by surprise, I stood rooted to the spot, cut off at the legs, I couldn't budge" (CS, 186).

Her heart broken, Gitanette considered both murder and suicide, but ironically, fell too ill to carry out either. Reflecting on the relative ease with which the woman recalls her death wish/threat, the narrator comments, "She speaks calmly of killing, or of dying, all the time turning her spoon in the cup of cold coffee. This simple girl, who lives so close to nature, knows full well that all that is required to sever the threads of misery is one single act, so easy, hardly an act of violence. A person is dead, just as a person is alive, except that death is a state that can be chosen, whereas a person is not free to choose their own life" (CS, 187). Although she admits that she is just as sad now as she was when she first learned of her lover's treachery, Gitanette insists that she wants to cling to her sorrow, for it keeps her company.

Inconstancy in love, a shocking scene of revelation exposing the betrayal, heartache that leads to illness but is subsequently viewed as a source of sustenance by the scorned woman—these are all stock plot elements easily recognized by any devoted reader of Colette's fiction. Yet, in her stories, the abortive relationships that follow the pattern outlined above are almost always heterosexual. What is the effect, then, of retelling the time-tested tale with a pair of lesbian lovers in the place of their heterosexual counterparts? One could argue that, by mirroring both the situations and the psychological responses of the heterosexual lovers in Colette's fiction, this story valorizes homosexual relations by underscoring their reassuring similarity to the heterosexual "model." Just as the tranquil complacency of a man and woman in love can be shaken by the sudden appearance of the "other" woman, so a lesbian affair can be threatened by a seductive interloper. While the personal pronouns may change, the fundamental terms of description remain the same.

Without denying the appropriateness of this interpretation, I would maintain that the implications of the story extend beyond the rather mundane "naturalization" of homosexuality. To a certain extent the story reifies cultural definitions of gender roles, since Gitanette, who plays the witch role in the dance numbers that the couple performs, exhibits "masculine" traits, assuming the authority for the pair and handling their financial affairs. Rita, on the other hand, is stereotypically "feminine"; flighty and unreliable, she easily switches allegiances, dependent first on the protective Gitanette, then on the boisterous Lucie. Yet, as Judith Butler stresses, the presence of stereotypical gender categories in homosexual contexts need not be viewed as evidence of "the pernicious insistence of heterosexist constructs within gay sexuality and identity." On the contrary, "the replication of heterosexual constructs in nonheterosexual frames brings into relief the utterly constructed status of the so-called heterosexual original. Thus, gay is to straight *not* as copy is to original, but, rather, as copy is to copy."⁴³ When considered in this light, "Gitanette" "denaturalizes" gender typologies by exposing the arbitrary character of the heterosexual model.

While the stories discussed thus far focus on the cultural implications of homosexuality, "Sleepless Nights," from the collection entitled *The Tendrils of the Vine*, explores homoerotic desire, but so subtly that an inattentive reader may mistake the lesbian lovers for a heterosexual couple. The story can be divided into three sections: the first, a plea addressed by the narrator to the bed she shares with her lover, asking for relief from their desire-induced insomnia; the second, a recollection of the day the two spent frolicking in the garden; and finally, a prophetic passage anticipating the "sensual satisfaction" the dawn will bring. The first few sentences, describing the "chaste, white" bed and its surroundings, stage a confrontation between the judgments of others (visitors to the couple's home, the reader) and the circumstances of the pair's shared existence. Despite its "honest candor," exposed as it is to both daylight and the insistent glare of an unshaded lamp, the bed does not reveal its most important truth: that it nightly welcomes the lovers' two "united" bodies. By structuring the passage around negative terms (e.g., "*no* drapery veils its honest candor," "We do *not* find there the well-devised shade of a lace canopy . . . ," "Fixed star, *never* rising or setting, our bed *never* ceases to gleam . . ." [CS, 91, emphasis added]), the narrator underscores both the unashamed openness of the couple and the incomprehension with which their frank voluptuousness is met by outsiders.

Furthermore, the initial description of the bed as both "chaste" and "white" sets in motion a series of associations that link the pure and virginal to the erotic and sensual. The French title of the story, "Nuit blanche," literally "white night," establishes a continuity between the unsated desire responsible for the lovers' insomnia and the "unsullied" bed in which they seek relief from mounting sexual tension. At the same time, the title calls to mind a semantically related expression, *"mariage blanc,"* meaning an unconsummated marriage and thus implying sexual abstinence. While the sleeplessness in the story is temporarily allied with abstinence, the entire passage pulsates with the promise of sensual pleasure to come. Thus, the common link between whiteness and purity is not subverted, but rather expanded to include the "sovereign exorcism" of lesbian lovemaking.

The narrator next evokes the aromas floating up from the entwined bodies: her lover's odor of tobacco, her own aura of sandalwood and the shared odor of grasses, retained from their day spent reveling in the outdoors. Confounding conventionally accepted associations between the sexes and particular smells, this passage includes a male-identified aroma (tobacco), a fragrance often used by both men and women (sandalwood), and a neutral odor evoking nature in its untamed state ("the wild odor of crushed grasses" [CS, 91]). Because the last emanates from both women, it stresses not the difference, but rather the similarity drawing the two lovers together.

The following, long paragraph, recalling the joys of a spring day spent in the garden, reinforces the couple's desire through a series of suggestive images appealing to the sensory perceptions: an elusive, "velvety" butterfly, a "keen and insistent" breeze, the "powerful and spicy" sap whose taste sums up the potent sensuality of the entire day. Serving to intensify the lovers' "quivering exhaustion," their encounter with nature leads to a communion rather than a confrontation with external forces. The narrative tension thus created through the impression of increasing desire is the product of a mingling of self and other, a wearing away at the division between the internal and external domains of experience. The easy passage from the intoxicating delights of a oneness with nature to the erotic joy of sexual excitement is a clear mark of what might be called Colette's "pansensualism," her recognition of the limitless and expanding sources of physical pleasure.

In the final section of the story, the narrator envisions what will happen at daybreak, when her feverish restlessness will be soothed by sexual satisfaction, "You will accord me sensual pleasure, bending over me voluptuously, maternally, you will seek in your impassioned loved one the child you never had" (CS, 93). Although never specified in the English translation, the gender of the person to whom the identifiably female narrator addresses this lyrical piece is revealed in the last sentence of the original French by a feminine marker, a final "e" on the past participle *"penchée"* (literally "bent over"). Clearly present in the original manuscript, this ending is frequently omitted by publishers, who are apparently apprehensive about negative public perceptions of homosexuality. The reader who unsuspectingly comes across the telltale grammatical marker will be obliged to examine the expectations he or she brought to the story, as a result of the discovery that it is an account of lesbian rather than heterosexual lovers.

Since the fulfillment of desire is only imagined in the future, the story necessarily ends before the sexual tension has been dissipated. But, even before the act can be imagined, the narrator produces a mental image that superimposes the couple of mother and child on the lesbian lovers. At this point, all the complexities raised by Colette's treatment of lesbianism come into play. One might be tempted to view the story's final sentence as an indication that, for Colette, lesbian relationships are but a poor substitute for other choices denied to some women: motherhood and / or a caring relationship with a man. Thus, the lover bestows her maternal feelings on the child-substitute who seems to welcome the opportunity to be enfolded in a motherly embrace.[44]

Yet the rest of the story, in which the couple freely enjoys a complete, intimate relationship, with no hint of regret or bitterness, belies this interpretation. I would like to suggest that the explanation for the story's somewhat puzzling ending is to be found in an underlying sensual continuity that leads the narrator to effortlessly displace her desire from velvety butterflies to white-skinned lover, from the garden "aflame with iris" to the bedroom in its blue obscurity. When read in conjunction with the two stories that follow it in the collection, with which it was bound in a small volume dedicated to "M" (Missy), "Sleepless Nights" can be understood to initiate a circulation of desire that flows naturally from past to present, from the treasured preoedipal mother to the generous "maternal" lover.

The last sentence of the story announces the nostalgia for the maternal presence that is the central focus of "Gray Days," which directly follows. In this latter story, the narrator's longing for someone "who possessed me before all others, before you, before I was a woman" (CS, 95) overwhelms her, as she rejects both her lover and her lover's "country," the seaside which stands in such sharp contrast to the wooded landscape of her native Burgundy. Only at the story's end, after evoking in terms a forsaken suitor might use the charms of her lost childhood paradise, does she mentally retrace her steps, relinquishing her desire for that which she knows is forever beyond her grasp, and substituting in its place a renewed passion for the present.

In "The Last Fire," the third story in the trilogy, the arrival of spring triggers the narrator's memories of the first bouquets of February violets she so coveted as a young country girl. In response to her lover's expression of concern over these futile dreams of an "unreachable kingdom," the narrator exclaims, "Do not feel sorry for me, beautiful pathetic eyes, for evoking so vividly what I long for! My voracious longing creates what it is missing and feeds on it. I am the one who smiles kindly at your idle hands, empty of flowers" (CS, 98). Instead of mourning the loss of her past, and the object of longing forever beyond her grasp, the narrator replaces her unsatisfied desire with a fitting stand-in. When considered together, then, the three stories do not simply highlight the unique qualities of lesbian relationships, but instead place homosexual and heterosexual desire on an unbroken continuum, ignoring arbitrary dividing lines separating differing orders of sexual and sensual pleasures. Through a series of temporal displacements, the stories establish a continuous and nonhierarchical circuit of desire that floats among past, present, and future, from the homoerotic to the filial, from flower to forest—and back again.

Between Women and Men

Both "Mirror Games," with its debasing exercises in self-concealment practiced beneath the male gaze, and "The Portrait," with its sorrowful images of women's lives constricted by the male presence, raise the general question of what transpires in the perilous boundary zone dividing men from women. Although many of her stories (including several already discussed) indirectly explore this hazardous territory, a few develop the theme in greater depth. The most exemplary of these is the title story from the collection *The Other Woman*, which in the English version is called "The Hidden Woman," a literal translation of the French title, *"La Femme cachée."* The story is a web of untruths, intricately woven and then unwoven before the reader's eyes. A doctor tells his wife, Irene, that he will not be able to go through with their plans to attend the Opera Ball because he must call on one of his patients outside of the city. When he encourages her to go to the ball without him, she trembles with disgust and protests, "Oh, no! Can you see me in a crowd, all those hands . . . What can I do? It's not that I'm a prude, it's . . . it makes my skin crawl. There's nothing I can do about it" (CS, 235–36).

Despite his pronouncement, the husband attends the ball, carefully disguised so as not to get caught in his "schoolboy lie." Surveying the masked revelers, he soon spies a woman in a Pierrot costume whose mannerisms and voice are suspiciously similar to his wife's. She scratches her thigh "with a free and uninhibited gesture," and he breathes a sigh of relief, convinced his wife could never behave so indecently. But when the Pierrot checks her lipstick in the mirror of an antique snuffbox she takes from her pocket, he immediately recognizes the gift he gave Irene on her last birthday, and he is forced to face up to the shocking truth: if he has deceived his wife, he in turn has been deceived. As he follows his wife's movements, his incredulity turns to horror, for he is confronted with the actions of an openly sensual woman who indiscriminately welcomes the embraces of every man she passes. Hands grab for her and, as she slithers through the crowd of eager men, she laughs with abandon at their advances.

The husband's sense of betrayal is complete when he realizes his wife has not come to the ball for a prearranged rendezvous, but is simply seeking physical satisfaction with passing strangers:

> He was sure that she was not waiting for anyone, that the lips she held beneath her own like a crushed grape, she would abandon, leave again the next minute, then wander about again, gather up some other passer-by, forget him, until she felt tired and it was time to go back home, tasting only the monstrous pleasure of being alone, free, honest, in her native brutality, of being the one who is unknown, forever solitary and without shame, whom a little mask and a hermetic costume had restored to her irremediable solitude and her immodest innocence. (CS, 237–38)

The last sentence of the story, cited above, provides remarkable insight into the importance given to masks and role-playing in Colette's short fiction. In a final twist, capping the subtle ironies of this story, the woman's masquerade allows her to retrieve her original nature, buried until that point beneath the role of modest, respectable doctor's wife. Her sexual expression is thus unleashed by the mask that paradoxically reveals rather than conceals. The title of the story in French neatly synthesizes the complexity of female identity at issue in this short piece, for the word *"femme"* can be translated into English as either "woman" or "wife." The story's message seems to be that the two meanings of *"femme"* are mutually exclusive, that the woman's fundamental sensuality is stifled by the socially accepted role she assumes as "wife." Once the "wife" is obscured by the mask and costume, the woman can then enjoy a brief fling, secure in the knowledge that her public image will not be compromised.

Although written in the third person, the story is, for the most part, told from the point of view of the deceiving, then deceived husband. The narrative registers his reactions to the guests at the ball, his thoughts as he discovers Pierrot's concealed identity, and his ultimate dismay at his wife's voluptuousness. Introduced by the clause, "He was sure that . . . ," the final sentence, which seems to record what the husband imagines are his wife's motivations, is at the same time infiltrated by a narrative voice whose understanding of the situation surpasses the narrow view of the betrayed spouse. Such adjectives as "free and honest," and the expressions with which the sentence terminates, "irremediable solitude" and "immodest innocence" suggest a complex blending of two distinct angles of vision, one dictated by the husband's (and no doubt society's) censorious judgment of the wife's "promiscuous" behavior, the other guided by an insider's understanding of female sexuality.

A closer look at the last two words of the story will help clarify the sophisticated modulations in narrative point of view marking this passage. The French adjective, *"déshonnête,"* translated here as "immodest," but also meaning "unseemly" or "indecent," expresses the condemnation which the wife's actions would inevitably elicit from the social circles she frequents, while the noun "innocence" mitigates the harshness of this indictment with the narrator's implicit championing of the woman's legitimate claim to sexual pleasure. In the French version, the adjective precedes the noun, rather than occupying what could be considered its normal position after the noun, a stylistic choice that allows the sentence and, in fact, the story itself, to end with the word "innocence." The reader is therefore left with the impression that, far from compromising her innocence, the wife's unabashed display of sexuality represents the "free and honest" expression of her desire. The unexpected juxtaposition of the adjective and noun, each supplying a distinctly different perspective on Irene's conduct, is a microcosmic example of the confrontation between two separate worlds that, as I have insisted, is a frequent hallmark of Colette's short fiction.

Irene's appearance in the disguise of the male pantomime figure, Pierrot, suggests two important issues that arise elsewhere in Colette's short fiction: the blurring of gender lines and the instability of female sexual identity. The seductive appeal of the costume is, as the following description makes clear, heightened by a melding of gendered attributes, creating a provocative indeterminacy:

> He turned around and saw someone in a long and impenetrable disguise, sitting sidesaddle on the balustrade, Pierrot by the look of the huge-sleeved tunic, the loose-fitting pantalons, the skullcap, the plasterlike whiteness coating the little bit of skin visible above the half-mask bearded with lace. The fabric of the costume and skullcap, woven of dark violet and silver, glistened like the conger eel fished for by night with iron hooks, in boats with resin lanterns. . . . The Pierrot-Eel, seated, casual, tapped the marble balusters with a dangling heel, revealing only its two satin slippers and the black-gloved hand bent back against one hip. The two oblique slits in the mask, carefully covered over with a tulle mesh, allowed only a smothered fire of indeterminate color to pass through (CS, 236).

Part man, part woman, part silently implacable theatrical icon, part slippery denizen of the deep, the creature whose presence the husband finds so troubling appears frighteningly unknowable. With her partially veiled eyes of indistinct color obscured by a mask *bearded* with lace, she brazenly sits sidesaddle (in French *"en amazone,"* or amazon-style), taunting the male gaze by scandalously confusing gender differences. Irene's masquerade, implying gender and sexual ambiguities, raises issues that have recently been the subject of considerable debate, opened up by psychoanalyst Joan Rivière's 1929 article, "Womanliness as Masquerade."

Extending the theories of Freud and Ernest Jones, Rivière argues that for some women "feminine" behavior functions as a defense mechanism, a cover-up designed to hide what they recognize will be regarded by men as menacing masculine traits, and to avert any reprisals that might result from the discovery of those traits.[45] For Rivière, then, femininity is nothing more than an act, a representation constructed in accordance with man's desire and concealing an unconscious masculinity. What is important to underscore is that she makes no distinction between womanliness and the masquerade; her analysis allows for no essential female identity that predates the playacting. The capacity for womanliness (as for masculinity) functions either as a device for avoiding anxiety or a mode of sexual enjoyment and should not be viewed as an essential component of the individual psychosexual makeup. Irene, who masquerades as a submissive, modest bourgeois wife, seems in some ways to exemplify Rivière's explanation of female sexuality. The frank and open sensuality to which she is "restored" by her multiply gendered disguise serves as proof that she is posturing at feminine respectability as defined within patriarchal society. Furthermore, her pursuit of sexual pleasure, undertaken by means of transvestism, constitutes a challenge to both gender and sexual binarism. Small wonder that her husband is horrified by the "monstrous pleasure" her freedom allows her, for she has managed, at least for the moment, to elude his oppressive gaze.

"Châ," another story in the same collection, is a literary illustration of Rivière's assessment of the "hidden dangers" men perceive lurking behind the feminine masquerade. Describing the striking comparison André Issard perceives between a group of "doll-like" Cambodian dancers performing at a private party and his tall, imposing wife, whose "virile blue eyes" are "accustomed to judging all things from above," the story traces the husband's surprised discovery of Madame Issard's troubling masculinity. Watching her from a distance as she methodically plots his career advancements, "her chin working like a tribune's, her closed fist beating out the rhythm of her sentence on the back of a chair," he observes, "She looks like a man. How is it I hadn't noticed it before?" (CS, 295).

Although she is able to convince influential guests at the large dinner party of her husband's promise, her aggressive conduct wins his condemnation, "She's a man. I was wondering what it was I had against her, unjustly . . . That's what it is, my wife is a man—and what a man! I only have what I deserve; I should have realized it sooner" (CS, 295). In contrast, he is mesmerized by the dancers, exclaiming in total admiration, "They're pretty . . . They're new . . . They're feminine, really feminine." Acknowledging the stereotypical colonial male's conflation of the erotic and the exotic, the story points out in clear terms his preference for a womanliness that gives no hint of what might lie behind the mask. On the other hand, Madame Issard, who seems oblivious to the importance of feminine role-playing, merits disdain as an object of desire, eliciting the very reprisal that, according to Rivière, prompts women to engage in the masquerade.

In "Armande," published in the collection entitled *The Kepi*, Colette presents yet another story in which the relation between the sexes is portrayed as an elaborate game of playacting, requiring the players to exercise considerable skills of dissimulation. The story, one of a very few written by Colette in the third person from the point of view of the male character, recounts the efforts of the timid Maxime Degouthe, a doctor who is a returning war veteran, to rekindle the flame of his relationship with a "comfortably rich orphan," Armande Fauconnier. A woman who, according to Maxime, has a tendency to shrink away from "anything that can be tasted or touched or smelled," she is the antithesis of the uninhibited Irene, who, at least when disguised, actively pursues the satisfaction of her sensual pleasures. Irritated by Armande's inscrutable facade, Maxime searches in vain for some proof of her love, all the while overlooking the wealth of subtle signs revealing her devotion to him. His misreadings of her feelings, which to the reader seem so blatantly obvious, are evidence of the absence of communication between the two, both of whom squander every opportunity for sincere conversation by indulging in defensive posturing.

While Armande's assessment of this unfortunate romantic impasse is never disclosed, Maxime's frustration is clearly expressed in his recurring fantasies of overpowering, subduing, and ultimately conquering the woman he believes to be resisting his "fretful desire" (CS, 459). Finally, a freak accident helps him to achieve his goal. As he is leaving Armande's after an abortive visit has brought him no closer to discovering the secrets of her heart, the chandelier in the hallway, having been jarred loose by Armande's violent tugging on the unresponsive front door, crashes down on his head. Momentarily knocked unconscious, Maxime takes advantage of the situation to feign a more serious injury so that he can surreptitiously observe Armande's reaction to his plight. What he sees and hears, her frantic cries for help, her clumsy efforts to bandage his head wound, her repeated cries of "my darling," convinces him that he has emerged victorious. The last paragraph of the story leaves no doubt that Maxime views this misadventure as a conquest. As he is carried down the imposing front stairway of Armande's home, she remains behind, "but at the bottom of the steps, Maxime summoned her with a gesture and a look: 'come . . . I know you now. I've got you. Come, we'll finish that timid little kiss you began. Stay with me. Acknowledge me . . .' She walked down the steps and gave him her hand. Then she adapted her step to that of the stretcher-bearers and walked meekly beside him, all stained and disheveled, as if she had come straight from the hands of love" (CS, 468).

Having dropped the protective veil of decorum, having revealed, in spite of herself, the depth of her attachment to this man, Armande must now yield meekly to his summoning gestures. Not only is she "tamed," as Maxime aptly puts it, she is also sullied by this inadvertent admission of a love which, even before it is consummated, leaves its indelible mark on her. Here, the woman's dilemma is unmistakably clear: she either guards herself against the man's disarming advances by masking her feelings or she accepts the subservient role that the acknowledgment of love reserves for her. Although it is true, as Elaine Marks suggests, that Maxime's accident releases Armande from the constraints of her "false apparent self,"[46] the self that emerges immediately loses the hide-and-seek game that the men and women in Colette's stories so often play with one another.[47]

Gender Role-Playing

Recognizing the dangers inherent in assuming that the slippery categories of sexuality and gender represent stable sites of signification, I would like to clarify the admittedly elusive definitions that underlie my discussion in this section. In her lucid analysis of the issues raised in assigning fixed meanings to the intersections of sex, gender, and desire, Judith Butler asserts that a matrix of power and discursive relations both creates and monitors the operation of these concepts.[48] Exposing both gender and sex as cultural inventions, she enumerates the false assumptions that allow us to found notions of identity on such illusory distinctions: "Gender can denote a *unity* of experience, of sex, gender and desire, only when sex can be understood in some sense to necessitate gender—where gender is a psychic and / or cultural designation of the self—and desire—where desire is heterosexual and therefore differentiates itself through an oppositional relation to that other gender it desires."[49] As the notion of neatly symmetrical, prediscursive alignments of sex, gender, and desire is interrogated with ever increasing intensity, such binary oppositions need to be regarded as fundamentally suspect.[50] In the stories to be discussed in this section, Colette challenges the rigidity of the arbitrary frontier separating masculine and feminine experience, by calling into question not only accepted gender definitions but the narrative conventions to which they gave rise in late nineteenth- and early twentieth-century French fiction.

The clearest example of a story that problematizes the confining gender roles dominating life and literature at the turn of the century is "Chance Acquaintances," published in 1940.[51] At first glance, this story, one of the longest Colette wrote, represents little more than a reworking of a standard nineteenth-century plot, calling to mind any number of consumer novels produced by the collaborative efforts of the "stable" of writers deftly managed by Colette's first husband, Willy.

The details of the plot can be easily summarized: a distraught husband, confined to a resort hotel where his wife is taking the cure, prevails upon a reluctant Colette, a fellow vacationer whom he has met quite by chance, to visit his mistress in Paris, in order to find out why he has not heard from her in over two weeks. When Colette returns with the news that his mistress has disappeared without a trace, the philandering husband is so shaken that he attempts suicide. Bungling the affair badly by taking a massive dose of an emetic poison, he survives only to become involved in another romantic liaison, this time with an opportunistic dancer to whom Colette has introduced him. In the end, the dancer, whose life is a series of calamities, dies of blood poisoning contracted from a neck wound probably inflicted by one of her lovers. All the while, the wife, occupied alternately by her profligate spouse, her illness, and her intricate needlework, remains a paragon of female virtue.

The story has the predictable, stock characters found in several novels published under Willy's name, such as *Une Passade* or *Maîtresse d'esthètes*,[52] which trace the amorous adventures of naïve men who fall victim to what Claude Pichois refers to as "vampire women,"[53] a uniformly rapacious lot. The prototypical predatory woman, represented in Colette's story by both mistresses of the male character, Gérard Haume, finds her opposite in Haume's wife, Antoinette, an exemplary model of the saintly, patient woman, whose most noteworthy quality is a silent passivity in the face of adversity.

Some contemporary literary critics have come to view the tendency of male authors either to exalt or denigrate female characters as a manifestation of psychosexual phenomena considered the direct outgrowth of the limitations imposed by rigidly determined gender roles. Isabelle de Courtivron, for example, suggests that a sublimated struggle between the fear of and wish for castration leads to men's deeply rooted ambivalence towards their own and female sexuality.[54] She goes on to argue that, in playing out his "wish to be a woman" (an impulse thwarted by narrowly defined sex roles in patriarchal societies), the male writer creates the cruel, sadistic woman to check what he recognizes as a dangerous fantasy.[55]

Object-relations theorists, stressing the primacy of the mother-child relationship in both male and female ego formation, consider the particular circumstances in which the masculine personality is formed to produce an unavoidable ambivalence towards women. According to this account, the male child must establish his identity by breaking the pre-Oedipal bond with the mother, a separation that, throughout the Oedipal stage, necessarily involves a simultaneous reinforcement and repression of the infantile, heterosexual love. As a result, in order to reaffirm their independent identities, men must strive at all costs to deny their connections with femininity, continuing all the while to harbor nostalgic fantasies of their "lost union with mother-as-flesh."[56]

Whatever the explanation for the predilection among male writers to depict women as either passively angelic or aggressively malevolent, it is clear that "Chance Acquaintances," despite a plot and characters based on a vision that is gendered masculine, departs significantly from the model. The reliance upon a first-person narrator, Colette, whose complex relation to the events (and her narration of the events) is central to the story's impact, allows for consideration of such fundamental issues as the inadequacies of generally accepted gender differences and the multiplicity of the female self. In the stock stories representative of the prevailing traditions discussed above, the male narrator is more often than not an experienced member of a rigidly defined world in which men are invariably victimized by scheming, unscrupulous women. The narrator of Colette's story is soon revealed to be an equally experienced woman who belongs to a world where such easy, unambiguous categories no longer hold sway. Through the interventions of Colette, who in the guise of intermediary (she refers to herself as a "proxy" [CS, 291] participates in the action, and who in the role of narrator both discloses and decodes other characters and events, the strict adherence to sex role stereotypes on which the plot seems at first to be founded, gradually crumbles away.

The narrator, who from the outset expresses her hesitation to get involved with chance acquaintances, is nonetheless drawn by natural curiosity towards the couple she meets at the hotel. Motivated by an almost simultaneous fear of indifference and involvement, she modifies her judgments of the other characters throughout the course of the story. As a result, the portraits of the three central characters that gradually emerge are altered in such a way as to dismantle the fixed triangle in which one might expect to find a victimized and sympathetic male balanced precariously between a "good" and a "bad" woman.

Colette opens the story with a description of Lucette d'Orgeville, a performer rejected by the true music hall artists who scorn her lack of professionalism. In her initial appearance, Lucette conforms to the model of the destructive woman. Compared by the narrator to a parasitic mollusk, she is representative of a human type Colette disdainfully refers to as "envoys from the nether world" (CA, 225) who, through the exercise of mysterious powers of attraction, succeed in luring their victims into unpleasant situations.

The image of Lucette as a quixotic and self-centered, predatory

47

woman is, however, modulated over time by the narrator, as she brings to light the hidden costs of Lucette's lifestyle. In describing Lucette adorned with the jewels lavished upon her by her current lover, the narrator notes, "she raised both her arms together as though they were handcuffed" (CA, 230) and remembers her later "weakly raising her fetters of diamonds" (CA, 291). Through the interpretive interjections of the narrator, the manipulative fortune hunter is unmasked to reveal a woman imprisoned by a role that forces her into economic dependence upon men to whom she remains emotionally indifferent.

Although in "Chance Acquaintances" Colette claims her narrative has little to do with Lucette ("It is quite unnecessary for the purposes of this story to dwell for long on the subject of Mlle d'Orgeville" [CA, 226]), she nevertheless develops her portrait over several pages. Now, it is almost always the case in Colette's short fiction that apparently gratuitous digressions, even when labeled as such by a disingenuous narrator, serve to reinforce the overall narrative design. Colette's strategic showcasing of a parasitic woman, prone to easy liaisons for which she is usually rewarded materially, is an illustration of this general rule. The story begins with Lucette's description and ends with her sordid death. The account of Gérard Haume's misadventures, regularly punctuated by reminders of his wife's stoic passivity, is thus framed by Lucette's story, with which it eventually becomes entangled. In fact, as the plot unfolds the focus of interest shifts from the romantic foibles of the male protagonist to the constellation of exemplary women whose complexly drawn characters stand in sharp contrast to the rather dull, undifferentiated Gérard.

Lucette's central position in the story is justified towards the end of the narrative when she responds to Colette's complaints about her involvement with a married man. In a defense completely devoid of moral considerations, Lucette explains that Gérard was simply, "the chap at the end of the wire. The wire of the electric bell. Haven't you ever been tempted by the button of a door-bell, when you're in a strange place? I am, often I say to myself, 'I'd like to know what's at the end of that wire. Suppose I press that button? Perhaps it'll bring the police or cause an explosion, or a peal of God's thunder . . .' " (CA, 306).

By acknowledging that she has at times succumbed in much the same way to her own curiosity, the narrator implicitly recognizes a link between the respectable, middle-aged writer whose legitimacy is insured by the confident and authoritative tone of her narrative voice and Lucette, the destructive Eve figure. Like Eve, both women are seekers of truth, ready to disregard the risks they may encounter in their thirst for knowledge.

The portrait of Antoinette, the long-suffering wife, also evolves throughout the course of the story, allowing the narrator to add nuances to the stereotypical image of the virtuous and submissive woman. At first, Antoinette is presented as a representative of the "eternal feminine," who, for better or for worse, in sickness or in health, remains ever patient and silent. Yet, there is another side to Antoinette. Struck from their first meeting by her masculine physical traits ("a husky, virile voice" and "powerful wrists") Colette is also impressed both by the woman's courage in the face of illness and her husband's infidelity, and by her considerable patience: "She never complained. I like courage in women . . . I admired Antoinette's patience and the way she would sit without speaking, wrapped up against the wind in a little shawl of patterned satin, edged with mink, which I thought atrocious, while she cut the pages of a novel. Her wisdom appealed to me in much the same was as her powerful wrists, her strong and by no means ugly mouth, her firm, thick neck—a smooth column instinct with exceptional power" (CA, 247).

By linking virility to patience, to the capacity to endure life's injustices, Colette suggests a realignment of the traditionally accepted views of femininity and masculinity. In contrast to her husband, whose high voice and delicate hands are signs of his fragility and inconstancy, Antoinette displays remarkable resilience and strength. Gérard Haume is, in fact, one of the best examples in Colette's short fiction of her view of the "eternal masculine."[57] Weak in character, narcissistic, and indecisive, he fails in his only attempt at independently initiated action, his suicide. Yet, if the narrator, through her assessment of the characters, liberates them from the constraints of conventional roles dictated by past literary practices, she does not replace these conventional figures with other fixed and ostensibly objective portraits. In key passages, Colette invites the reader to question her judgment, admitting, for example, that certain circumstances may have compromised her impartiality.

The narrator's uncertainty in sorting out her observations is underscored by a recurrent motif that casts her in the role of a decipherer who tries, often unsuccessfully, to penetrate the mysteries other people present to her. One significant element of the story that tests Colette's decoding skills is Antoinette's needlework, with which she is continually occupied. Although her friend repeats the name of her embroidery several times, the narrator is unable to recall the word, drawn from a realm of experience that she admits is foreign to her. At this point in the text, the narrator appears to view the embroidery as a symbol of Antoinette's infinite patience, a virtue Colette recognizes that she herself neither enjoys nor fully understands.

Expressing both admiration and incomprehension for Antoinette's patience, Colette exploits all the contradictory metaphorical possibilities of sewing as a literary motif. Viewed as an exclusively domestic activity, needlework can be considered a trivial feminine occupation or, alternatively, a means for powerful women like Penelope to "exercise their art subversively and quietly in order to control the lives of men."[58] In a chapter of *My Mother's House* entitled "The Seamstress," Colette mentions the potential for disruption lurking within this seemingly harmless feminine art. Confessing that she might have preferred that her daughter not learn how to sew, she recognizes the threat posed by the dangerous currents accessible to a mind left free to think: "It would seem that with this needle-play she has discovered the perfect means of adventuring, stitch by stitch, point by point, along a road of risks and temptations" (CS, 312).

In another short piece, Colette debates the importance of needlework with her "friend Valentine," who maintains that teaching young girls to sew is a way of reaffirming old-fashioned moral values. While Valentine views sewing as a means of taming the female spirit ("a young lady who plies her needle isn't looking for trouble" [CS, 57]), Colette sees it as a potentially seditious activity, affording the young girl the opportunity to give free rein to her lively imagination: "For a solitary little girl, what immoral book can equal the long silence, the unbridled reverie over the openwork muslin or the rosewood loom? Overly precise, a bad book might frighten, or disappoint. But the bold daydream soars up, sly, impudent, varied to the rhythm of the needle as it bites the silk; it grows, beats the silence with burning wings, inflames the pale little hand, the cheek where the shadow of the eyelashes flutters" (CS, 60). In this passage, the calm and conciliatory posture of the sewing child is undermined by the suggestion that an unfettered spirit pulsates beneath her serene exterior. Similarly, Antoinette's embroidery carries a double message, representing at once feminine passivity and courage.

In hesitating to attach a fixed identity to Antoinette and Lucette, the narrator may inadvertently be acknowledging a phenomenon Freud termed the "undecidability" of the female self. According to Sarah Kofman, Freud was troubled by what he observed to be a pattern of fluctuation between active and passive tendencies in women, a signal for him of an underlying ambivalence in feminine sexuality. Kofman's analysis dismisses Freud's explanation with the suggestion that woman's resistance to any essentialist notion of her femininity lies precisely in her oscillation between opposites.[59] The evolving portraits of the female characters in "Chance Acquaintances" do in fact trace a swing between opposing forces. Lucette balances between independent, assertive action and a dependency induced, at least in part, by economic necessity. Antoinette, although a model of feminine passivity, reveals an inner reserve of "virile" resilience. In a discussion of the images of complex sexual types that Colette develops in a fascinating book entitled *The Pure and the Impure*, Ann Cothran explains the process by which Colette challenges received ideas about sexuality. "[T]o many readers these portraits seem separate and distinct, a reaction no doubt due to the general social tendency to classify human sexuality in rigid, polarized categories. However, a close textual analysis of the ways in which meaning is communicated and organized . . . reveals that Colette has altered our conventional perceptions by breaking down and reassembling those categories."[60]

Colette engages in a similar sort of dismantling and restructuring of categories in "Chance Acquaintances," resulting in the systematic deconstruction of stereotypes representing gender differences as static and unchanging. As categorical opposites are conflated and formerly rigid boundaries are increasingly blurred, the subtly nuanced portraits of the three women (Lucette, Antoinette, and Colette) emerge as the central focus of the story, thrusting the male character into the shadows, where he becomes little more than a pretext for the exploration of the intricate complexities of the female self.

I have already suggested that these portraits are, to a large extent, molded by the judgments of the narrator, but they are also altered by the often striking contrasts that surface through their juxtaposition. In fact, Colette's short fiction includes a number of stories in which one or several female characters fulfill contrasting gender roles, encouraging a reexamination of widely held beliefs concerning acceptable lifestyles for women. In one of these stories, entitled "The Photographer's Wife," the juxtaposition of two single, economically productive working women with a married woman who is troubled by her own idleness, invites a comparison that becomes a central issue of the text.

As is so often the case in Colette's short fiction, the narrator of "The Photographer's Wife" (once again the writer "Colette") intertwines personal reminiscences with the characters and events of her story, impeding the forward flow of the narrative with digressions that may, at first glance, appear irrelevant to the story's main concerns. In fact, the tale is dominated by the presence of the narrator, who pauses along the way to relate almost everything she sees and hears to her own past experiences and present perceptions. In the opening paragraph, with a few short, economical sentences, Colette manages to convey important clues to the direction the story will take: "When the woman they called 'the photographer's wife' decided to put an end to her days, she set about realizing her project with much sincerity and painstaking care. But having no experience whatever of poisons, thank heaven, she failed. At which the inhabitants of the entire building rejoiced, and so did I, though I did not live in the neighborhood" (CS, 532).

By using the pronoun "they" (in French, the even more neutral *on* or "one") in the opening sentence, the narrator establishes herself as an outsider, someone not from "the neighborhood," and therefore removed from the milieu of those who provide her with her first introduction to the central character. Next, by referring to Mme Armand as the "photographer's wife," she underscores the woman's subordination to her husband, most particularly in his role as a productive wage earner. The appellation is significant because Mme Armand's attempt at suicide results directly from her perception of herself as a useless and superfluous appendage to her husband. In explaining to the narrator why she tried to kill herself, she enumerates the unimportant chores that mark her daily existence, all undertaken to lend support to her husband, providing for either his physical or professional needs. Numbed by the monotonous routine, she finally asked herself, "Is that all? Is that the whole of my day, today, yesterday, tomorrow?" (CS, 553). The frightening, unspoken answer convinces her that suicide is the only option left to her.

The early disclosure of the story's major event and its outcome encourages the reader's interest to shift away from a concern with plot development and towards the diffuse blend of personal commentary and anecdote that constitutes the majority of the text. Following her initial reference to the photographer's wife, the narrator turns her attentions to Mlle Devoidy, a pearl stringer whose apartment shares a landing with the Armands'. Admitting that she seizes the opportunity afforded her by a broken string of pearls to visit Mlle Devoidy, Colette takes pleasure in socializing with this native of the same region in Burgundy where she was born and raised. Emphasizing at every opportunity the common heritage she shares with the pearl stringer, the narrator also underscores the bond linking them as working women. Only after thoroughly expressing her admiration for Mlle Devoidy's high degree of professionalism ("I . . . had a friendly feeling for the details and peculiarities of a craft that demanded two years' apprenticeship, a special manual dexterity, and a slightly contemptuous attitude towards jewels" [CS, 534]), does the narrator move on to a description of Mme Armand. The implicit comparison between the two productive, self-sufficient women and the dissatisfied housewife who pronounces her life "trivial" quickly emerges as one of the story's dominant motifs, sustained throughout the narrative by subsequent passages reinforcing the striking contrast.

The extended visits Colette pays to her "compatriot" provide her with numerous anecdotes about the pearl stringer's varied customers. One of these episodes concerns a distraught woman who asks Mlle Devoidy to verify the authenticity of a set of pearls she has received as a gift from her lover. When Mlle Devoidy claims she is incapable of assessing the pearls, the woman takes matters into her own hands and, seizing a lump of metal used by the stringer to secure her threaded needles, brings it down on one of the pearls, crushing it into tiny bits. As the deceived woman bustles from the apartment, Colette asks Mlle Devoidy if this is the first time she has witnessed such an occurrence. The latter answers that, once before, a man had asked her to authenticate what turned out to be a real string of pearls, which his wife claimed to have purchased for fifteen francs.

In "The Photographer's Wife," the several references to real and sham pearls seem to suggest an analogy with the contrast between the practical working women and the ineffectual housewife (so concerned with appearances that she leaves her boots on as she prepares for her imminent death in order to hide unsightly corns on her feet). Mme Armand's extended first-person account of her misadventure certainly lends weight to the parallel, as she rambles on about the trivial details of her daily existence. In light of the narrator's generally unfavorable presentation of the photographer's wife's often foolish weaknesses, Colette's final judgment about what we might have thought to be Mme Armand's "inauthenticity" comes as a surprise. If Mme Armand is to be reproached for anything, the narrator concludes, it is her blindness to her own virtues. The last sentence of the story restores to the photographer's wife the "banal heroism"[61] to which so many of Colette's heroines lay claim. "Whenever I think of her, I always see her shored up by those scruples she modestly called fidgets and sustained by the sheer force of humble, everyday feminine greatness; that unrecognized greatness she had misnamed 'a very trivial life' " (CS, 557).

Primed from the story's beginning to dismiss the idle photographer's wife as inconsequential, the reader is finally obliged to revise his or her judgment and consider Mme Armand, along with the two other female characters, as a representative of "humble, everyday feminine greatness." The fact that such greatness can transcend the confines of the often contradictory roles women are called upon to play attests to their fundamental resilience, a quality Mme Armand proves to have in great abundance when she finally decides to abandon her plan to take her own life, because, as she puts it quite directly, "suicide can't be the slightest use to me" (CS, 557).

On the Threshold of Old Age

Mme Armand's dismissal of suicide is representative of an attitude shared by all of Colette's female characters, who show none of the fascination or preoccupation with death exhibited by some of their male counterparts. While Colette's fictional women would tend to agree with the protagonist of *Break of Day* when she proclaims, "Death does not interest me—even my own,"[62] they are at times much less sanguine about the aging process, for in most cases, they understand the daunting threats to their sexuality posed by advancing age. Registering the harsh judgment levied by early twentieth-century France on women who had passed the first blush of youth, Colette's stories chronicle the bitter disappointments of those who either regret the loss of desire signaled by advancing age, or who must renounce their still active desires because they are no longer viewed by men as sexual beings. The importance of youth in determining the status of French women at the turn of the century cannot be overestimated, "Should her thigh in its fetching garter wither and yellow with age, should her adorable face begin to show signs of fatigue, or the onset of menopause, the female became a non-being, odious in every respect."[63]

In "The Bracelet," one of the stories included in *The Other Woman*, the 50-year-old Madame Augelier's regret over the passage of time is triggered by an anniversary gift from her husband, commemorating the twenty-ninth year of their marriage. Reviewing the series of anniversary presents her husband has given her (27 old enamel plaques mounted on a belt, 28 jade bowls, and the last, 29 pavé diamonds set in a bracelet), she suddenly has a vision of a magical moment from her childhood, bathed in the iridescent light passing through a treasured blue glass bangle. The next day, she heads out in search of a replica, hoping to recover the magical moment from her youth. She finally locates a bracelet similar to the one that haunts her memories, only to encounter disappointment when the object fails to arouse the same sensuous response she wistfully recalls. Resigned to the restrictions imposed on her by her "advanced" age, Madame Augelier bids farewell to the child she once was, a stranger wearing a bracelet of blue glass.

Although she is never able to fully articulate the source of her longing, it becomes clear to the reader that Madame Augelier seeks the crude trinket as a means of retrieving not only her lost youth, but more importantly, the desire that the years have gradually stripped away from her. While she remains only vaguely aware of the origins of her sense of loss, her strange restlessness eventually divulges the true nature of her dimly remembered "nameless pleasure": "Madame Augelier craved a visual pleasure which would involve the sense of taste as well; the unexpected sight of a lemon, the unbearable squeaking of the knife cutting it in half, makes the mouth water with desire . . ." (CS, 298). The concerted appeal to the senses (sight, taste, hearing) grounds the memory in physicality, making it clear that what Madame Augelier regrets above all is the "powerful and sensuous genius" (CS, 299) of her youthful desire, that miraculously imparted a new and excitingly provocative shape to all objects and experiences that fell under its spell.

A later story, "The Kepi," appearing in the volume of the same name, explores the devastating consequences of advancing age for a woman blithely unaware of the limitations imposed on her expression of sexuality by the larger society. As she does so frequently, Colette, as self-declared narrator, takes a detour through the meandering pathways of her own past before approaching the central plot line in her story. Set in 1898, during her first marriage, but recounted many years later, the story is dominated by the distinctively mature voice of its narrator, yet accords a pivotal role in the development of the action to another Colette, the stylish young Parisian wife. Through a mutual friend, Paul Masson, the young Colette makes the acquaintance of the story's main character, Marco, a woman who earns her living ghostwriting novels at the paltry rate of one sou per line. Divorced from a man who replaced her given name with one he deemed more appropriate for the wife of a rising artist, Marco is described by Masson as "of a certain age." When Marco receives an unexpected windfall from her ex-husband, Colette leads her through a fashion makeover, complete with a new wardrobe and a surprise discovery of her substantial feminine charms.

One evening, Colette, Masson, and Marco decide on a whim to compose letters in response to a personal ad placed in the paper by an army lieutenant looking to "maintain correspondence with an intelligent, affectionate woman," and to send the best of the three letters to the young man. Marco's letter easily wins the contest and is forthwith dispatched to the unsuspecting lieutenant. His reply sets in motion a love affair that transforms Marco, "the virtuous victim of belated love and suddenly awakened sensuality" (CS, 520). She first loses weight, then gains a bit, passing into what Masson refers to as "the phase of the odalisque." In one of Colette's characteristic revealing moments that occurs near the end of the story, Marco playfully dons the lieutenant's military cap after passionate lovemaking, and encounters her lover's horrified expression as, emerging from the thrall of ecstasy, he is struck by "her leathery, furrowed neck, the red patches on the skin below the ears, the chin left to its own devices and long past hope" (CS, 528), all incontrovertible proof of her 46 years.

Beating a quick retreat, the lieutenant leaves Marco, who eases into what Masson calls "the phase of the priest": "when a woman, hitherto extremely feminine, begins to look like a priest, it's the sign that she no longer expects either kindness or ill-treatment from the opposite sex" (CS, 530). Although Marco returns to her solitary task of ghostwriting, her brief interlude of happiness has not left her life unchanged, for as Masson cynically remarks, she now earns two sous a line. Offering their assessment of Marco's mishandling of the affair, Masson and Willy define a strict code of behavior for the aging woman who engages in sexual exchange, "a child of three would tell you . . . , that Marco's first, most urgent duty was to remain slender, charming, elusive, a twilight creature beaded with raindrops, not to be bursting with health and frightening people in the streets by shouting, 'I've done it! I've done it! I've . . .' " (CS, 524). Having let herself degenerate into "the phase known as the brewer's dray horse" ("when a gazelle turns into a brood mare"), the foolhardy woman deserves no sympathy, for she has, as Masson argues, "compromised" her lieutenant.

The narrator quickly dismisses this outdated view as simply a manifestation of the way, "around 1900, intelligent, bitter, frustrated men maintained their self-esteem" (CS, 524), and then offers her own interpretation of her friend's downfall: "Marco had brought down the sword of Damocles by putting on the fatal kepi, and at the worst possible moment. At the moment when the man is a melancholy, still-vibrating harp, an explorer returning from a promised land, half-glimpsed but not attained, a lucid penitent swearing 'I'll never do it again' on bruised and bended knee" (CS, 529). The men's analysis is no doubt an accurate reflection of turn-of-the-century attitudes towards female sexuality and aging. The prescription is nothing if not predictable. In order to be desirable, a "mature" woman must walk a dangerous tightrope: she must be physically attractive, yet understated in her sexual drives. When she oversteps the bounds, by either compromising her beauty or honestly expressing her desires, she becomes a ridiculous and pitiable parody of the ideal sex object.

Colette's succinct yet insightful assessment of male sexuality is, of course, a good deal more interesting. Shifting her focus from Marco's shortcomings to an analysis of the lieutenant's psychological state, she shrewdly represents male desire in surprisingly modern terms: continually denied satisfaction, the desiring subject meets with ceaseless disappointments as he pursues his quest for elusive fulfillment. Returning from the half-glimpsed but ultimately unattainable promised land, the lieutenant looks upon Marco with the de-eroticized gaze of the disillusioned, sobered by the discovery that full present satisfaction of his desire is beyond his grasp.[64]

Masson's disparaging definitions of the "phases" in a woman's life, determined primarily by changes in her physical appearance, clearly represent a dominant view in early twentieth-century French culture that remains uncontested in the stories discussed thus far. There is, however, an alternative image of the older woman in Colette's short fiction, one based on a sharply different pattern of the stages marking women's life history. The best examples illustrating the more positive effects of aging on women are to be found in the autobiographical vignettes of *Sido* and *My Mother's House*, or in the lyrical, personal essays written near the end of her career. Whether the admirably strong older woman is represented by the narrator or her "model," Sido, her wise authoritative presence dispels the image of the forlorn and forgotten "nonbeing," relegated to the margins of society by her fading appeal as a sexual object.

In fact, Colette's short fiction is replete with examples of women whose dynamic life stages have little, if anything, in common with Masson's static, stereotypical "phases." Much more inclined to trace the course of a woman's life as she frees herself from such inflexible sexual roles, Colette's work, in Erica Eisinger's words, tends to follow "the journey of a pure protagonist away from the androgynous paradise of youth, through the impurity of rigid sex assignments, and back towards an ideal which unifies male and female. . . . Thus a woman will experience androgyny in phases: first in the gender-free world of childhood and adolescence, then in the liberating world of work such as the music-hall, and finally through time, in the androgynous harmony of aging."[65]

In subsequent sections, I explore Colette's view of the emancipating possibilities of childhood and the music hall. For the moment, I would like to focus on an inference drawn from Eisinger's observations that is particularly relevant to an examination of the implications of aging for the women in her short fiction: the link between liberation from rigid gender roles and the circular pattern of female psychosexual development. While it is true that for some of Colette's women characters, growing old signifies a debilitating loss of "womanliness," for those who succeed in negotiating the treacherous passage from youth to full maturity, the process is largely beneficial, leading them back to their reassuring origins.

As I have already indicated, no character exemplifies the unabashed confidence of advanced age more than the narrator herself, who musters her creative energy as writer to establish a perfectly harmonious model for mature womanhood. One particularly fine example of this model emerges from "Flora and Pomona," first published in 1943. In this curiously protean first-person story, what begins as Colette's homage to plant life (hence the title, referring to the Roman goddesses of flowers and gardens) ends up as her reflection on the integrative power that the memory and imagination of a self-confident older woman can exercise over experience. Vowing to sow her daydreams, memories, and schemes for the future side-by-side in her garden of tomorrow, Colette as narrator intertwines the natural world with her past, present, and future, gliding smoothly from gardening to remembering and writing, from objects (plants cultivated and animals nurtured) to the words an author calls upon to evoke these objects. Her intermingling of these disparate domains in the same textual space insures the continuous, free-flowing exchange among objects, words, desires, and perceptions that so distinguishes her literary universe.

Recuperating her past by resurrecting the gardens she has known, the narrator progresses from the provincial gardens of her childhood to the Parisian gardens of her mature years, and finally to the garden of the future, which she acknowledges will be nurtured only in her imagination. While the underlying movement of the narrative is established by the backward tug of nostalgia, its title posits spring as an implicit reference point, introducing a counterbalancing forward motion. Colette's longing to rediscover the mother / earth, the simplicity of provincial life represented by the gardens of her childhood, is thus accompanied by the promise of renewal, sustained, when all is said and done, by her recuperative return to the rootedness of her past.

For the mature woman in Colette's short fiction, then, regression to her origins can have decidedly salutary consequences, offering her rewards that far surpass the illusory plenitude that psychoanalyst Jacques Lacan allots to the Imaginary register. According to Lacan, during early infancy the child, believing that it is part of the mother, is unaware of any separation between herself and the world. Her sense of identity and presence is thus based on a dyadic relationship with the other that is eventually disrupted when the child takes up her place in the Symbolic Order, accepting the father's prohibition of access to the mother's body. Colette's literalized reappropriation of the lost paradise of youth, a retrospective gesture that nevertheless allows her to maintain her sense of being separate, also offers the tantalizing possibility of the oneness of the maternal bond. The reassuring accommodation between her past and present selves that takes place, at least on a textual level, serves to fortify her as she faces her present and future.[66] Once again, the path Colette's women follow deviates from the one many theorists, influenced by conventional notions about male experience, have proposed. Noting the pitfalls of the critical establishment's frequent indifference to questions of gender, Nancy K. Miller cites as an example the following description of the fate of the "modern individual," as one who is "rejected from the maternal breast, marked with the sign of the *ego* condemned to wandering and conquest (the transformation of the world) . . ."[67]

As Miller observes, Colette's autobiographical narrator, whose writing is grounded in a matrilinear culture, does not suffer the same intense alienation. Consequently, her purposeful journey backward in time and place has as its ultimate goal not the transformation of the world, but rather the "endless rememorization of the female 'I.' "[68] While the narrator of "Flora and Pomona," or of other Colette short stories, may never manage to complete the process of self-recuperation, her efforts are buoyed by her decision to ground that process in the enduring and, for Colette, inseparable presences of mother and nature.

Colette's short fiction thus offers contradictory views on the significance of the aging process for women, based, no doubt, on conflicting notions of womanhood. Reflecting the prevailing judgment of woman's unchanging status in patriarchal society as a sexual object, her female characters who remain bound by narrow gender roles find their identity severely compromised as they grow older. When the life of a woman is viewed as cyclical, however, advancing age can liberate her from complete submission to phallic rule, allowing her to reappropriate herself as subject of a desire that still enjoys full expression, even if only in her own discourse.

Right and Wrong:
Shifting Moral Grounds

> I haven't got the blind certainty with which you blissfully examined both "good" and "evil," nor your art of giving new names, according to your code, to embittered old virtues and poor sins that have been waiting for centuries for their share of paradise. What you shunned in virtue was pestilential austerity.[69]

Guided by the real and imagined model provided by her mother (to whom the above passage is addressed), Colette continually challenged the accepted moral codes of her day. In the story "Green Sealing Wax," discussed above, Sido's surprising disregard for the legal and ethical implications of Mme Hervouët's cold-blooded murder of her husband for material gain typifies the attitude towards imposed moralities that prevails in many of Colette's short stories. Condemning the widow for her megalomania, Sido concludes that the worst of Mme Hervouët's transgressions is neither murder nor forgery, but a failure to recognize the limits of her own powers. Since, in this case, it is Sido's voice that lends moral authority to the text, her final words carry great weight. The lesson she proposes to the young Colette is one that ignores established codes of conduct, which is to say the laws of patriarchal society, in order to call upon a highly personal, if not idiosyncratic, set of principles. Unconcerned about conforming to externally defined rules, Sido nevertheless demands a no less rigorous adherence to individually initiated constraints based on self-knowledge.[70] She thus replaces the dominant system of beliefs with a matrilineal counterorder, stressing independence, cooperation among women, and a profoundly lucid pragmatism.

In the stories based on her experiences as a music hall mime, Colette subverts the Belle Époque's disapproval of what was generally considered the stage performer's loose and immoral lifestyle. Although certain stories in *Music Hall Sidelights* depict the deprivation and exploitation of this marginalized group, others focus on the often ignored advantages of their situation: the true friendship and solidarity fostered by shared adversity, the liberation from rigidly defined social norms that their status affords them, and the respectability earned through honest hard work. One of these stories, "Bastienne's Child," brings to the surface the beauty and essential human dignity of a woman whose unconventional life as an unwed mother and dance hall ballerina no doubt constituted an affront to established middle-class values in early twentieth-century France. Less a short story than a subtly drawn portrait, "Bastienne's Child" first introduces its subject as a young dancer abandoned by the father of the child with which she is five months pregnant. Despite the fact that she is near starvation, often foregoing dinner in order to pay her hotel bills, Bastienne never succumbs to despair, for she is sustained by the support of the other "motherless ballerinas," who, like her, lead an "indigent, happy-go-lucky but hardworking life" (CS, 148).

In the latter half of the story, Bastienne's portrait is expanded to include descriptions of her infant daughter, who enjoys, "despite her environment, the gorgeous childhood of a fairy-tale princess. Ethiopian slaves in coffee-colored tights, Egyptian girls hung with blue jewelry, houris stripped to the waist, bend over her cot and let her play with their necklaces, their feather fans, their veils that change the color of the light" (CS, 149). In a glowing tableau that celebrates the earthy wholesomeness of maternity, the narrator describes Bastienne's hurried return from the stage to tend to her child. "In comes Bastienne, breathless, smoothing her tense billowing skirts with the tips of her fingers, and runs straight to the tray of the old traveling trunk. Without waiting to sit down or unfasten her low-cut bodice, she uses both hands to free from its pressure a swollen breast, blue in color from its generous veins. Leaning over, one foot lifted in the dancer's classical pose, her flared skirts like a luminous wheel around her, she suckles her child" (CS, 149).

When fate favors Bastienne with a benefactor, who offers both mother and child regular meals and warm lodgings, she remains unchanged by her good fortune, faithful to the principles that guided her in more troubled times. "Life, for a now flourishing though once misery-racked Bastienne, means dancing in the first place, then working, in the humble and domestic sense of the word given it by the race of thrifty females" (CS, 151). By emphasizing Bastienne's adherence to a strict work ethic, her maternal and domestic leanings and the warm and supportive atmosphere provided by her music hall family, Colette proposes a broadening of community standards defining motherhood and childrearing.

In another story, "The Patriarch," published in *Bella-Vista*, Colette imbeds a similarly indulgent view of the natural beauty of mothers and infants, whether legitimate or illegitimate, a disquieting scene of incest, a practice that even the most liberal moral code would undoubtedly question. Adopting a characteristic narrative tack, she launches into the story with an anecdote drawn from her own past, recalling the experiences of her handsome half-brother, Achille, when he was a young country doctor. From the beginning, Colette systematically wears away at received notions concerning distinctions between man and nature by comparing her brother, hardworking and uncomplaining, to another "remarkable creature": his reliable grey mare. With a professional curiosity rivaled only by the inquisitiveness about natural phenomena that he inherited from Sido, Achille is portrayed as the young Colette's role model and kindred spirit.

Having thus prepared the reader for the unconventional, Colette recounts what she describes as a "warm idyll," her brother's seduction by a young farm girl who brazenly sets out to ensnare the good-looking doctor by feigning pregnancy in order to trick him into giving her a "thorough" examination. This "living statue of the young Republic" (CS, 323), serene and confident in her victory over the unsuspecting Achille, returns for " 'consultations' " frequently, and according to what Sido has confided to Colette, "from these almost silent encounters, a very beautiful child was born" (CS, 324). Steeped in the passionate admiration for life and nature exuded by the Sido / Colette dyad, the illegitimate birth is almost reverentially celebrated, rather than condemned as a flagrant offense to traditional views of marriage and the family.

The second episode Colette relates deals with an indisputably more controversial form of illegitimacy, one that severely tests both Sido's and her daughter's tolerance for transgression. Having been summoned by a "robust, grizzled father of a family" to deliver the baby of his 14-and-a-half-year-old daughter, Achille learns that the widower, the patriarch of the story's title, is the infant's father. It soon becomes clear that the man has also had incestuous relations with his three other daughters. Oddly enough, the reader's horror is somewhat attenuated by the obvious fine health of the baby boy, the high spirits of the new mother, who emerges from childbirth "gay and laughing," and the immaculate, cozy atmosphere of the country home. By comparing the Binard girls to graceful antelope, Colette stresses their closeness to nature, in contrast, of course, to the very "unnaturalness" of their relationship with their father.

While neither Colette nor Achille comment directly on "The Monsieur Binard story," Sido's voice emerges in the last paragraph, providing at best an inconclusive guide to the moral judgment the story promotes. "Sido did not like this story, which she often turned over in her mind. Sometimes she spoke violently about Monsieur Binard, calling him bitterly 'the corrupt widower,' sometimes she let herself go off into commentaries after which she would blush. 'Their house is very well kept. The child of the youngest one has eyelashes as long as that. I saw her the other day, she was suckling her baby on the doorstep, it was enchanting. Whatever am I saying? It was abominable, of course, when one knows the facts" (CS, 325–26). Pausing for a moment to consider the issue further, she adds a final half-expressed thought, "After all, the ancient patriarchs . . ."

Sido's definitive opinion of the "Monsieur Binard story" remains unclear. Although she accepts, in principle, society's stringent sanctions against incest, it seems that she is nevertheless captivated by the unquestionable beauty that confronts her. Perhaps, as Jacob Stockinger suggests, the ambivalence with which the story ends can be attributed to Colette's natural tendency to "condemn the normal and normalize the aberrant," developing "a narrative vision that is, by prescriptive social standards, amoral in its stance toward humans, animals, and plants."[71] I think it could also be argued, though, that Sido's almost wistful evocation of the ancient patriarchs' acceptance of incestuous relations suggests another, not necessarily contradictory, conclusion. Without dismissing the abhorrent aspects of incest, Sido is, in spite of herself, attracted to at least the abstract possibility of closing the domestic circle off to menacing incursions from without. Her fantasies of solidifying the primal familial bonds that provide the child with protection from the dangers of the world beyond momentarily blind her to the terrible implications of the Binards' situation.

As the analysis of the stories included in the first section indicates, Sido and her fictional counterparts are prone to see the family, and particularly the mother-daughter relationship as a refuge, a safe haven protecting the young from the unspecified, though very real, threat posed by strangers, who are defined by Sido as anyone who is not a blood relation. When Colette's half-sister, Juliette, married, the distressed Sido complained that the young woman had been all but abducted by "a man she hardly knows" (CS, 42). It is perhaps reasonable to assume, then, that in "The Patriarch," Sido's strong maternal impulse to keep the child safely enclosed within the confines of the domestic sphere collides with a societal proscription she cannot ignore. Her hesitation to condemn, slight though it may be, indicates that both she and her interpreter, Colette, will continue to scrutinize imposed values according to their own unconventional, yet highly consistent ethical standards, redefining as they go the boundaries between such fixed categories as "pure" and "impure," or "natural" and "unnatural."

Revisions of the Real

The title of the collection, *The Hidden Woman*, suggests a theme common to much of Colette's short fiction, in which, as Elaine Marks puts it, the author is "dealing with the problem of reality and appearances" (Marks, 152). While it is true that a number of Colette's stories are concerned with the often ill-defined boundary between appearances (sometimes more clearly expressed as illusions originating in the mind / eye of the beholder) and conventional reality, I would argue that they actually explore the often jarring confrontation between two conflicting realities, each the product of a distinct signifying system imposing its own particular order and meaning on the world. The results of this contact between opposing worldviews vary from one work of short fiction to the next, but in most cases, though an uneasy accommodation between the forces representing the two "realities" is often proposed, there is seldom a definitive resolution of the conflict.

The concept of dual realities can probably be best understood through a discussion of a very short piece, "The Priest on the Wall," often cited by critics to illustrate Colette's unique relationship to language. In this autobiographical vignette, Colette writes about her own sobering initiation into an adult world that imposes limits on the free exercise of a child's imagination. As a small girl, she recalls, she was fascinated by the word "presbytery," which she had heard repeated by the adults around her. Taken with the magical powers that the odd syllables conjured up for her, she would scramble to the top of the garden wall and chant the word from her privileged vantage point, reveling in the possibilities that the strange but provocative sounds presented to her. Colette continues the story by noting that soon after she first learned the word, she became convinced "presbytery" was the scientific name for a small striped snail commonly found in the family garden, and triumphantly related her discovery to her mother.

When her mother, chiding her for not calling things by their proper names, explained that "presbytery" referred to the house occupied by Monsieur Millot, the local priest, the child was infuriated and balked at the restriction of her power to name: "I fought against the intrusion,

67

closely hugging the tatters of my absurdity. I longed to compel Monsieur Millot, during my pleasure, to inhabit the empty shell of the little "presbytery" snail . . ." (MH, 46). Despite her initial defiance, Colette eventually capitulated: "I was craven and I compromised with my disappointment. Throwing away the fragments of the little broken snail shell, I picked up the enchanting word and, climbing on to my narrow terrace, shaded by the old lilac trees and adorned with polished pebbles and scraps of colored glass like a thieving magpie's nest—I christened it the Presbytery and inducted myself as Priest on the wall" (MH, 46).

As Joan Stewart pertinently explains, the young Colette's efforts to create a world with "free-floating signifiers" are thwarted here by arbitrary codes that come into direct conflict with what the child imagines to be her complete autonomy as she presides over her own privileged universe where "words are material, tactile, voluptuous, and mutable."[72] The child's bold claim to her right to assign meanings to words comes into direct conflict with the laws governing signification imposed by the adult world, in order to suppress the proliferation of multiple meanings that constitute a threat to hegemonic discourse. As a result of the sobering admonishments of her beloved mother, the child is obliged to realize the overwhelming force of the set of rules designed to structure her experience, which she has until then valiantly tried to ignore.

Yet, through the magical possibilities of language, the child is able to preserve the illusion of her autonomy while at the same time gesturing brazenly toward the rules enforced by the world on the other side of the garden wall. If "presbytery" must mean "priest's house," then she will transform the rather ordinary concept into the lofty perch of a thieving magpie. Like the magpie who fashions his nest by appropriating polished stones and shards of glass, the child steals the word and makes it her own, spiriting it away to her exclusive vantage point, from which she can continue to reign, albeit always within sight of what lies beyond. The child's precarious position underscores the instability of the accommodation between the two worlds, the uncompromising adult domain that seeks to impose fixed meanings on things and the charmed, yet transitory realm of childhood, with its seemingly limitless power to create private signifying codes.

Citing the linguistic theories of Julia Kristeva, Nicole Ward Jouve has interpreted "The Priest on the Wall" as proof that, by taking pleasure in the sheer sound of a word, the child affirms her ties with what Kristeva has defined as the "semiotic" function of language, in which "the signifier functions independently from the signified, carrying archaic [instinctual and maternal] drives," while neatly sidestepping participation in the "symbolic," which marks entry into established codes of signification.[73] If, by renaming her shaded terrace in response to the threat from the symbolic order that lurks beyond the garden wall, the child has made a small concession to the forces without, accepting the discrete meanings upon which the paternal law insists, she has nevertheless exploited the possibilities of language so as to redefine the object, reducing its role to that of correlative or support for her own desire and pleasure.

The issue at stake here, as in other stories to be considered in this section, is less the revealing of reality according to objective standards, than the jealous guarding of a closed experience through which reality is obliged to take on the colors of the perceiving consciousness.[74] The extent to which Colette as a character succeeds in shaping the "real" through the intervention of her senses and the mediation of desire varies from one story to the next, yet in each case, the exercise itself serves to call into question the premises upon which conventional distinctions between reality and illusion are founded.

In "The Sick Child," another story in which the interplay between language, the world, and the self is at issue, a dangerously high fever threatens the life of a young boy suffering from polio. Jean, the bedridden child, weakened by his prolonged illness, floats in and out of consciousness. As his distraught mother, whom he calls "Madame Mamma," hovers at his bedside, his imagination, spurred on by fever-induced hallucinations, soars off beyond the mundane confines of his room. Freed from the cause and effect logic of the waking world, his sensory organs respond to several categories of stimuli. "He excelled in making a magical and paradoxical use of his senses. For him, the white muslin curtains gave out a pink sound when the sun struck them about ten in the morning" (CS, 328).

Caught up in this oneiric world, governed by the principle of synesthesia, in which sounds bring forth colors and smells evoke sounds, the child becomes so disconnected from his surroundings that a complete separation (brought on by death) seems inevitable. But, just as his perceptions are on the verge of dissolving into chaos, the syllables forming the words "Crisis, salutary but severe" invade his delusionary world, and he awakens to the relieved exclamations of his mother, who has been assured by the doctor, that her son is on his way to recovery.

As he reluctantly relinquishes the limitless mobility of his liberated imagination, Jean longs for the "visible sounds, the tangible images, the navigable air" he has had to forego.

His regret echoes that of the child, Colette, who must renounce her universe of infinite possibilities in which a priest's house can be transformed at will into a small, striped snail. Yet, deprived of the young Colette's linguistic strategies, Jean's renunciation seems complete and irrevocable, and so his disillusionment is profound. "With the wave of his hand, Jean said farewell to his angel-haired reflection. The other returned his greeting from the depths of an earthly night shorn of all marvels, the only night allowed to children whom death lets go and who fall asleep, assenting, cured, and disappointed" (CS, 346). While the young Colette can successfully negotiate between her realm of independently assigned meanings and the immutable reality of the adult world by relying upon desire to direct her as she imparts meaning to objects, Jean is bombarded with intoxicating sensory data, mediated only by his unfocused, semiconscious impulse to take refuge in the experience.[75]

In another, very short story entitled "The Hand," Colette presents a particularly cynical vision of a woman's rite of passage, a young bride's initiation into marriage, a transition that, in Colette's universe, inevitably leads to her disappointment and eventual submission. The story opens with the scene of the newlyweds in bed, two weeks after their wedding, following a brief courtship of one month. Excited and surprised to find herself tasting "the joys of living with someone unknown and with whom she is in love" (CS, 246), the adolescent girl awakens during the night to savor the thought of her "conjugal adventure." As she admiringly takes a silent inventory of her husband's physical attractions, her attention is suddenly riveted by his large hand, transformed beneath her persistent stare into a monstrous creature threatening to take on a life all its own. Her anxiety mounts as the hand of the sleeping man appears to react to her disgust: "It regrouped its forces, opened wide, and splayed its tendons, lumps, and red fur like battle dress, then slowly drawing itself in again, grabbed a fistful of the sheet, dug into it with its curved fingers, and squeezed, squeezed with the methodical pleasure of a strangler" (CS, 247–48).

Although her revulsion subsides when the hand disappears beneath the bed sheets, it returns with even greater intensity the following morning, during breakfast, when she is forced to look at the hand once more, "with its red hair and red skin, and the ghastly thumb curving out over the handle of a knife" (CS, 248). In a concerted exercise of self-control, she hides her true feelings, "and, beginning her life of duplicity, of resignation, and of lowly, delicate diplomacy, she leaned over and humbly kissed the monstrous hand" (CS, 248).

The wife's resignation here calls to mind Jean's reluctant reconciliation to the constrictions of the waking world and the young Colette's bitter response to the competing authority that challenges her from beyond the garden wall. In this case, what triggers the bride's accommodation with a devastating reality is the sudden and unanticipated retreat of desire. The male protagonist of her exciting adventure is dramatically de-eroticized in the three brief pages of the story when he is stripped of the glow projected by his wife's infatuation. The stark contrast between the two closely juxtaposed visions serves to underscore once again the primordial role desire plays in mediating between the self and the world in Colette's short fiction.

In fact, desire, or rather, its absence, emerges as the key to an understanding of what may at first appear to be a disconcerting organizational lapse in "Bella-Vista," a longer story published in a volume with several others in 1937 and based on a seemingly bizarre "personal" anecdote. Claiming the events of the story unfolded during what she calls a "blank period" in her life, an interlude when she was not in love, Colette hastens to underscore the indifference accompanying her relationship to the events and characters she describes in "Bella-Vista." Her insistence that the subject matter is a de-eroticized experience suggests that the shape and texture of the narrative may differ significantly from much of her short fiction, written under the sign of desire.

In "Bella-Vista," Colette claims to relate events from her past, when she was obliged to spend some time in a pension in the south of France while workmen were renovating a house she had recently purchased in the environs. Her narrative records the steps in her discovery of at least the partial truth surrounding the proprietors of the hotel, Mme Suzanne and Mme Ruby, and one of their mysteriously sinister guests, a certain M. Daste. Colette soon guesses that Mme Suzanne, an attractive, middle-aged woman who shoulders the major responsibilities of running the establishment, and Mme Ruby, a "virile" American in her fifties, who limits her contributions to lifting heavy suitcases and doing minor repair work, enjoy an intimate relationship. Through a series of surprising revelations, the reader learns that Mme Ruby is actually a man named Richard, concealing his true identity because he is wanted by the police for a crime the nature of which remains undisclosed. As for M. Daste, the reader is left to speculate in horror at his diabolical nature, since he disappears at the story's end after having brutally murdered all 19 of Mme Ruby / Richard's pet parakeets.

Although revisions Colette made between the time the story first appeared in installments and its publications in volume form testify to her effort to pare down its prose, the story seems to be curiously lacking in structure.[76] The two principal plot lines, one following the relationship between the hotel proprietors, and the other concerned with the sadistic behavior of M. Daste, intersect only minimally, when Daste and Mme Ruby / Richard clash briefly during a card game. The disagreement might account for M. Daste's final murderous gesture as an act of revenge, but there is nothing explicit in the story to support this conclusion. Furthermore, the plot does not terminate in resolution, for in the end, Colette, having learned just enough to assure herself that she wants nothing more do to with the people she has met at the Bella-Vista, hastily departs, leaving behind almost as many unanswered questions as she found at the beginning of her stay.

Closer examination of the story suggests that its loose organizational framework may be related to another of its features, that distinguishes it significantly from the majority of Colette's writing: the privileging of sight above the other senses. Passages in which light and dark are contrasted, plot developments that depend upon what is seen (and not seen), metaphors equating vision with insight or understanding, and even the title of the story (substituted before publication for the original one, "*Belle Encontre*")[77] serve to reinforce the primacy of sight. Furthermore, an inspection of manuscript variants reveals that, although Colette introduced few changes into the original version, she did consistently replace abstract terms with words drawn from the visual domain. Faced at the outset with what she refers to in her introduction as characters who are "unreadable," Colette makes unsuccessful attempts to discover the true nature of the three enigmatic people she meets. That she should liken the experience to the act of reading underscores the extent to which the visual directs her inquiry.

When Colette arrives at the pension, she immediately asks to change the room she has been assigned for one with a southwest exposure. From the vantage of her window, she has a direct view of the garage where the hapless parakeets are sheltered and the terrace-courtyard, scene of a significant exchange of glances between Mme Ruby / Richard and Lucie, the young maid who has caught his fancy. Although she only hears the conversation between Mme Ruby and Mme Suzanne during which the former's identity is unmasked, the revelation is accompanied by the passage of light from the couple's bedroom to Colette's through her window, marking the exact moment of the narrator's (and the reader's) "illumination." The progress of the narrative thus relies upon what the narrator, as detached spectator, has seen with her own eyes. In fact, although in several stories discussed earlier Colette insists upon her role as distanced observer, in no other does she succeed to the same degree in avoiding any direct involvement in the events that unfold around her.

The effect of her detachment is most dramatically evident on a stylistic level, in several descriptive passages of the seacoast. Colette is quick to establish her indifference to the Mediterranean, which, in her judgment, compares unfavorably to the teeming, tumultuous Atlantic she has come to know in Brittany. The Mediterranean she claims, is "the empty sea, over which shadows of white clouds skimmed in dark green patches," characterized by "feeble waves that rose and fell without advancing or retreating" (CS, 570). Drawing principally on visual perceptions, her descriptions convey an impression of immobility, of impermeable surfaces concealing, beneath their smooth, unchanging exteriors, a sterile emptiness.

Colette's cool dismissal of the southern coast in "Bella-Vista" stands in sharp contrast to the following passage taken from her novel, *The Break of Day*, in which her description of the same region shares more with the complex interaction between language and the external world encountered in the other stories discussed in this section. "We have walked on the coast road, its most populated part, the narrow flowery marsh where hemp agrimony, statice, and scabious contribute three shades of mauve, the tall flowering reed its cluster of brown edible seeds, the myrtle its white scent—white, white and bitter, prickling the tonsils, white to the point of causing nausea and ecstasy—the tamarisk its rosy mist and the bulrush its beaver-furred club."[78]

The passage, which continues for a page or more, dispels any notion of the sterile and impassive seascape described in "Bella-Vista," while at the same time conveying the narrator's susceptibility to its appeal. In fact, the synesthesia (e.g., "white scent—white to the point of causing nausea and ecstasy") underlying the imagery here is evidence of the narrator's total involvement in the experience, enriched by the active participation of all her senses. Unlike the perplexed narrator of "Bella-Vista," the Colette of *Break of Day* perceptively grasps the interpretative powers she wields in her symbiotic relationship with the world, as the following quotation indicates. "Dawn comes, the wind falls. From yesterday's rain, in the shade, a new perfume is born; or is it I who am once again going to discover the world and apply new senses to it? . . ."[79]

The dynamic engagement of the self with the world intrinsic to so much of Colette's fiction is thwarted in "Bella-Vista" by the distanced, detached gaze of a disaffected narrator. This fact invites a more general consideration of the story's privileging of sight. Vision, which since the Greeks has been directly linked to knowledge in Western thought, has long been accorded a superior status among the senses. The position sight has enjoyed as "the most discriminating and trustworthy of the sensual mediators between man and the world"[80] can be explained by certain features distinguishing it from the other senses. "Sight does not require our being part of the material world in the way feeling by touch does. . . . The directness of seeing when contrasted with hearing, its non-involvement with the object when contrasted with feeling by touching, and its apparent temporal immediacy when contrasted with both feeling and hearing are features that may partly explain the belief that sight is the most excellent of the senses."[81]

Nevertheless, the very properties that have insured the primacy of sight among the senses can, from a different angle, be understood as inhibiting perception and distorting reality. A number of twentieth-century French thinkers, including Luce Irigaray, Hélène Cixous and Michel Foucault, have in fact begun to examine the problematic implications of according a superior status to vision. This interrogation of vision has been so pervasive that at least one critic has concluded, "it is legitimate to talk of a discursive or paradigm shift in twentieth century French thought in which the denigration of vision supplanted its previous celebration."[82]

Among feminist critics there has been a particular insistence on the inadequacy of the "male logic" of the visual to translate female experience. Cixous, for example, argues that the emphasis on visibility which is the cornerstone of Freud's explanation of sexual difference serves to devalue feminine desire.[83] In a similar vein, Irigaray reasons that "the prevalence of the gaze, discrimination of form, and individualization of form is particularly foreign to female eroticism," suggesting that for women, the primary locus of pleasure is touch rather than sight.[84] In assessing the philosophical pertinence of French feminist critiques of ocular-centrism, Evelyn Fox Keller and Christine Grontowski find the hierarchical advantage enjoyed by sight in traditional Western thought less troubling than the sustained emphasis on the "de-eroticization of the visual." They maintain that a definition of knowledge founded, even if only metaphorically, on the atemporal, objectifying aspects of sight denies that seeing is a dynamic process permitting the possibility of exchange. Such a static, disengaged notion of the transparent gaze rules out the "latent eroticism" of visual experience, thus safeguarding knowledge from desire.[85]

As the comparison cited above suggests, the de-eroticized gaze that prevails in "Bella-Vista," because it plays down the communicative capacity of vision through the exchange of glances, and ignores the active role of sight, is fundamentally at odds with the kind of knowing derived from mingling the self with the external world through experience that is commonly found in Colette's short fiction.

The need to sort out appearances from reality provides a pretext for the narrative, as Colette's search for the elusive truth prolongs her interest in the characters and events. Yet, as the story line becomes more and more diffuse, the reader's attention is inevitably diverted by the imposing, inescapable presence of the narrator to the processes of Colette's interrogation. The focus of interest thus shifts from what she knows to how she knows, or perhaps more accurately, to the point of intersection between the two. How does the manner in which she knows come to shape what she knows?

Presenting the narrator with certain enigmas, each character also offers differing degrees of resistance to her inquiring gaze. Mme Suzanne, described as "a striking person, one of those who make an instant, detailed physical impression" (CS, 561), appears to be the most easily decipherable. Colette's initial impression of the woman, stressing her openness, is couched in visual references. "Before I had even spoken to her, I already knew by heart the pleasant shape of her hands baked by the sun and much cooking, her gold signet ring, her small wide-nostriled nose, her piercing glance which plunged straight into one's own eyes . . ." (CS, 561).

Intrigued by Mme Ruby's androgynous qualities, Colette seems to have greater difficulty determining her nature. At first, she is quite taken with her masculine qualities, remarking, "There was something definitely attractive about her wide, grey eyes, her unassuming nose, her big mouth with its seemingly indestructible teeth, and her skin, which was freckled over the cheekbones" (CS, 562). As we have seen in other stories, Colette draws here upon the figures of paradox and oxymoron to launch a subtle challenge of cultural norms, describing Mme Ruby at first as "scandalous and personable, pleasantly virile" (CS, 562, my translation). Underscoring the seductive appeal of the cross-dresser's sexual ambiguity, which is produced through concealment, Colette's positive response is later tempered when she observes Mme Ruby brushing her hand over Lucie's hair, "Far from avoiding my look, Mme Ruby's own took on a victorious malice which drew attention to Lucie's distress so indiscreetly that, for a moment, I ceased to find the boyish woman sympathetic" (CS, 573). The narrator's prescient disaffection, confirmed by Mme Ruby's unmasking, is caused by what the reader is encouraged to regard as Richard's *real* perversion: his *staging* of lesbianism.

In contrast, the narrator makes almost no headway at all in unraveling the mystery of M. Daste, who continually thwarts her efforts to comprehend his character. When her curiosity is first aroused by this strange man, she innocently asks Mme Suzanne, "And who is M. Daste?" The simple woman naïvely replies, "A very nice man . . . I believe what I see. It's the best way, don't you think? . . . Have you seen him, by the way?" (CS, 568). Colette's answer, the single word, "poorly," quite clearly reveals her tendency here to confuse seeing and understanding.

M. Daste seems, in fact, to be impervious to her insistent stare, to lack color and contour: "He was neither ugly nor deformed, only rather mediocre, made to attract as little attention as possible . . ." (CS, 568); "he gave a general appearance of grayness, gray suit, gray hair, and a grayish tinge in his small-featured face . . ." (CS, 566); "he had a stingy face which looked all the more stingy when his eyelids were closed" (CS, 568). Surprising him near the parakeets' cage, she suspects foul play and scans his face for signs of malice: "His gaze wandered from the birds to me and back again. I could read nothing in that pleasant neutral face, as far removed from ugliness as it was from beauty . . ." (CS, 576).

M. Daste is not the first of Colette's male characters to resist a woman's probing gaze. As Marcelle Biolley-Godino demonstrates in her thorough study, descriptions of men in Colette's fiction frequently seem to play over apparently impenetrable surfaces. For example, in the novel *Chéri*, an aging courtesan perceives her younger lover as an enigmatic, inaccessible marble statue. "An unreadable thought rose in the depths of his eyes whose form, whose gilliflower color, whose alternating severe or sad brilliance only aided him in conquering rather than revealing his mind. His nude torso, large through the shoulders, slim about the waist, emerged from the mussed sheets as from foam and all his being breathed forth the melancholy of perfect things."[86]

While the description may disclose precious little about this young Adonis, by deflecting her adoring gaze back onto the heroine, it speaks volumes about her desire. Filtering experiences and perceptions through its refracting lense, desire gives coherence to the narrative. Deprived of such a unifying thread, the narrator of "Bella-Vista" is no more capable of breaking through the barrier M. Daste presents to her than she is able to fathom the depths of the passively resistant Mediterranean.

On only one occasion does Colette sense a more agreable side to M. Daste, previously concealed from her gaze. When he returns from a daytrip with an odd wound on his cheek (inflicted, he admits mysteriously and ominously, by a bird), she finds something curiously comforting in his appearance. "The bruise which was now clearly visible around the little triangular wound on his cheek made him seem, for some reason, likeable, less definitely human. I like a fox terrier to have a round spot by its eye and a tortoiseshell cat to show an orange crescent or a black patch on its temple" (CS, 587). It is important to note here that the narrator finds both M. Daste and Mme Ruby / Richard more sympathetic when at least their appearance suggests that they are contradicting established norms, and in so doing, transgressing fixed boundaries. As he momentarily hovers between the human and nonhuman, M. Daste gains fleeting approval. While masquerading as a woman, Richard exhibits appealing androgynous qualities that are ultimately betrayed the moment he is revealed to be nothing more than an aging lethario, in drag only to avoid police detection.

In her efforts to sort through the appearances that confound her, Colette is foiled by her reliance upon cognitive, rational processes that equate seeing with knowing. She remains alienated, so incapable of deriving meaning from what she has witnessed, so disengaged from the world of false appearances, that the only recourse left to her is retreat. Although the narrator's alienation is conveyed by the story's neutral tone, the text also offers brief glimpses of another kind of discourse that finds its source in the affective domain of experience. Explaining the private code of communication she established with her dog Pati, Colette writes, "She was called Pati when it was necessary for us both to be on our best behavior, Pati-Pati when it was time for her walk, Pati-Pati-Pati and even more when we were playing. Thus we had adapted her name to all the essential circumstances of our life" (CS, 563).

Her use of language to expand meaning in this instance appears to coincide rather closely with Julia Kristeva's observations on women's writing practice. "All my reading of women's texts leaves me with the impression that the notion of the signifier as a network of distinctive marks is insufficient, because each of these marks is loaded, beyond its discriminatory value, with a libidinal or emotional force that, strictly speaking, is not signified but rather remains latent in the phonic invocation or in the inscribing gesture."[87] In Kristeva's terminology, then, Colette modulates meaning by overloading the signifier (Pati) with latent affective content derived from shared experience. A powerfully expressive undercurrent sets the communication described in this passage apart from the other uses of language in the story, offering a startling alternative to the transparent system of signification that prevails throughout the rest of the text. The neutral tone of the visually dominated discourse in "Bella-Vista" is punctuated here by the sort of "loaded" language that characterizes most of Colette's writing, a language suggesting that the self may achieve an accommodation with the world through the intervention of desire.

According to the critic Yannick Resch, what draws the reader into Colette's "pleasure text" is not the writer's accurate evocation of the real, but the seductive claim she lays on the world through the concerted application of her senses. As Resch puts it, "[Colette's] work is infiltrated with a hunger, an impatience to appropriate the sensory world, which gives her writing a certain emotional quality. . . . For her, capturing the real takes on the guise of a project: to fix a fleeting impression, sensation, or moment. The reader becomes engaged in a sort of jubilatory exploration of the real, which often strikes a familiar chord with something in his or her own experience."[88]

Bewildered by the discrete, undifferentiated visual messages she receives, the narrator of "Bella-Vista" cannot enlist her desire in the cause of interpreting experience. Her confusion heightens the reader's own alienation (linked through identification with the narrator) from the story's uncommon perversions: sadistic acts against the natural world and homosexuality as masquerade. The total disengagement of the narrator, who encounters a world that by her strictly amoral standards is both unnatural and perverse, deprives looking of its pleasure. The reader's "jubilatory exploration" is thus thwarted by an emotional detachment that pervades the text, and which thus indirectly valorizes the eroticized experience that is generally a source of knowledge and understanding in Colette's fiction.

The Narrator as Quick-Change Artist

In Colette's short fiction, objective reality is repeatedly subordinated to knowledge gained through the collaborative effort of the senses. In the process the object, whether a garden-variety snail or a handsome yet vacuous lover, is reduced to the role of supporting the subject's desire, longing, pleasure, or anguish. In "Flora and Pomona," published in the same volume as "The Photographer's Wife" and "The Sick Child," Colette claims that the orchids she describes defy scientific labels, for they are "creatures mad for imitation, disguised as birds, hymenoptera, open wounds, sex organs."[89] Seduced into questioning an easy allegiance to "reality" by this highly evocative and suggestive set of images, the reader is at the same time not permitted to forget the existence of the actual flowers thus "disguised." Their material immutability, lying outside of the charmed circle inscribed by the writer's eroticized gaze, is affirmed through the litany of their scientific names ("miltonia," "aristolochia," etc.).

The gap separating the technical terms for flowers from their polysemic poetic images, or the accepted sense of "presbytery" from the meaning conjured up by the untrammeled imagination of a young child, is inhabited by a desire or longing that transforms objects without, however, completely abolishing their material models. The nagging resistance of those models to the attack launched by the perceiving subject is accomplished on a narrative level by a shifting perspective, which places the narrator (and the reader) simultaneously in two positions that are nevertheless separated by an insuperable distance.[90] In "The Abduction," discussed in the section devoted to mother / daughter relations, the narrator declares herself to be a mother recounting her experiences as a little girl. She therefore identifies with both the small child whose erotic dream of abduction excludes its implicit dangers, and the mother with whom she shares an understanding gained from adult knowledge of the world. Her tone, her choice of language, her subtly shifting voice, allow her to speak at once for both the rebellious child, who stubbornly defends her right to an existence (and a language) outside the Symbolic order (the world "out there" threatening to coerce her into submission to the codes and constraints of culture), and the gently mocking alter ego of the maternal law enforcer.

Gliding effortlessly between the roles of object and observer, the narrator of Colette's short stories often ably negotiates between these two poles without identifying exclusively with either one. In the texts cited above, the positions of subject and object are clearly delineated in recognizable roles (mother, child, mature and authoritative writer) as well as by the "real life" author's relation to each. In other stories, in which the tie between subject and alter ego is less obvious, or the position of the narrator more elusive, the "cat-and-mouse" game of shifting perspectives and doubled voices leaves the reader uncertain about how to establish meaning.

One such story, whose complex narrative perspective has encouraged varying and often contradictory interpretations since it was first published in the collection entitled *Bella-Vista* in 1937, is "The Rendezvous," one of the rare third-person narratives among Colette's longer works of short fiction. The story, set in Morocco, is ostensibly told from the point of view of Bernard Bonnemains, an architect vacationing with Cyril and Odette Bessier and their recently widowed sister-in-law, Rose. Bernard, who is "exactly thirty, [with] no rich clients and not much money" (CS, 471), has an amorous liaison with Rose which, out of fear of family opposition, he is struggling to keep secret, hoping that Cyril will ask him to become his partner, thus taking the place of the deceased younger Bessier. His seething antagonism towards the Bessiers, particularly towards Odette, whom he views as an aggressive, interfering "female," is surpassed only by his reluctance to compromise his position by offending them.

Frustrated in his efforts to pursue his affair with Rose, Bernard finally arranges, through a series of subterfuges whose success is dependent on Rose's complete complicity, for a late-night assignation. The two slip out of their hotel rooms and, trembling with pent-up desire, hasten to a clearing chosen earlier in the day by Bernard. While inspecting the ground before spreading out Rose's raincoat, Bernard comes across the body of a man bleeding from a knife wound to the arm. On closer inspection, he discovers Ahmed, a young Arab boy employed at their hotel, who has apparently had a fight with a rival over the affections of a local woman.

After bandaging the injured man's wounds with strips of cloth torn from his shirt, Bernard tries to convince Rose to go for help. By refusing to risk exposing her indiscretion for fear of scandal, Rose provokes

Bernard's anger, and with an embittered outburst directed at both Rose and the "bourgeois" Bessiers, he sends her packing. The story ends with an apparently complacent Bernard "[watching] the morning dawn and [tasting] a contentment, a surprise as fresh as love but less restricted and totally detached from sex" (CS, 496). As he waits beside a sleeping Ahmed for help to arrive, he dismisses the woman he desired so fervently with the thought, "She was my woman but this one here is my counterpart. It's queer that I had to come all the way to Tangiers to find my counterpart, the only person to make me proud of him and proud of myself. With a woman, it's so easy to be a little ashamed, either of her or of oneself. My wonderful counterpart! He had only to appear . . ." (CS, 496).

Judging from review articles written in 1937 and 1938, most of Colette's contemporaries were considerably less puzzled by the story than modern-day readers, for they naively assumed a perfect concordance between the protagonist, narrator and author. Lauding Colette's accurate depiction of recognizable female types, one critic characterized Odette as a "vulgar woman" of the sort encountered all too frequently "in Paris and elsewhere," while another found Rose representative of the "incredible stupidity and monstrous selfishness of the infatuated European woman, who would rather leave an Arab to die than risk soiling her coat or her reputation." For yet another, Colette's negative portraits of the two sisters-in-law confirmed her underlying misogyny.

The story's denouement was often viewed as championing the superiority of "fraternity" over less rewarding romantic liaisons with frivolous or vulgar women. Witness the following summary of the story's message: "A handsome chap suddenly discovers that the woman whom he desired, and even thought he loved, is much less important to him than the combined comradery, fraternity, devotion, and charity that he encounters under circumstances in which, finally delivered from sensuality, he has the opportunity to dedicate himself to another man." The redemptive quality of Bernard's decision was generally underscored, as critics contrasted the purity of his gesture with the baseness and mediocrity of the two women.[91]

Among the readers emphasizing the theme of homosociality was Colette's third husband, Maurice Goudeket, who rhapsodized about his wife's success in painting so accurate a picture of male bonding.

> This short story has, within Colette's work, a unique resonance. At the site of a rendezvous, at the very moment when between a man

and a woman the ritual of love-making is about to take place, a weak cry reveals the presence of a young native, wounded during a fight. This single cry suspends all desires in the man's heart except the urge to come to the aid of his fellow man in distress, even if he is only an insignificant youth. And so, he lets his female companion take off, in a rage.

I wasn't the only one to admire the fact that a woman could write such a virile story. This secret between men, this strong solidarity which is fostered by war and the rallying of troops, this complicity, which we imagine to be beyond women's understanding, was not sheltered from Colette's penetrating gaze.[92]

Other readers, attributing more self-interested motives to Bernard's supposedly humanitarian gesture, deplored the signs of a veiled homosexuality they found in the story. For example, in his review for *Mercure de France* in 1938, John Carpentier remarked "If the hero of 'The Rendezvous' accomplishes an act of humanity which releases him from a degrading passion, he only frees himself through sensuality. The escape proposed to him by his guardian angel, so to speak, is on a par with animality."[93] Carpentier's reference to the story's homoerotic overtones signals his implicit understanding that the exotic North African setting, suggesting all that the "Orient" had symbolized for centuries in the imagination of the average French reader, would have an inevitable erotic appeal. Serving as a reminder of the beautiful, young Arab boys that awaken the protagonist of Gide's *The Immoralist* to the possibilities of physical pleasure, Ahmed is an inseparable element of the sensual phantasm that the Moroccan decor calls forth. Carpentier's moral outrage notwithstanding, his reading certainly builds upon well-known literary commonplaces.

Given the certainty with which her contemporaries approached this story, in spite of their often diametrically opposed conclusions, a reader attuned to Colette's careful manipulation of narrative perspective may be less certain of interpreting "The Rendezvous" correctly. My own initial notes are peppered with questions. "Do the insights into Bernard's thoughts, the only subjectivity the story allows for, invite sympathy with his denigration of women? Is the story to be read as a transposition into male terms of the positive female bonding experience that figures so prominently in other Colette stories? And what of the class and racial implications of 'The Rendezvous' "?

The difficulty of answering these questions definitively was brought home to me when, in trying to write an objective plot summary of the story, I discovered its unstable perspective; the indeterminacy of both characters and events made even this straightforward task problematic. For example, the reference to Bernard's financial circumstances is taken from a passage relating Odette's frequent reminders of his inferior social and economic status: " 'Bernard had better not count his chickens before they are hatched,' Odette was in the habit of saying, whenever she thought it expedient to recall the fact that Bonnemains was exactly thirty, had no rich clients and not much money." The only information about Bernard's background supplied by the narrative is thus colored by the caustic irony of a character who is herself presented, for the most part, negatively *and* from the protagonist's limited viewpoint.

The complex handling of the story's narrative perspective encourages multiple readings, undermining the assumptions of unitary point of view that guided Colette's contemporaries. For example, despite Bernard's humane act and defiant dismissal of the bourgeois prejudices and crass self-interest of his traveling companions, he seems unlikely as a self-sacrificing hero, able to achieve a certain transcendence through solidarity with other men. There are too many inconsistencies between Bernard's final gesture, described in his own words and thoughts, which stress its sincerity and egalitarian thrust, and the occasional glimpses of a less appealing side to his personality.

For example, Bonnemains only permits his suppressed anger to surface in rare, unexpected outbursts that, because they are not explained, make him seem like a small child in the throes of a temper tantrum. On more than one occasion, his unrealized fantasies highlight his reticence to take any action that might compromise his financial stability. Speculating about what might happen if he were to unleash the fury of his sexual frustration on the insensitive Odette, he thinks, " 'If I didn't control myself, I'd remind her there was such a thing as decency.' But he did control himself, wincing like a starving man reminded of food" (CS, 471). Bernard's recurring daydreams of taking a stand, speaking his mind to the Bessiers, overpowering Rose as a means of seeking revenge on "the others," never materialize, leaving an overall impression of weakness and impotence that is never fully effaced by his last, defiant act.

The hint of self-delusion that emerges from the scene in which Bernard exchanges a passionate glance with Rose under the watchful eye of Odette, and then turns away from her "with a cowardice which he told himself was discretion" (CS, 474), serves to raise the specter of doubt about the motivations underlying Bernard's surprising choice at the end of the story. High-minded and noble as his gesture may appear, the parting image is that of Bernard, liberated from the chafing role of frustrated suitor and subservient fortune seeker, eager to assume the dominant position in a self-declared alliance with his unlikely "counterpart."

The last paragraph brings together the contradictory motives animating Bernard, leaving the reader the difficult task of sorting through them. "Before lifting Ahmed, Bonnemains tested the knots of his amateur dressing. Then he wrapped his arms around the sleeping boy, inhaled the sandalwood scent of his black hair, and clumsily kissed his cheek, which was already virile and rough. He estimated the young man's weight as he might have done that of a child of his own flesh or that of a quarry one kills only once in a lifetime" (CS, 497). Although the second sentence of the passage cited above conveys a suggestion of homoerotic desire, it also appears to contradict Bernard's assertion that his attraction to his "counterpart" (in French, the word is *semblable*, meaning literally "fellow," or "equal") is based on the bond of similarity. In fact, Ahmed's odor of sandalwood and his black hair, both evoking the exotic, call attention to his otherness as the main feature of his appeal. Furthermore, the two analogies in the last sentence conjure up vastly different images, the first evoking protective tenderness and selfless love (that of a parent for a defenseless child, or that of a lover enthralled by the touch and smell of his cherished loved one), the other suggesting control, conquest, and domination (of hunter over prey).

If the insights into Bernard's character provided by the narrative favor the second image, making his gesture a self-serving quest for power by an ineffectual man, parallels with other Colette short stories support the first image, in which escape from adversity is achieved through solidarity with fellow women. Bernard's retreat from love recalls the novella, *The Toutounier* (1939) and the collection of vignettes, *The Tendrils of the Vine* (1908), in which female characters assuage the pain they have suffered in heterosexual relations gone awry by establishing intimacy with other women. In short, Colette's story leaves unanswered the question of whether Bernard is a good Samaritan who finds comfort in identifying with his "counterpart," a dissatisfied middle-class Frenchman who discovers, in the stereotypical "sensuality" of an African setting, the pleasures of either homosocial or homosexual relations, or, as Marie-Christine Bellosta would have it, "a failed painter, an unsuccessful architect," whose sudden commitment to male solidarity is his way of compensating for feelings of frustration and powerlessness.[94]

As one of a collection of stories that interrogate community attitudes towards gender and sexuality ("Bella-Vista"), incest ("The Patriarch"), and abortion ("Gribiche"), "The Rendezvous," while flirting with such potentially controversial issues as homosexuality, colonial myths of the Orient, and bourgeois complacency, resists espousing any particular moral position. The reader cannot comfortably seek answers to the questions that have been posed from an authoritative narrative voice, since its position has been effectively destabilized. As a result, the very openness of the text, its polysemic ambiguity, serves as a challenge to the rigid social codes upon which a linear reading of the story might otherwise be predicated.

In "Rainy Moon," published in 1940 in the volume entitled *Chance Acquaintances*, the image of the narrator's past self is revived through the introduction of a textual alter ego, a technique that results in a proliferation of narrative "I's." Here, the doubling effect leads to an intermingling of the self (or selves, since the ghost of the younger Colette is called forth) and the other. As narrator / protagonist, Colette is forced to confront painful memories when she discovers Rosita Barberet, the typist whom she has recently hired, lives in the same apartment that she, Colette, occupied following the breakup of a romantic relationship. The coincidence is compounded after Colette meets Rosita's sister, Délia, who is nursing emotional wounds inflicted by an unfaithful husband. Colette is immediately drawn to Délia, whom she envisions at times as a reflection of her younger self. Her attraction for this eerie reminder of her past is tempered by her reluctance to relive the suffering with which it is inextricably allied.

When Colette arrives one day at the Barberet apartment and finds Délia lying inert before the front door, Rosita accounts for her sister's bizarre behavior with oblique references to black magic and the occult. She finally confesses to Colette that Délia is plotting to kill her husband, Eugène. Having attempted to "summon" him by repeating his name, she has taken to weaving an evil spell (Rosita hints darkly at sharp needles dipped in foul substances). Unsettled by these strange occurrences, Colette renounces further contact with the troubling, yet strangely fascinating sisters, vowing to turn them into a memory. Despite her decision to avoid the Barberets, she catches a glimpse of Délia quite by chance on several occasions, looking "pale and diminished, like a convalescent who is out too soon" (CS, 386). At the story's end, the narrator runs across a visibly restored Délia, devouring a large bag of fried potatoes with obvious gusto. Her apparently calm and complacent demeanor is in contrast to her apparel, a black dress and hat, adorned with the unmistakable white crepe band of a widow.

Colette prefaces the story by calling attention to her role as writer, comparing her own affinity for the past to the preferences of Proust. "Marcel Proust, gasping with asthma amid the bluish haze of fumigations and the shower of pages dropping from him one by one, pursued a bygone and completed time. It is neither the true concern nor the natural inclination of writers to love the future. They have quite enough to do with being incessantly forced to invent their characters' future, which, in any case, they draw from the well of their own past. Mine, whenever I plunge into it, makes me dizzy." In light of Colette's self-proclaimed aversion for theoretical pronouncements (or for pronouncements of any kind, for that matter) on the craft of writing, this brief passage, in which she casually aligns herself with one of the most accomplished French writers of her time, should give the reader pause. For Colette is foregrounding at once both the autobiographical (conventionally understood as referential) underpinnings of the tale she is about to tell and its status as invention, by calling attention to herself as a writer who creates characters and their futures.

Referentiality is emphasized here, as in many of the stories previously discussed, by liberally incorporating elements of verifiable reality into the fictional narrative. For example, the Colette character prepares stories for publication in periodicals the names of which would be immediately recognizable to the reading public of her time, and she goes on carefree picnics in the Bois de Boulogne with her real friend, Annie de Pène. Historical grounding is further reinforced by passing references to Colette's contemporaries, Proust, Francis Carco, and Pierre Veber.

On the other hand, several passages counteract easy referentiality with reminders of the artifice of fiction, stressing the act of writing. Remarking that, despite her efforts, she was never able to complete the serial novelette she had initially asked Rosita to type, Colette admits to a loathing for the " 'action' and swift adventure" that are requisite elements of successful popular fiction. The unwritten story to which she alludes stands in sharp contrast to the written one, "Rainy Moon," with its rambling, disjointed structure, its discursive insouciance, and its penchant for subtle detail. The implicit comparison heightens the reader's awareness of the story's divergence from established convention, suggesting that an alternative reading approach may be needed. In a passage that modestly plays down her literary imagination, Colette confesses that her "rational view of things" makes her cling to the distinction "between fact and possibility, between an event and the narration of it" (CS, 358). Her praise for those writers who succeed in conflating these seemingly contradictory terms serves ironically to direct attention to boundaries that, in the majority of her stories, are carefully and cleverly concealed.

If self-reflexivity is clearly not a hallmark of Colette's short fiction, neither are black magic and the occult. Yet interestingly, the intersection of these two apparently anomalous features of "Rainy Moon," when considered in the light of Freudian psychoanalytic theory, furnishes one key to approaching the story.[95] In a 1919 article, Freud used the German word "*unheimlich*," literally "not of the home," to define a phenomenon he described as "that class of the frightening which leads back to what is known of old and long familiar."[96] Since the word's opposite, "*heimlich*," can signify both "familiar, agreeable" and "concealed, out of sight, or unfamiliar," Freud notes that the term, which in its positive form suggests the familiar, may contain within it hidden, fear-provoking dangers. The uncanny, as the phenomenon has come to be called in English translations of Freud, is therefore "something which is familiar and old-established in the mind and which has become alienated from it only through the process of repression."[97] One important characteristic of repressed material is that, while it is subject to the repulsion of the consciousness, it also exercises a counterbalancing attraction "upon everything with which it can establish a connection,"[98] thus accounting for the involuntary recurrence of uncanny effects.

There are two other points in Freud's essay that help elucidate "Rainy Moon." First, in enumerating the categories of the uncanny, among the most prominent themes that emerge is the figure of the double, possessing "knowledge, feelings and experience" in common with the subject. By identifying with another, Freud explains, the self seeks protection from the threatening effects of the operations of the conscience, a critical agency capable of treating the rest of the ego like an object. By ascribing unrealized, and potentially dangerous, fantasies to the figure of the double, the self takes a protective measure that allows it to project outward that which has been repressed. Second, in evaluating the functioning of the uncanny in literature, Freud maintains that only works that profess to "move in the world of common reality" can have uncanny effects, resulting from the shock created when the imaginary is inserted into a realistic setting.[99] Thus purely fantastic literature, such as fairy tales, cannot produce uncanny effects.

The implications of Freud's essay for "Rainy Moon" are suggestive. It would be hard to imagine a more *"heimlich"* atmosphere, in the full and contradictory sense of the term, than the one that pervades "Rainy Moon," from the moment the narrator arrives at the Barberets' apartment. Although Colette used to live in the same neighborhood, she is so disoriented by the changes that have taken place since her departure that she cannot even locate her street, which has either disappeared or changed its name. As she looks out the window in an attempt to get her bearings, her hand falls upon its unmistakably familiar hasp, shaped like a mermaid, and the unanticipated jolt of memory elicits "the rather pleasant giddiness that accompanies dreams of falling and flying" (CS, 348). From then on, the past continues "to raise its dripping mermaid's head" (CS, 351), reinforcing the alienating homeliness of the place: the wallpaper with its "ghost of a bunch of flowers, repeated a hundred times all over the walls" (CS, 348), the ceiling rose, and the "rainy moon," the narrator's fond name for a prism of rainbow colors projected on the wall by sunlight passing through a flaw in the windowpane.

The impression of unfamiliar familiarity intensifies when Colette leaves the apartment after her first visit: "From the pavement, I studied my house, unrecognizable under a heavy makeup of mortar. The hall, too, was well disguised and now, with its dado of pink and green tiles, reminded me of the baleful chilliness of those mass-produced villas on the Riviera" (CS, 350). Exuding pungent memories of a poorly buried past, the apartment and its environs are disguised not only by the changes introduced over time but also, undoubtedly, by the imperfect veiling of repression. In the dreamlike state brought on by the confused messages she is receiving, Colette's estrangement surfaces with a textual *"frisson,"* expressed in the "baleful chilliness" of those undifferentiated Provençal houses that are devoid of both memories and meaning.

The uncanniness of the experience is heightened when Colette finally meets Rosita's sister, whose mirroring function is presaged when Rosita remarks that Délia has changed her name, roughly inverting the syllables of her christened name, Adèle.[100] Entering the bedroom she recognizes as formerly hers, Colette is taken aback, "For a second, I had that experience only dreams dare conjure up: I saw before me, hostile, hurt, stubbornly hoping, the young self I should never be again, whom I never ceased disowning and regretting" (CS, 360). Colette's response reenacts the dual movement of repression, as she at once disavows and yearns for this vision of her former self, "that sad form stuck like a petal between two pages, to the walls of an ill-starred refuge" (CS, 367). Admitting that she has been continually haunted by the nightmare of coming face-to-face with her alter ego, Colette explicitly acknowledges what she most fears: dredging up old disappointments in love. "They are the least worthy of being brought back to mind, but sometimes they behave just like a cut in which a fragment of hair is hidden; they heal badly" (CS, 352). The comparison is an apt image for the nagging return of the repressed. Colette's description of her state of mind when she met the Barberets suggests the concealed presence of that "sad form" from her past, which continues to worry the wound inflicted by her own painful love affair: "a private life that was clouded and uncertain, a solitude that bore no resemblance to peace . . ." (CS, 362).

Délia is further allied with the uncanny when it becomes clear that she is engaging in the practice of witchcraft. According to Freud, techniques of magic are linked to that which is "familiar and old-established" because they revive residues of the previously surmounted animistic belief in the omnipotence of thought and imagination (i.e., the idea that wishing something can make it happen) (Freud, 240). When an exasperated Colette criticizes Délia for her apparent indolence, she protests that the "work" she is doing in her head is every bit as grueling as her sister's. Pressed to explain the exact nature of her work, she replies enigmatically that she is creating something "a bit like a novel, only better" (CS, 368).

Using supernatural powers to summon her husband, casting a spell on him, causing him to weaken and finally die, Délia expresses primitive, or perhaps infantile beliefs in the individual's mastery of the universe. There is not such a great distance, after all, separating Délia's (fictionlike) control of her husband's fate and the young Colette's (fanciful) victory over threats to the free exercise of her imagination (and her will) posed by the adult world. Like the child's dream of abduction, the story Délia is conjuring up asserts its creator's fervent desire to rewrite the drama in which she participates.

That drama is rewritten with the help of the most unlikely fatal instruments: sewing needles contaminated with poisonous substances, materializing Délia's vengeful feelings towards her husband. To reiterate a point made earlier in my discussion of "Chance Acquaintances," although needlework is traditionally a symbol of feminine domesticity and docility, in Colette's short fiction this seemingly innocuous activity more often than not masks subversive, or even, unlawful thoughts. In the case of "Rainy Moon," they are spectacularly realized. Here, Délia's handiwork proves to be a good deal more than the clever talent of an idle woman; Délia's self-declared "profession," her bead work, aided and abetted by her ritualistic repetition of her husband's name, succeeds in killing him.

As narrator / protagonist, Colette is particularly implicated in the tale of her character's exploits, since she so clearly acknowledges her undeniable link with Délia. Despite the narrator's efforts to maintain a distanced attitude towards the disturbing young woman during periods of wakefulness, her dreams divulge the extent to which her life is intermingled with Délia's on the level of the unconscious. "I kept relapsing into a nightmare in which I was now my real self, now identified with Délia. Half reclining like her on our own divan-bed, in the dark part of our room, I 'convoked' with a powerful summons, with a thousand repetitions of his name, a man who was not called Eugène" (CS, 385).

To fully explore the complex implications of the Colette / Délia connection, as well as its central importance in the story, I will need to return briefly to Freud, and specifically to his 1917 essay entitled "Mourning and Melancholia." In comparing the two complexes, Freud notes that in melancholia "the occasions which give rise to the illness extend for the most part beyond the clear case of a loss by death, and include all those situations of being slighted, neglected or disappointed."[101] In this account of the neurotic functioning of melancholia, the subject shifts reproaches against the loved object onto its own ego through narcissistic identification. Although a similar libidinal investment in the lost object also occurs during the mourning process, the subject in mourning can usually free its libido from the lost object, eventually mending the ego that was divided against itself by self-reproaches. With melancholia, recuperation is arrested by the subject's inability to resolve ambivalent feelings towards the (not fully) lost object. Thus, as Flieger concludes, "successful mourning seems to result in an identification that heals the ego, assimilating and integrating the fantoms that haunt it, while melancholia exacerbates the split in the ego, the internal warfare among ghosts, fraught with guilt and anguish."[102]

Freud illustrates the pernicious effects of this essentially negative process with an analogy particularly pertinent to "Rainy Moon" when he writes that "the complex of melancholia behaves like an open wound."[103] The narrator's explicit acknowledgment of her agitated state (a life "clouded and uncertain," a solitude that bears "no resemblance to peace"), the comparison of disappointments in love with "cuts that heal badly," her nightmares centering around the lost love object, and her immediate identification with an alter ego whose anguish "uncannily" mirrors and magnifies her own, paint a picture faithful to Freud's description of the melancholic subject. If the story is interpreted as a case study in melancholia, then the murder of the absent loved one opens the door for the healing of the injured ego, for with his death and utter disappearance, the true mourning process can begin. But, the question remains, what does Délia's rehabilitation, so clearly signalled by her robust appearance and healthy appetite in the final scene, have to do with the narrator? Is the reader to conclude that Eugène's death lays to rest the unnamed *revenant* from the narrator's past? If so, by what black (and white?) magic is the double murder accomplished?

By the end of the story, the attentive reader will discover that failed relationships are not the only thing the two central characters have in common. Just as Délia conquers the phantoms of her past, using the magical powers of the spoken word to seduce her errant husband into her web of witchcraft and deadly needles to sew up his sorry fate, the narrator exorcises the specter "not called Eugène" by weaving a text with her own tools of seduction: the written word and the pen. The therapeutic value of the story becomes explicit when the narrator places it in the category of "a particular kind of unremarkable and soothing event," reminiscent of "the dressing of wet clay and bits of twig, the marvelous little splint the snipe binds around its foot when a shot has broken it" (CS, 357). While this second reference to the narrator's painful wound is further proof that, like her counterpart, she still suffers from the "internal warfare among ghosts" characteristic of melancholia, the soothing effect that the story has on her implies a healing process that parallels Délia's.

Since the work of mourning is an active labor (remember that Délia contends she calls upon all her energies to achieve her goal), the narrator's role as storyteller must be asserted, so that she can reap the psychic benefits of her own creative act. In other words, for the narrator's story to serve her as a "snipe's bandage," she must affirm her authority over its production and in a sense, exposing the text's unconscious. By interspersing gentle reminders of the story's status as fiction into a narrative that nevertheless makes manifest its referential underpinnings, the narrator cleverly manages to preserve the conditions necessary for the uncanny to perform its work, while at the same time dropping tantalizing hints of her own collusion in inventing the events she describes.

Despite the detailed alibi the narrator offers to absolve herself from responsibility for the plot that unfolds, she occasionally allows the reader to see through her veil of innocence. For example, she remarks offhandedly that she refrained from telling Annie de Pène about the "Barberet story," for fear that her wise friend might guess the reason for her interest in the young women: "Would not Annie's subtle ear and lively bronze eyes have weighed and condemned everything in my narrative that revealed no more than the craving to go over old ground again, to deck out what was over and done with a new coat of paint?" (CS, 357). Furthermore, although the narrator staunchly clings to her rational skepticism in the face of the supernatural happenings with which she is confronted, she infiltrates the uncanny effects into the text in such a way as to lull the reader into accepting them, strange though they may seem. From the eerie projection of refracted light to the proliferation of coincidences, the narrative provides an accumulation of evidence that ultimately undermines the storyteller's level-headed rejection of the unexplained.

The narrator first creates a character who acts as her surrogate, and then, by cagily positioning herself in relation to the double's story, furnishes a "novellike" conclusion to her own pain and suffering. Although she cautiously disassociates herself from Délia's darker side, she is, in fact, the unindicted coconspirator of Délia's crime, chasing her own personal demons while shirking responsibility for her character's unlawful act. In a stunning demonstration of what Freud calls the storyteller's "peculiarly directive power,"[104] the law-abiding narrator exorcises the ghosts from her own past by telling the daring story of her fictional character's bold, defiant gesture.

The reader will recall that in "Green Sealing Wax" there is a similar doubling of the narrator with a female character whose personal account complements the autobiographical story line. While the Colette / Délia rapport is more clearly articulated than the link between the adolescent girl and the impetuous widow of "Green Sealing Wax," their shared circumstances should be evident from the previous discussion. In both stories, the deviant, sinister, and distinctly aggressive actions of the double, an unmistakable transgressor against the Law, provide a contrasting backdrop for the more conventional behavior of the narrator, whose discretion and common sense keep her safely within the bounds of accepted feminine conduct. Challenging the increasingly elusive dividing line between autobiography and fiction, author and character, subject and object, self and other, woman and writer, past and present, "Rainy Moon" is perhaps one of the most exemplary short stories in Colette's extraordinarily rich repertoire.

Conclusion

This study has endeavored to show that Colette, renowned as a novelist, whose bittersweet tales of love explore the deepest recesses of sensual pleasure, also deserves to be remembered as an accomplished and innovative short story writer. With great lyricism, coupled perhaps paradoxically with studied stylistic precision, she successfully molded this literary form to her own particular voice and vision. As her stories interrogate culturally sanctioned systems of meaning (moral, political, sexual, gendered, epistemological), they often challenge the time-honored rules governing the behavior of men and women in society. Yet Colette's writing never takes on a moralistic or preachy tone. Instead, through the orchestrated interplay of an unsettlingly mobile point of view with the brilliantly crafted language "of multiple desire,"[105] her stories invite readers to wonder, to speculate, and finally to call into question some of their most fundamental beliefs about human experience.

Many of the issues raised by the stories discussed in this study also surface in Colette's novels. For example, *Chéri*, the story of a middle-aged courtesan and her young lover, deals with the question of women and aging, while *Break of Day*, a cross between a memoir, a novel, and a prose poem, travels over the familiar terrain of mother-daughter relations, the aging process, and writing the self. Yet, Colette exploits the formal constraints (concision, brevity, economy) and the greater latitude for stylistic variation (including highly allusive, figural prose and elliptical language) provided by the short story in order to treat these themes with even greater acuity and insight.

A story like "The Abduction," for example, permits multiple, overlapping readings, all of which owe their force to the consummate skill with which the narrative unfolds. An engaging blend of earthy dialogue, loving reminiscence, and playful humor, the story counters romantic childhood fantasy with parental nightmares, a vivid pictorial representation of a kidnapping with a no less vivid (and a no less fictitious) literary version. In less than four pages, the text manages to convey the robust flavor of provincial life, the threatening yet enticing aura of erotic adventure, as well as the storyteller's inescapable presence in the temporal space encompassed between the first and last lines. Despite this story's brevity, readers who return to it for a second and third time will no doubt discover seemingly insignificant details that serve to enhance or modify their reading experience. The preceding analysis has sought to show that the same observation can be made about the majority of Colette's short fiction. If decoding her stories, situated as they are at the crossroads of gender, social origins, and genre, is dependent upon a reappraisal of conventional interpretive strategies, it is their very ambiguity and indeterminacy, their precarious location in ill-defined yet always potentially dangerous boundary zones, that ultimately contribute to their enduring literary interest.

Future studies of Colette's short fiction might benefit from a systematically sustained intertextual approach, as exemplified by certain passages excerpted from Lynne Huffer's book, *Another Colette*, included in Part Three of this book. Since my central purpose has been to provide an introduction to Colette's short stories, I have concentrated my efforts on close readings of individual texts, although I have occasionally alluded to fruitful points of comparison. Nevertheless, the remarkable unity of Colette's oeuvre suggests that contrasting the deployment of common themes or rhetorical figures in several stories would open them up to productive, new interpretations.

Notes to Part 1

1. Jacob Stockinger, "Impurity and Sexual Politics in the Provinces," *Women's Studies* 8 (1981): 359.

2. See the article by Gary M. Olson, Robert L. Mack, and Susan A. Duffy entitled "Cognitive Aspects of Genre," *Poetics* 10 (1981) for an informative discussion of strategies and expectations of short story readers.

3. Mary Louise Pratt, "The Long and the Short of It," *Poetics* 10 (1981): 176.

4. Marie-Laure Ryan, "On the Why, What and How of Generic Taxonomy," *Poetics* 10 (1981): 111–12.

5. *The Complete Works of Edgar Allen Poe*, XI, ed. James A. Harrison (1902; rpt. New York: AMS Press, 1965): 108.

6. *Henry James and H. G. Wells: A Record of their Friendship, their Debate on the Art of Fiction, and their Quarrel*, eds. Leon Edel and Gordon N. Ray (Urbana: University of Illinois Press, 1958), 140. As cited in Valerie Shaw, *The Short Story: A Critical Introduction* (New York: Longman, 1983), 48.

7. Ross Chambers, *Story and Situation* (Minneapolis: University of Minnesota Press, 1984), 4.

8. James Moffett and Kenneth R. McElheny, eds. *Points of View: An Anthology of Short Stories* (New York: Signet Classics, 1966), 147. As cited in Shaw, 83.

9. Marks, *Colette* (New Jersey, Rutgers University Press, 1960), 155.

10. Shaw, 192.

11. Frank O'Connor, *The Lonely Voice: A Study of the Short Story* (Cleveland and New York: World Publishing Co., 1962), 39.

12. Marks, *Colette*, 52.

13. Michèle Sarde, *Colette, Free and Fettered*, trans. Richard Miller (New York: William Morrow and Co., 1980).

14. Herbert Lottman, *Colette: A Life* (Boston: Little Brown and Co., 1991), 9.

15. *Ibid.*, 12.

16. "The Abduction," in *My Mother's House*, trans. Roger Senhouse (New York: Penguin Books, 1966), 42.

17. *Looking Backwards*, trans. David Le Vay (Bloomington: Indiana University Press), 17.

18. Joanna Richardson, *Colette* (New York: Franklin Watts, 1984), 7.

19. *Ibid.*, 8.

20. *My Apprenticeships*, trans. Helen Beauclerk (London: Secker and Warburg, 1978). Hereafter referred to as MA.

21. Lottman, 49.

22. Maurice Goudeket, *Close to Colette* (New York: Farrar, Straus, and Giroux, 1957), 155.

23. The *'nouvelle'* is undoubtedly no easier to define than the short story, and, to complicate matters, Colette's interpretation of the form probably represents an amalgam of several definitions. In *Le Grand Robert de la langue française* (2ᵉ edition, vi, 1985), the *'nouvelle'* is described as "a generally short narrative dramatically constructed, presenting few characters whose psychology is only studied to the extent that they react to the event that is at the center of the narrative." The nineteenth-century literary historian, Albert Thibaudet, in his *Histoire de la littérature française*, offers the following definition: "in the *'nouvelle,'* there is generally a focus on the presence or the passage of a traveler, of a witness who recounts, of a curious person who observes, of an artist who paints. In the novel . . . the novelist jumps into the water and swims. . . . The author of the *'nouvelle'* remains on the bank, with his easel and his canvas" (211). While Colette's stories generally underscore the role of the witness / narrator, who more often than not keeps her distance from events, her detachment is never complete. The significant consequences of Colette's unique approach to narrative voice in her short fiction will be analyzed in the following chapter.

24. Sarde, 22, 39.

25. Mari McCarty, "Possessing Female Space: 'The Tender Shoot,' " *Women's Studies* 8 (1981): 368.

26. *The Collected Stories of Colette*, ed. Robert Phelps (New York: Farrar, Straus, Giroux, 1983), xii. Hereafter referred to as CS.

27. "The Abduction," in *My Mother's House* (England: Penguin Books, 1966), 42–43. Hereafter referred to as MH.

28. The analysis that follows represents a revised version of my article, "Colette's 'La Cire verte': Breaking the Law," *Modern Language Studies* (Winter 1991), 37–44. Copyright © Northeast Modern Language Association 1991. Reproduced by permission of the publisher.

29. Sigmund Freud, "The Relationship of the Poet to Daydreaming," (1908) in *On Creativity and the Unconscious*, trans. I. F. Grant Duff (New York: Harper, 1958), 47.

30. *Oeuvres* II (Paris: Editions de la Pléiade, 1986), lii–liii.

31. McCarty, 367.

32. The title of the story in French is "*Le Tendron*," which can be translated as both "tender shoot" and "young girl."

33. McCarty, 373.

34. Colin Francome, *Abortion Freedom: A Worldwide Movement* (London: George Allen and Unwin, 1984), 33–34.

35. *Le deuxième sexe*, I (Paris: Gallimard, 1949), "Introduction," 12–35.

36. Reference to the inescapable gaze staring down from the photograph

brings to mind the historical portraits hanging in the museum in Bouville that so unsettle Roquentin, the existentialist hero of Sartre's *Nausea*. As Roquentin walks through the museum, he senses that the immutable presence of the portraits compromises his right to exist, transforming him into an object, or, to use Sartrean terminology, a "thing-in-itself." Jean-Paul Sartre, *La Nausée* (Paris: Gallimard, 1938), 122.

37. *The Other One*, trans. Elizabeth Tait and Roger Senhouse (New York: Farrar, Straus and Giroux, 1960).

38. *My Apprenticeships*, 19.

39. Stephen Heath, "Difference," *Screen* 19 (1978): 107–8.

40. I borrow this apt term from Judith Butler, *Gender Trouble: Feminism and the Subversion of Identity* (New York: Routledge, 1990), 32.

41. *Paysages et Portraits* (Paris: Flammarion, 1958).

42. Lynne Huffer, *Another Colette* (Ann Arbor: University of Michigan Press, 1992), 107–115.

43. Butler, 31.

44. Such an interpretation is offered by Michel Mercier in his editorial comments on *The Tendrils of the Vine*, when he concludes that the true meaning of Colette's liaison with Missy is revealed in the story's denouement: "a mutual need for refuge and, on Missy's part, a sort of fundamental dissatisfaction that is nothing more than the painful expression of a maternal desire, which chance had prevented her from realizing." In *Oeuvres* I, 1538 (my translation).

45. Joan Rivière, "Womanliness as Masquerade," in *Formations of Fantasy*, ed. Victor Burgin, James Donald and Cora Caplan (London and New York: Methuen, 1986), 38.

46. Marks, *Colette*, 155.

47. In fact, the chapter Marks devotes to Colette's short stories is called "Hide-and-Seek." Marks sees Armande's disclosure of her affection for Maxime and Irène's interlude of open self-expression as liberating experiences for the two women. It is important to note, however, that Armande's apparent "escape" is immediately transformed into another sort of entrapment, and Irène's freedom is equally transitory. (See Marks, *Colette*, 155–56.)

48. Butler, 32.

49. *Ibid.*, 22.

50. As one example of the challenges to these categories being launched by contemporary thinkers, Butler cites Foucault's proposition that sexuality produces "sex" as "an artificial concept which effectively extends and disguises the power relations responsible for its genesis." *Ibid.*, 92.

51. In *Three Short Novels by Colette*, trans. Patrick Leigh Fermor (New York: Farrar, Straus and Young, 1952). Hereafter referred to as CA. The analysis that follows is revised from my article, "The 'Third Woman' in Colette's 'Chance Acquaintances,' " *Studies in Short Fiction* 29 (Fall 1992):

499–508. Copyright © 1992 by Newberry College. Reproduced by permission of the publisher.

52. *Une Passade* (Paris: Calmann-Lévy, 1894); *Maîtresse d'esthètes* (Paris: Simonis Empis, 1897).

53. In *Oeuvres* 1 (Paris: Editions de la pléiade, 1984), lxxvi.

54. Isabelle de Courtivron, "Weak Men and Fatal Women: The Sand Image," in *Homosexualities and French Literature*, ed. Elaine Marks and George Stambolian (Ithaca: Cornell University Press, 1979), 223. Courtivron's explanations are based on the theories of Karen Horney.

55. *Ibid.*, 220.

56. Coppélia Kahn, "The Hand that Rocks the Cradle: Recent Gender Theories and Their Implications," in *The (M)other Tongue: Essays in Feminist Psychoanalytic Interpretation*, ed. Shirley Nelson Garner, Claire Kahane, and Madelon Sprengnether (Ithaca: Cornell University Press, 1985), 77. The most often cited proponent of object-relations theory is Nancy Chodorow, *The Reproducing of Mothering: Psychoanalysis and the Sociology of Gender* (Berkeley: University of California Press, 1978).

57. See Marcelle Biolley-Godino, *L'homme objet chez Colette* (Paris: Klincksieck, 1972) for a full discussion of the male image in Colette's work.

58. Sandra Gilbert and Susan Gubar, *The Madwoman in the Attic: The Woman Writer and the Nineteenth Century Literary Imagination* (New Haven: Yale University Press, 1979), 521.

59. See, for example, Sarah Kofman, *L'énigme de la femme: la femme dans les textes de Freud* (Paris: Galilée, 1980) for a cogent feminist analysis of Freud's interpretation of female sexuality.

60. Ann Cothran, "The Pure and the Impure: Codes and Constructs," *Women's Studies* 8 (1981): 335–36.

61. Quoting this expression taken from Colette's novel *Mitsou*, Joan Stewart in *Colette*, 111 notes that understated heroic qualities are common to the female characters in Colette's short fiction.

62. *Break of Day*, trans. Enid McLeod (New York: Farrar, Straus, and Giroux, 1961), 51.

63. Sarde, 160.

64. See Sigmund Freud, "Beyond the Pleasure Principle," in *The Freud Reader*, ed. Peter Gay (New York: W. W. Norton and Co., 1989), 594–626, for a discussion of the tragic link between sexual energy (the desire for gratification) and the death drive. See also the summary of Lacanian theory in Toril Moi, *Sexual / Textual Politics* (New York: Routledge, 1985), 99–101.

65. Erica Eisinger, "*The Vagabond*: A Vision of Androgyny," in Eisinger and McCarty, 96.

66. The reader will recall that the positive effects of continuity between mother and daughter were discussed in the analysis of "Green Sealing Wax." Several feminist critics have proposed theoretical reevaluations of the Imaginary

realm that are supported by the "empirical" evidence cited here. See, for example, Naomi Schor, "*Eugénie Grandet*: Mirrors and Melancholia," in *The (M)other Tongue*, 217–37.

67. Michel Beaujour, "Autobiographie et autoportrait," *Poétique* 32 (Nov. 1977): 453, as cited in Nancy K. Miller, "The Anamnesis of a Female 'I': In the Margins of Self-Portrayal," in Eisinger and McCarty, 173.

68. Miller, "The Anamnesis," 173.

69. *Break of Day*, 66–67.

70. The preceding discussion is summarized from Dana Strand, "Colette's "La Cire verte": Breaking the Law," in *MLS*, 42.

71. Stockinger, 365.

72. Stewart, 1.

73. Nicole Ward Jouve, *Colette* (Bloomington: Indiana University Press, 1987), 141.

74. See Suzanne Relyea, "Polymorphic Perversity: Colette's Illusory 'Real,' " in *Colette, the Woman, the Writer*, eds. Erica Eisinger and Mari McCarty (University Park: Pennsylvania State University Press, 1981), 150–63, for an excellent discussion of this aspect of Colette's writing, which she refers to as "the eroticization of the signifier."

75. Jean's disappointment at abandoning his feverish state, accompanied as it is by intermittent immobilizing pain filtering through his trancelike fantasies, may initially be baffling. Nevertheless, a theory establishing a link between physical pain and pleasure, proposed by Freud in his essay "On Narcissism," suggests that the body part associated with pain becomes endowed with libido that has been withdrawn from love objects. As a result, pain sends to the mind sexually exciting stimuli that are psychically invested. Thus, Jean's recovery, so thankfully greeted by his devoted mother, signals to him that he must forego the self-investment in his pain as a source of pleasure. See Sigmund Freud, *The Freud Reader*, ed. Peter Gay (New York: W. W. Norton and Co., 1989), 551.

76. For a summary of the publication history and variants of "Bella-Vista," see *Oeuvres* III, ed. Claude Pichois (Paris: Editions de la pléiade, 1991), 1844–49.

77. Bibliothèque nationale, Paris, Catalogue de l'exposition "Colette" (253), 1973.

78. *Break of Day*, p. 51.

79. *Ibid.*, 141.

80. Martin Jay, "In the Empire of the Gaze: Foucault and the Denigration of Vision in Twentieth Century Thought," in *Foucault: A Critical Reader*, ed. David Couzens Hoy (New York: Basil Blackwell Inc., 1980), 176.

81. G. N. A. Vesey, "Vision," *Encyclopedia of Philosophy*, VIII (New York: Macmillan, 1967) as quoted in Evelyn Fox Keller and Christine R. Grontkowski, "The Mind's Eye," in *Discovering Reality: Feminist Perspectives*

in Epistemology, Metaphysics, Methodology and Philosophy of Science, ed. Sandra Harding and Merrill B. Hintikka (Dordecht: Reidel, 1983), 221.

82. Jay, 178.

83. Hélène Cixous, "Sorties," in *La jeune née* (Paris: Union générale d'éditions, 10 / 18: 1975), as quoted in *New French Feminisms*, ed. Elaine Marks and Isabelle de Courtivron (New York: Schocken, 1981), 95.

84. Luce Irigaray, *Ce sexe que n'en est pas un*, as quoted in *New French Feminisms*, eds. Isabelle de Courtivron and Elaine Marks (New York: Schocken, 1981), 101. More recent critiques of women and sexuality have attacked the theories of Irigaray and others for essentializing women by assuming an innate pattern of feminine sexual response. For these critics, such narrow definitions of what constitutes "normal" female sexuality severely curtail the range of possibilities for sexual expression available to women. While I take their point, I would simply stress that Irigaray's analysis does not overestimate the potential (and actual) oppressive effects of the male gaze, which is central to my argument here. See, for example, Carol S. Vance's introductory article, "Pleasure and Danger: Towards a Politics of Sexuality," in her edited volume, *Pleasure and Danger: Exploring Female Sexuality* (London: Pandora Press, 1989), 1–27, for a cogent summary of the constructionist versus essentialist debate.

85. Keller and Grontowski, 220.

86. *Chéri* (New York: Albert and Charles Boni, 1929), trans. Janet Flanner, 204.

87. "Questions à Julia Kristeva," *Revue des sciences humaines* 168 (1977): 597 (my translation).

88. Yannick Resch, "Colette ou le plaisir-texte," in *Colette: Nouvelles approches critiques*, Actes du colloque de Sarrebruck (Paris: Nizet, 1986), 170 (my translation).

89. In *Gigi* (Paris: Hachette, 1960), 146 (my translation).

90. Among the critics who have examined the importance of shifting perspective in Colette's writing are Jerry Aline Flieger in *Colette and the Fantom Subject of Autobiography* (Ithaca: Cornell University Press, 1992) and Marie-Christine Bellosta in her introduction to "The Rendezvous" in *Oeuvres* III, 1881–91.

91. François Porché, "La Vie littéraire: L'art infaillible de Colette," *Le Jour*, 15 décembre 1937, 2; Robert Kemp, "Les Livres," *La Liberté*, 28 décembre 1937, 4; Pierre Loewen, "La Vie littéraire: 'Bella-Vista' par Colette," *L'Ordre*, 27 décembre 1937, 2; Robert Brasillach, "Causerie littéraire: Colette, 'Bella-Vista' [. . .]," *L'Action française*, 9 décembre 1937, 5, (my translations). For a complete summary of critical reaction to "The Rendezvous," from which I have selected the preceding references, see Marie-Christine Bellosta's introduction to the story, in *Oeuvres* III, 1881–91.

92. Maurice Goudeket, preface to *Fleurs du désert* (Flowers of the Desert), as cited in *Oeuvres* III, 1888 (my translation).

93. As cited in *Oeuvres* III, 1887 (my translation).

94. Marie-Christine Bellosta, in her introduction to "The Rendezvous," *Oeuvre* III, 1890.

95. Jerry Aline Flieger's cogent analysis of the relevance of Freudian theory to selected autobiographical works by Colette has contributed significantly to my analysis of "Rainy Moon." See her *Colette and the Fantom Subject of Autobiography*.

96. Sigmund Freud, "The Uncanny," in *The Complete Psychological Works of Sigmund Freud*, trans. James Strachey, 17 (London: The Hogarth Press, 1955), 220.

97. *Ibid.*, 241.

98. Sigmund Freud, "Repression," *The Freud Reader*, 570.

99. Sigmund Freud, "The Uncanny," in *The Complete Psychological Works of Sigmund Freud*, 250.

100. Several critics have noted the rapport between the reflexive name of another Colette character, Renée Néré, the protagonist of the novel *The Vagabond* and her project of self-analysis. See, for example, Joan Hinde Stewart, *Colette* (Boston: Twayne Publishers, 1983), 47. In this story, of course, Délia gives the narrator the same opportunity for self-appraisal afforded other Colette women characters by their reflections in mirrors.

101. Sigmund Freud, "Mourning and Melancholia," in Gay, *The Freud Reader*, 588.

102. Flieger, 201. Flieger convincingly presents this line of reasoning in much greater detail in tracing the mourning process of Colette's autobiographical subject, who must overcome melancholic identification with her lost parents.

103. Sigmund Freud, "Mourning and Melancholia," in Gay, *The Freud Reader*, 589.

104. Sigmund Freud, "The Uncanny," in *The Complete Psychological Works of Sigmund Freud*, 251.

105. Nancy K. Miller, *Subject to Change: Reading Feminist Writing* (New York: Columbia University Press, 1988), 259.

Part 2

THE WRITER

Colette on Writing

As a music hall performer and, later, a well-known literary personality, whose life was more than occasionally touched by controversy, Colette often found herself in the public limelight. The numerous photographs, taken from the early days of her marriage through her middle years, which show her in every imaginable pose, setting, and costume, suggest that she thoroughly enjoyed occupying center stage. Furthermore, her highly autobiographical writings, in which she frequently assumed a role as principal character in a self-revealing drama, reinforce the image of an outspoken woman, willing to "tell all."

Yet, despite the candor that characterized her private life and public letters, Colette was always very reluctant to talk about her views on the creative process of writing. In fact, throughout her career, she systematically shunned invitations from critics and journalists to make theoretical pronouncements on her craft. Like her friend, the writer Renée Vivien, whom she praised for her refusal to "talk shop," Colette was by her own admission "sparing of words" when it came to the subject of literature.[1] Modest and self-effacing, at least in her role as writer, she never missed an opportunity to mock those who took it for granted that she believed in the "lofty" nature of her professional calling. Once, when asked in an interview what profession she would choose if she had to start over, she quickly replied, "Grocer. One writes, but the only good thing is living."[2] While the response seems a bit disingenuous, considering the unrelenting diligence with which she approached her writing (even during her later years, when financial pressures no longer propelled her literary output), it is nevertheless consistent with her continued efforts to demystify her craft.

Even Colette's considerable correspondence, including many letters written to other notable writers of her day, provides precious little insight into her views on writing. As Michèle Sarde has noted, "Colette's correspondence has nothing in common with the correspondence of Gide or Flaubert; there are no grand ideas, aesthetics, politics or philosophy discussed in her letters, and even a paucity of allusions to literature."[3] When pressed in an interview to expound on some of the great theoretical issues that captivated her contemporaries, she brushed off the question with characteristic directness, "There are three things in particular that suit me very ill: feathered hats, general ideas, and earrings. I shall therefore avoid them now as I do at all other times. And in any case, is it possible for poetry and poets ever to accommodate themselves to general ideas?"[4]

What little evidence we have of Colette's views on the writing process indicates that she did indeed avoid excessive conceptualizing, her vast stores of creative imagination checked at all times by her unwavering commitment to precision. Aware that her work habits seemed unorthodox, particularly when compared to the highly intellectual approach of some of her (male) contemporaries, she acknowledged her absence of method by recounting the following self-deprecating anecdote. "Among my notes . . . What notes? I shan't leave a single one behind me. Oh, I've tried! Everything I wrote down became as sad as the skin of a dead frog, sad as a plan for a novel. Following the example of those writers who do make notes, I had made notes on a sheet of paper, and lost the paper. So I bought a notebook, American style, and lost the notebook, after which I felt free, forgetful, and willing to answer for my forgetfulness."[5]

Despite Colette's frank aversion to expounding her personal opinions on her craft, it is nevertheless possible to piece together her decidedly unconventional views on writing from brief allusions found in her essays, letters, memoirs, and creative works. Perhaps the most comprehensive statement Colette made about her prose writing can be found in a very short article, published in *Le Figaro* in 1937, during the period in which she was producing the majority of her short fiction.

> I think that, as a writer, I was born—to employ an expression so overused that it turns ones stomach—I was born "under the sign" of passivity. I have chronicled my obscure beginnings, under a stifling tutelage that turned writing into a chore. When I emerged from that obscurity, I did not escape all controlling influences, and I remember that, when I began *Chéri*, a charming man, who was a writer himself, said to me, "You have no understanding of how to construct a book. I'll show you how to organize it." He did, and I confess contritely that, faced with a structure of twenty-two irreproachably logical chapters, solid as a rock, varied as a prairie in May, I suddenly and inexplicably broke down in foolish tears. The outline was torn up, and I was abandoned to the humiliating fate of an author who is unsure, before writing, of what he will write.

Do I claim, in confiding this to you, the privileges of independence, a quixotic humor, and that sort of carelessness that, when I was young, was called artistic temperament? No, it's a far cry from this fantasy to the regular, persistent work that finds its only joy in the sources from which it draws. My sources don't run the risk of drying up, and I will die on their banks before exhausting them. They are called nature and love. They have sated others greedier than I. There are not—as luck would have it—two loves the same nor two leaves alike. There are no two creatures, no two seasons that are identical. . . . I don't recall having endured humdrum disappointments in love, nor having called a loved one by a name that was not his own.

Having thus acknowledged at once her distaste for rigorous structure and the discipline she brought to bear on the arduous task of writing, Colette went on to admit the extent to which the creative process escapes the control of the artist. Literary characters, for example, soon take on a mind and a life of their own:

I know only too well from experience that heroes of novels, patiently and ploddingly provided with character traits, faces, crimes and virtues, only depend so long on the will of the author. At a certain point, they are grown up enough to take off on their own. . . . Such a wresting of power does not take place without a struggle, although it does have its pleasant side. For every writer, who cold and stubborn, fought against himself, pulling along the weight of his recalcitrant heroes for pages and pages, I wish—it's a little miracle of the common sort—I wish that one lovely night, he might see his disobedient creatures imperceptibly take over from him, deliberate among themselves, and set out on a path that he has not chosen.[6]

As the above article suggests, any discussion of Colette's self-conscious statements on her art must begin, perhaps ironically, with her assertion that she came to writing reluctantly. As she put it:

[I]n my youth, I never, *never* wanted to write. No I did not get up at night in secret to write verses in pencil on the lid of a shoe-box! No, I did not get nineteen or twenty for style in an exercise between the ages of twelve and fifteen! For I felt, more so every day, I felt that I was made precisely *not* to write. I never sent essays promising a pretty amateur talent to a famous writer; yet today everyone does, for I never cease to receive manuscripts. I was, then, the only one of my kind, the only one brought into the world not to write.[7]

Reflecting on the invaluable opportunity to discover the world that her safe, but gloriously free childhood afforded her, Colette saw the absence of a calling as liberating, allowing her apprehension of the world to remain unsullied:

> What leisure I enjoyed at such a lack of literary vocation! My childhood, my free and solitary adolescence, both preserved from the cares of self-expression, were both uniquely occupied with directing their subtle antennae towards whatever contemplates and listens to itself, probes itself and breathes. Limited deserts, without dangers; imprints of birds and hare on the snow; lakes covered with ice or veiled with warm summer mist; assuredly, you gave me as many joys as I could contain. Must I call my school a school? No, but a sort of rude paradise where ruffled angels broke the wood in the morning to light the stove and ate, in the guise of heavenly manna, thick "tartines" of red haricot beans, cooked in a wine sauce, spread on the grey bread kneaded by the farmers' wives . . . [. . .] In my own family, no money, but books. No gifts, but tenderness. No comfort, but freedom. No voice borrowed the sound of the wind to whisper in my ear, with a small chill breath, the advice to write and to write again, to tarnish, in writing, my soaring or tranquil perception of the living universe. . . .[8]

The above quotation, while succinctly summarizing the unfettered freedom of Colette's initial contacts with the world, also reveals her attitude towards language as a form of constraint, attenuating the force of her perceptually based experiences. One of Colette's many fictional alter ego's, Renée Néré, the writer turned actress who is the principal character of the 1907 novel, *The Vagabond*, echoes her creator's frustrating struggles with language, through this sobering assessment of the act of writing. "To write is to pour one's innermost self passionately upon the tempting paper, at such frantic speed that sometimes one's hand struggles and rebels, overdriven by the impatient god who guides it—and to find, next day, in place of the golden bough that bloomed miraculously in that dazzling hour, a withered bramble and stunted flower."[9] Comparing music to writing, Colette explains the limitations of language, which is more likely than music to lose its evocative powers through repeated prosaic usage:

The dancing light, the flutter of the music's wing, the fragments of melody that haunted and evaded me in the nighttime, have been replaced, little by little, by the more pressing appeal of words. The melodic and the written phrase both spring from the same elusive and immortal pair—sound and rhythm. To write, instead of composing, is to pursue the same search, but in a trance that is less intensely inspired and that has a lesser reward. If I had composed music instead of prose, I should despise what I have done for forty years. For words are wearisome and worn, while the arabesques of music are forever new.[10]

In a sense, the process by which Colette became reconciled to writing over time can be likened to the passage she traces from childhood to maturity: in abandoning the lost paradise of her youth, she arrived at a gradual acceptance of inevitable limits to her autonomy; in accepting her role as an author, she faced up both to the difficulty of capturing in language her sensual contact with the world, and to the dangers inherent in a woman's frank and open self-expression through writing. In the opening story of *The Tendrils of the Vine*, Colette lyrically chronicles the almost simultaneous discovery of her voice as a writer, and of the necessity to temper it. She begins the passage with a fable that metaphorically prefigures her personal experience:

In bygone times, the nightingale did not sing at night. He had a sweet little thread of voice that he skillfully employed from morn to night with the coming of spring. He awoke with his comrades in the blue-gray dawn, and their flustered awakening startled the cockchafers sleeping on the underside of the lilac leaves.

He went to bed promptly at seven o'clock or half past seven, no matter where, often in the flowering grapevines that smelled of mignonette, and slept solidly until morning.

One night in the springtime he went to sleep while perched on a young vine shoot, his jabot fluffed up and his head bowed, as if afflicted with a graceful torticollis. While he slept, the vine's gimlet feelers—those imperious and clinging tendrils whose sharp taste, like that of fresh sorrel, acts as a stimulant and slakes the thirst—began to grow so thickly during the night that the bird woke up to find himself bound fast, his feet hobbled in strong withes, his wings powerless . . .

He thought he would die, but by struggling he managed after a great effort to liberate himself, and throughout the spring he swore never to sleep again, not until the tendrils of the vine had stopped growing.

From the next night onward he sang, to keep himself awake:

> *As long as the vine shoots grow, grow, grow,*
> > *I will sleep no more!*
> *As long as the vine shoots grow, grow, grow,*
> > *I will sleep no more!*

He varied his theme, embellishing it with vocalisations, became infatuated with his voice, became that wildly passionate and palpitating songster that one listens to with the unbearable longing to see him sing. (CS, 100–1)

She then tells her own story in the same terms used to describe the valiant nightingale's plight.

> Imperious, clinging, the tendrils of a bitter vine shackled me in my springtime while I slept a happy sleep, without misgivings. But with a frightened lunge I broke all those twisted threads that were already imbedded in my flesh, and I fled . . . When the torpor of a new night of honey weighed on my eyelids, I feared the tendrils of the vine and I uttered a loud lament that revealed my voice to me.
>
> All alone, after a wakeful night, I now observe the morose and voluptuous morning star rise before me . . . And to keep from falling again into a happy sleep, in the treacherous springtime when blossoms the gnarled vine, I listen to the sound of my voice. Sometimes I feverishly cry out what one customarily suppresses or whispers very low—then my voice dies down to a murmur, because I dare not go on . . .
>
> I want to tell, tell, tell everything I know, all my thoughts, all my surmises, everything that enchants or hurts or astounds me; but always, toward the dawn of this resonant night, a wise cool hand is laid across my mouth, and my cry, which had been passionately raised, subsides into moderate verbiage, the loquacity of the child who talks aloud to reassure himself and allay his fears.
>
> I no longer enjoy a happy sleep, but I no longer fear the tendrils of the vine. . . .

Inspired by the nightingale's plaintive song of survival, Colette as narrator rebels against the constraints shackling her. Yet, despite the freedom she derives from her newly found voice, she is fearful to tell all. Although she is committed to using her voice to stave off threats to her freedom, she is also acutely aware of the dangers of total candor.

The passage serves as a poignant statement of Colette's ambivalence towards writing: her recognition both of the need to safeguard her independence through empowering self-expression and of the inevitable risks of self-revelation.

The same ambivalence, the same competing impulses towards concealment and revelation are expressed by Colette in the guise of the narrator of her autobiographical novel, *Break of Day*.

> Why should I stop my hand from gliding over this paper to which for so many years I've confided what I know about myself, what I've tried to hide, what I've invented and what I've guessed? At no time has the catastrophe of love, in all its phases and consequences, formed a part of the true intimate life of a woman. Why do men— writers or so-called writers—still show surprise that a woman should so easily reveal to the public love-secrets and amorous lies and half-truths? By divulging these, she manages to hide other important and obscure secrets which she herself does not understand very well. The spotlight, the shameless eye which she obligingly operates, always explores the same sector of a woman's life, that sector tortured by bliss and discord round which the shades are thickest. But it is not in the illuminated zone that the darkest plots are woven. Man, my friend, you willingly make fun of women's writing because they can't help being autobiographical. On whom then were you relying to paint women for you, din them into your ears, debase them in your eyes, in short make you tired of them? On yourself?[11]

Drawn towards the security of reticence, haunted by the arduousness of writing, Colette nevertheless succumbs to the need to tell her story, however veiled and camouflaged it might be. The desire to create, the willingness to engage in tireless combat with words persists, and becomes stronger, eventually forcing her (but only near the end of her life) to acknowledge her vocation: "I don't know when I shall succeed in not writing; the obsession, the compulsion date back half a century. . . . Within me a tired mind continues with its gourmet's search, looks for a better word, and better than better. Fortunately, the idea is less demanding, and well-behaved provided she is well decked out. She is used to waiting, half asleep, for the fresh verbal fodder."[12]

The dominant imagery here, and elsewhere, serves to present writing as a natural, organic process, rather than a highly rational, intellectual activity. The "gourmet's search" for a word that will be added to the writer's "verbal fodder" brings to mind the imagery of the "golden bough" transformed, through the organic process of degeneration, into a "withered bramble and stunted flower," as well as the extended analogy drawn from nature that provides the basis for the fable of "The Tendrils of the Vine." Yet, it is important to note that, for Colette, the very "naturalness" of the writing process could only be achieved through hard work. Her admiring contemporaries were always surprised to learn that the seemingly effortless flow of her prose was accomplished through dogged application. The following remark by Somerset Maugham echoes the response of other fellow writers to her work: "I think no one in France now writes more admirably than Colette, and such is the ease of her expression that you cannot bring yourself to believe that she takes any trouble over it . . . I asked her. I was exceedingly surprised to hear that she wrote everything over and over again. She told me that she would often spend a whole morning working upon a single page."[13]

In fact, Colette's letters and memoirs include many references to the demanding task that writing was for her. Her account of her "apprenticeship" period, while married to her first husband, provides a candid record of some of the negative lessons she learned while under Willy's tutelage. Highly critical of the *Claudine* books she wrote during this earliest period of her career, she confesses, for example: "I do not like to rediscover, glancing through these very old books, the suppleness of mood that understood so well what was required of it, the submission to every hint and the already deft manner of avoiding difficulties. To kill off a character, for instance, whom I had come to detest, seems rather grossly casual. And I blame myself when I see how certain things in the *Claudines*—allusions, features that are caricatured yet recognizable, tales that come too near the truth—betray an utter disregard of doing harm."[14] Condemning the malleability and insouciance that accompanied her beginnings as a writer, Colette clearly learned to bring greater rigor to writing later in her life.

Although her initiation into the world of letters by Willy often taught her what *not* to do, she did take to heart some of her husband's early advice. "A few pages that were rather too poetical—there is no use looking for them, they no longer exist—brought my manuscript back to me, flung across the table with the acid comment of my reader-critic: 'I did not know that I had married the last of the lyric poets.' Hard words, but true, no doubt, and they were not wasted on me."[15]

Claiming that Willy confined her to her room with the admonition to fill the pages of her schoolgirl's notebook with tales of her childhood, Colette later attributed her careful work habits to her forced labor. "Under this regime I acquired, I developed and shaped within me, the ways and temper of a china-repairer."[16] In a letter to her friend, Marguerite Moreno, written while she was working on her novel *The Ripening Seed*, she reveals the meticulous care and concern for detail that no doubt dated from those early days learning her demanding art. "The last page cost my entire first day here and I defy you, when you read it, to suspect this. Alas, that a mere twenty lines, without fancy effects or embossing of any kind, should make such demands. It's the proportions that give me the greatest trouble. And I have such a horror of grandiloquent finales. . . ."[17]

Writing in a review of "Bella-Vista," that Colette "lacked a sense of the tragic," Colette's friend Edmond Jaloux clearly mistook the restraint she exercised with increasingly difficulty in her story writing for a natural penchant.[18] Colette quickly responded with a letter in which she protested: "and I, who hold back, who keep myself in check, who muzzle, tie up, strangle and gag myself in order to avoid the tragic, which comes all too easily to me."[19]

Another passage from a letter to her daughter refers to the internal struggle she faced in trying to harness her natural impatience to achieve the perfection she sought. "This is the nth time I have started again on a certain page of my miserable novel [*Break of Day*]. I work with ferocious patience, I who am usually so impatient! It's a battle between my two halves. Oh, what a métier writing is! It seems to me that when you've practiced any other craft for over thirty years, you feel a little confidence, a little mastery. With writing, it's the opposite."[20]

During the 1930s and 1940s, Colette turned away from the novel and began to devote her efforts to writing short stories. In his account of their years together, Maurice Goudeket cites a conversation he had with his wife that helps explain her shift to short fiction at this time:

> *Bella-Vista*, which appeared in 1937, is the first of her volumes of stories, and was followed by *Chance Acquaintances*, *Le Képi* and *Gigi*. This form, which thenceforth she preferred, was not the sign of any impoverishment in her, nor of less impatience, but of a desire for greater brevity. More and more she refused whatever was easy for her, descriptions of the country among other things. There are none to be found in "Gribiche" or in *Gigi*.

"Hello!" I would say to her. "Have you torn up what you wrote yesterday?"

"Yes, I found I was writing Colette."[21]

The following passage, included in an article entitled "The Poetry I Love," reveals in more specific terms the kind of control Colette continually sought to wield over the writing process, as she outlines her own vigilance against insidious poetic encroachments in her prose:

> For my part, I keep as close a watch as I can for the intrusion of unintentional lines of verse. I watch for them and I weed them out. You may tell me that my severity is excessive, that the ideal sentence is the one in which every word is irreplaceable, whether it goes on twelve feet or thirteen. But you must allow me to do it my own way; I know what I am about. If I were to relax the merciless control I inflict on my prose, I know perfectly well that I should soon cease to be the anxious and diligent prose writer that I am, and become nothing more than a bad poet, lacking in all restraint and as happy in my metronomic world as a tenor would be whose whole life was nothing but a pure and interminable high B flat! I am there, I am keeping watch.[22]

The great rigor Colette exercised in her writing and the importance to her of the smallest detail are reflected in the following comment, included in a letter to her good friend, Renée Hamon. "In my *Paris-Soir* piece on the deaf-mutes, the printer put in 'yeux purs' [pure eyes] instead of 'yeux pers' [sea-green eyes]. People have committed suicide for less. . . ."[23]

Colette stood firm against critics who sometimes questioned her choice of vocabulary, arguing that, on most occasions, only one term suited the exact circumstances she wished to describe. In *Chance Acquaintances*, she compared human nonentities to cerripedia (more commonly, barnacles), which prompted her friend Lucie Delarue-Mardrus to accuse her of pedantry: "You're proud of yourself because you stuck the word 'cerripedia' in your last book in order to impress us."[24] Colette was quick to leap to her own defense: " 'Cerripedia'? My dear creature, if you had seen cerripedia, you would know that cerripedia can only be compared to cerripedia. Besides, they are common, and can be found along our shores, o daughter of the sea! I am thrilled that you take issue with me, I want no other watchdog than you. What, you accept 'chrysoprase' [a term for a precious stone that appears in "The

Photographer's Wife"] but you chastise me for 'prasins' [ultra-green]? This 'prasin' which expresses so precisely the golden green of a cat's eyes?"[25]

Although she was reluctant to give advice to budding young writers, Colette did always insist on the essential honesty and simplicity she believed necessary for successful prose writing. For example, she counseled the detective novelist Georges Simenon (who submitted stories to her when she was an editor for *Le Matin* during the early twenties), "You must not be literary. Suppress all the literature and it will work."[26] Simenon later claimed it was the most useful advice he had ever had.

One final admonition could easily be appended to the above, illustrating again the modesty and pragmatic forthrightness Colette brought to her prose writing: "You should never use the word 'indescribable.' Since a writer's job is precisely to describe, the word 'indescribable' does not belong in his vocabulary."[27]

Notes to Part 2

1. *The Pure and the Impure*, trans. Herma Briffault (New York: Farrar, Straus and Giroux, 1966), 81.

2. Michèle Sarde, *Colette, Free and Fettered*, 408.

3. *Ibid.*, 387.

4. *Earthly Paradise: An Autobiography*, ed. Robert Phelps, trans. Herma Briffault, Derek Coltman, et al. (New York: Farrar, Straus and Giroux, 1966), 250.

5. *The Evening Star: Recollections*, trans. David Le Vay (London: Peter Owen, 1973), 96.

6. "My Ideas on the Novel," *Le Figaro*, 30 October 1937, as cited in Colette, *Oeuvres*, III, 1831–32 (my translation).

7. "The Footwarmer," in *Looking Backwards*, trans. David Le Vay (Bloomington: Indiana University Press, 1975), 16.

8. *Looking Backwards*, 16–17.

9. *The Vagabond*, trans. Enid McLeod (New York: Ballantine, 1955), 12.

10. *My Apprenticeships*, trans. Helen Beauclerk (London: Secker and Warburg, 1957), 125.

11. *Break of Day*, trans. Enid McLeod (New York: Farrar, Straus, and Giroux, 1961), 62–63.

12. *The Evening Star*, 143.

13. In *Belles Saisons: A Colette Scrapbook*, ed. Robert Phelps (New York: Farrar, Straus and Giroux, 1978), 258.

14. *My Apprenticeships*, 60.

15. *Ibid.*, 68.

16. *Ibid.*, 71.

17. In *Letters from Colette*, trans. Robert Phelps (New York: Farrar, Straus, and Giroux, 1980), 69–70.

18. In *L'Excelsior* 25 December 1937 as cited in *Lettres à ses pairs*, ed. Claude Pichois and Roberte Forbin (Paris: Flammarion, 1973), 308.

19. In *Lettres à ses pairs*, 308 (my translation).

20. In Phelps, *Belles saisons*, 181.

21. Maurice Goudeket, *Close to Colette*, 155.

22. In Phelps, *Earthly Paradise*, 252.

23. In *Letters from Colette*, 167.

24. *Ibid.*, 176.

25. *Ibid.*, 177.

26. In Phelps, *Belles saisons*, 151.

27. *Ibid.*, 225.

Part 3

THE CRITICS

Introduction

As I noted in my preface to this study, although critical interest in Colette, both the woman *and* the writer, has grown dramatically over the past 30 years, her short fiction has only recently begun to attract the attention of the critical establishment. The articles included in this section provide a sampling of critical approaches to Colette's short fiction. Elaine Marks' chapter on the short stories (from which I include extensive excerpts) is taken from her 1960 work that, as the first study published in English, constitutes an introduction for English-speaking readers to Colette's stories. Donna Norrell's article on "Rainy Moon," published in the 1981 collection, *Colette: The Woman, the Writer*, adopts a perspective somewhat different from the one that guides my discussion of the story. Her convincing argument, that the story invites the reader to open his or her mind to the existence of the occult, suggests that here again Colette hovers between two diametrically opposed positions, refusing to reject either out of hand. In her article on "The Tender Shoot," published in the special issue of *Women's Studies* devoted to Colette's works, Mari McCarty develops the important notion of female space, first suggested by the theologian Mary Daly. Writing in the same issue, Jacob Stockinger examines Colette's unorthodox attitude towards established moral codes in her story "The Patriarch," concluding that the digressive structure of the story has far-reaching ideological implications.

Finally, Lynne Huffer's analysis of stories from *My Mother's House*, excerpted from her book, *Another Colette*, seeks to sever the tie between the writer Colette and the fictionalized character who bears her name, by stressing the necessity of taking into account the important mediation of language in the creation of the textual "I." In the passages cited here, Huffer offers intertextual readings of several stories, a practice that yields significant insights into the complexity of Colette's textual strategies.

Elaine Marks*

"What did you say, my Dédé?"[1]
"Oh, nothing . . ."

The *nouvelle*, or short story, was originally an anecdote based on a real event, purportedly related by someone who was present at the time the event took place. Today, the short story is usually defined as a brief work of fiction, rigorously composed, concerned, as a rule, with a single episode and sustained by a unity of mood. Those of Colette's short stories in which "Colette" is the narrator, and they constitute by far the largest group, are all *nouvelles* in the original sense. Only eighteen of the twenty-two stories in *The Hidden Woman* [the title of the published translation is *The Other Woman*], five of the eleven stories in *La Fleur de l'âge*, "The Rendez-vous" in *Bella-Vista*, "Armande" in *Le Képi* and "The Sick Child" in *Gigi*[2] are short stories in the current sense of the term.

The title, *The Hidden Woman*, is to some extent misleading, for in these stories it is a question, not only of the "hidden woman," but also of the "hidden man," unless, of course, the title is to be read as implying that "to hide" is essentially a female trait. It is unsafe to think of the title which Colette gives to a group of stories as applying to them all. Almost always the book takes its name from the first story, but although this is the case in *The Hidden Woman*, the word "hidden" is nevertheless pertinent, not only to the theme of all the stories in this particular collection, but to Colette's other stories as well. In a very unpretentious and concrete manner, Colette is dealing with the problem of reality and appearance.

Most of the stories in *The Hidden Woman* range from three to four pages in length. Of these, seven are concerned with conjugal love, six with other forms of love, two with the lost paradise of childhood, one with the triumph of life over death as shown in the day of a painter,

*COLETTE by Elaine Marks, Copyright © 1960 by Rutgers, The State University. Reproduced by permission of Rutgers University Press, pp. 151–158; 180–184.

one with the relation between a woman and her critical butler and one with the semi-crazy people who haunt the offices of daily newspapers.

In each case, the story is a revelation, through an often trivial detail or incident, of what makes people love, fall out of love, go on living, kill, become jealous or heroic. A new hairdo, the constant movement of a thumb over lips, a hand lying on a sheet, a familiar whistle, an anniversary bracelet, an unknown song, a mildewed picture, an omelette, these are some of the seemingly unimportant details from which Colette produces her revelations.

As in the novels, though less often through dialogue, the reader is brought immediately into the action with only the vaguest suggestion of an introductory statement.

> "For a long time he had been watching the movement of the masked figures. . . ."[3]
> "The surgical suddenness of their rupture left him dumb."[4]
> "He had fallen asleep on his young wife's shoulder. . . ."[5]
> "He had taken her from another man. . . ."[6]
> "When Madame de la Hournerie returned home after a half day entirely consecrated to the hairdresser and the milliner. . . ."[7]
> "The access to the little villa was so easy that the robber wondered why and by what excess of prudence he had waited so long."[8]
> "The two young women separated as they had come together, without knowing why."[9]
> "When he had killed her, with one stroke of the little lump of lead under which she kept her wrapping paper, Louis became confused."[10]
> "The painter who wanted to die made the gesture, at the same time spontaneous and literary, of sketching a few lines before he killed himself."[11]

The factual, undramatic tone of these first sentences, whether they refer to a very ordinary or a very startling situation, sets the mood, and illustrates Colette's very particular, ironic point of view. In using the same tone for all the stories, Colette reduces the extraordinary to the ordinary and raises the ordinary to the extraordinary. Whether the principal character is a murderer, a widow, a bored married man, a newlywed wife, a robber, a Lesbian or a painter on the verge of suicide, becomes of little importance, and this in itself of a sufficient element of surprise to arrest the attention. The contrast between the unconventional status and role of some of the characters and the extreme situations in which some of them are found, and the rather conventional status, role and situation of others, is an all-important key to an understanding of these short stories.

Colette persistently forces acceptance of the fact that there may be no significant difference between the reactions of a perpetually irritated wife and the reactions of an unsuccessful robber. They are both victims of the annoying consequences of their actions, in one case marriage, in the other attempted theft, and they are both capable of a final, heroic silence in which they reveal a sense of compromise and propriety. Everything and anything human beings do is only a source of small vexations and small pleasures, which, depending on the angle of vision, may seem either very unimportant or very important. Colette is deliberately attempting an unromantic portrayal of human beings. She refuses to overdramatize murder, suicide, love, memory, to make of them anything but "facts." Aside from the very positive value she gives to silence, Colette is totally unconcerned with demonstrating anything other than the general notion that all lives are conditioned by details and that there is no relation between the apparent insignificance of the detail and the gigantic meaning it may assume as an instrument of revelation. Just as the novels explore variations on the theme of love, the short stories explore variations on the theme of the revealing detail. In the novels there is essentially one love, and in these short stories, because of the all-pervading unity of tone, there is essentially one human being, involved in a variety of situations, revealed by a variety of details.

In the title story of *The Hidden Woman* and in Colette's longer short stories, the theme of revelation is more fully developed. Irène in "The Hidden Woman," Bernard in "The Rendez-vous," Armande in "Armande" and Jean in "The Sick Child" reveal themselves as being very different either from the image they attempt to impose on others (Irène, Armande and Jean) or from the image they have of themselves (Bernard). Irène, Armande, and Bernard momentarily find a means of escaping from their apparent false selves to their true selves. Irène, at a masked ball, protected by her disguise, tastes for an instant "the monstrous pleasure of being alone, free, truthful in her native animality, of being the unknown woman, forever solitary and without shame, that a small mask and a hermetic costume have restored to her irremediable solitude and her dishonest innocence."[12] Armande, ordinarily prudish, becomes loving and caressing in gesture, intimate and vulgar in language, when her timid would-be lover, Maxime, is knocked unconscious by a falling chandelier while leaving her home. Bernard regains a sense of dignity when he helps a wounded Arab boy discovered at the place he and his mistress had chosen for a nocturnal meeting: "Poor Rose. . . . She was my woman, but he is my equal. It is curious that I had to come to Tangiers to meet my equal, the only one who can make me proud of him and proud of me. With a woman, one is easily a little ashamed, of her or of oneself."[13]

Ten-year-old Jean, in "The Sick Child," escapes through fever from the real world of his sickbed and the solicitous questions of Madame Maman to a fantastic, poetic world, composed of familiar objects metamorphosed, the existence of which he keeps hidden from those around him. Jean's recovery means the death of this world of perpetual revelation.

In each of these stories, and to a lesser degree in all the short stories of *The Hidden Woman* and *La Fleur de l'âge*, the characters are playing a game of hide-and-seek, alone and with others. In general, those who seek find something unexpected, and those who hide are discovered.

Irène's husband, who has deliberately not told his hitherto faithful wife that he is going to the masked ball and who in turn has been similarly deceived, finds her wandering from man to man, taking her fill of kisses. Although she does not recognize him, he recognizes her and allows her to betray herself. Maxime, who has failed miserably in his attempt at controlling his shyness in what he considers to be Armande's forbidding presence, pretends to be unconscious so as to enjoy the revelation of a sensual, affectionate Armande. Bernard, who is prepared for an evening of love, discovers that his mistress is essentially vulgar and that in binding Ahmed's wound with strips torn from his own jacket, he has given and received much more that that which he sought with Rose.

Jean is always beginning to play a game of hide-and-seek with Madame Maman and she with him, but neither of them can be trusted to close his eyes and count to twenty. "She thinks I'm asleep. . . . He thinks that I think he's asleep. . . . She thinks I'm not suffering. . . . How well he knows how to imitate a child who isn't suffering. . . ."[14]

Jean's important game of hide-and-seek is played with death. The further Jean goes in his exploration of a world in which he can fly on a paper knife or ride on a lavender smell, a world in which applesauce is transformed into "an acid young provincial girl of fifteen who, like other girls of the same age, had only disdain and arrogance for the ten-year-old boy,"[15] the further he moves from the real world, the closer he comes to death, which is what he is really seeking. Colette refuses Jean what might have been an empty revelation, the very unsatisfactory ending of a dangerous game. She brings him back to a world in which a paper knife cuts, lavender smells and applesauce is an often unattractive food. In abandoning, with Jean, her brief excursion into the world of imaginative revelation, Colette deliberately casts her choice for a world in which revelation is limited to that of the "hidden man" or the "hidden woman."

Anecdote and Meditation

The three chapters in *The Tendrils of the Vine* which compose the "Valentine" cycle are forerunners of Colette's longer first-person short stories: "Bella-Vista" in *Bella-Vista*, "Chance Acquaintances" and "Rainy Moon" in *Chance Acquaintances*, "The Képi" and "The Tender Shoot" in *The Képi* and "The Photographer's Wife" in *Gigi*. "It is insane to think that the periods without love are 'empty spaces' in a woman's existence. On the contrary. . . . These 'empty spaces' which took it upon themselves to furnish me with anecdotes, with troubled, lost, incomprehensible or simple characters who tugged at my sleeve, used me as witness, then let me go, I did not know then that they were more romantic interludes than my own personal dramas."[16]

Colette spent these "periods without love" in Paris or in French provincial hotels. The "romantic interludes" are transformed into short stories in which Colette appears as narrator, observer and character. Ostensibly these are "real" stories, based on real anecdotes, about people whom Colette meets in her travels; sometimes, as in the "Valentine" stories, "The Képi" and "The Tender Shoot," real friends supposedly tell Colette their past or present experiences. The air of authenticity is reinforced by the presence of other real people: Willy, Georges Wague, Annie de Pène, Paul Masson.

The atmosphere in these stories is always mysterious. What is Valentine's "disguised sorrow"? What is the connection between Monsieur Daste and the dead birds? What is Madame Ruby? Why does Monsieur Haume never stop looking at his watch? What is the strange relation between Colette's past and the two sisters who live in her old apartment? Why does the photographer's wife attempt to kill herself? Why does Albin Chaveriat, at the age of seventy, refuse the invitation of a friend whose household abounds in young girls?

Colette would have one believe that the people, each possessed of a particular secret, living a particular drama, a drama that would have passed unnoticed were it not for the writer who, observing the tics and the habits of her habitual or chance acquaintances, divines, intuits, imagines and creates. If one were to protest that a person such as madame Ruby, supposedly a Lesbian but really a man, or the series of coincidences that bring together the characters in "Chance Acquaintances" hardly seem ordinary, Colette would undoubtedly answer that the protest reveals inability to see, that everyone does have a secret, that everyone, at some time, fails to use such phrases as "the lover of young girls," or "the betrayed lover," or "the spinster," thereby implying that her characters belong to, and behave in a manner appropriate to, a general class of humanity.

That "Colette" attracts confidences and confessions, there can be no doubt. Her name is known even to chance acquaintances, and as she is a willing card player and a good listener, it is not very difficult to engage her socially. What is most revealing about "Colette" is that she is obviously unable to bear the solitude for which she pretends to yearn. Her arrival at a hotel is followed by a period of uneasiness caused by the strangeness of her room, the difference in the air and the necessity of speaking to unknown people. Her one desire is to return immediately to Paris. And yet, although she frequently reiterates that her acquaintances and their problems bore or annoy her, that she prefers the company of her dog or her cat to human contacts, once the initial presentations have been made, "Colette" quite willingly plays the role of detective or accomplice and soon finds that her room is livable, the air refreshing and the people interesting.

Her fear of solitude, a strong curiosity and a very real affection for human beings, an affection which "Colette" is often reluctant to admit, invariably propel her toward others. But it is not merely by chance that the secrets she discovers, the dramas in which she becomes entangled, reflect her own secrets, her own private dramas, that the "real" first-person short stories should bear so strong a resemblance to the invented third-person short stories. The "real" world of her experiences and her created world are very much the same. The only important difference between the two is that in the "real" world the revelation is double. A mystery is resolved, and "Colette" is partially unmasked. The moral of the story, and there is always a moral, supports the double revelation and becomes an apology for the drama, its actors and its narrator. "Whenever I think of her, I always see her firmly entrenched behind scruples that she modestly called annoyances and sustained by outbursts of feminine grandeur, humble and everyday, a grandeur which she misjudged by inflicting on it the name of 'a very small life.'[17]

The women, of which "my friend Valentine" is the first, are the unsuspecting heroines of Colette's first-person short stories. They are always courageous and always unaware of their courage, which, were it not for Colette, would have passed unnoticed. Colette lifts these women from oblivion, demonstrating once more that drama and heroism, far from being exceptions, are integral parts of many a "very small life."

The narrator, "Colette," also shares in this "feminine grandeur, humble and everyday." Her own daily life, her own "scruples," which she, too, modestly calls "annoyances," constitute in fact the second, complementary drama in these stories, a drama which she pretends to ignore. This lonely woman, so ready to apply the adjective "courageous" to others—is she not, by implication, the most courageous of all and her stories the proof of this courage that grapples with the daily adventure, attempting to give it a meaning and a value?

Aside from the very specific nature of the subject matter, "Music-Halls" in *The Tendrils of the Vine* and Colette's later music-hall anecdotes, *Music Hall Sidelights* and "Gribiche" in *Bella-Vista*, belong with the first-person short stories. In the music hall as in her chance acquaintanceships, "Colette" is both an outsider and a participant, more conscious of the task of illuminating the life of her companions than of the fact that she is revealing her own. Colette's music hall stories are documents on a world that no longer exists, sentimental tales in which the moral twist often seems excessive. One begins to wonder whether poverty and hard work are always attributes of heroism and dignity, whether intellectual mediocrity always implies moral superiority and whether Colette is not relying a little too much on her own facility to move from the particular to the general.

It is in the light of Colette's pre-music hall existence, her life with Monsieur Willy, that this emphasis on pride, dignity and morality is brought into proper focus. If it weakens the anecdotes, it nevertheless strengthened Colette. The music-hall stories, for all their local color, are essentially studies in the development of the character "Colette."

Quotations are from the *Oeuvres complètes de Colette* (Paris: Flammarion, 1948–1950).

Notes

1. "Châ," *La Femme cachée* [The Hidden Woman], 456.

2. "L'Enfant malade" ["The Sick Child"] was published for the first time with "Gigi," in 1945, although the story was written at an unknown, earlier date.

3. "La Femme cachée," *La Femme cachée*, 375.

4. "L'Aube" ["The Dawn"], *ibid.*, 380.

5. "La Main" ["The Hand"], *ibid.*, 389.

6. "L'Impasse" ["The Impasse"], *ibid.*, 393.

7. "Le Juge" ["The Judge], *ibid.*, 402.

8. "Le Cambrioleur" ["The Burglar"], *ibid.*, 421.

9. "L'Habitude" ["Habit"], *ibid.*, 469.

10. "L'Assassin" ["The Assassin"], *ibid.*, 432.

11. "Le Paysage" ["The Landscape"], *ibid.*, 441.

12. "La Femme cachée," *ibid.*, 379.

13. "Le rendez-vous," *Bella-Vista*, 269.

14. "L'Enfant malade," *Gigi*, 64.

15. *Ibid.*, 72.

16. *Bella-Vista*, 133.

17. "La Dame du photographe" ["The Photographer's Wife"], *Gigi*, 129.

Donna Norrell*

It has been generally accepted that Colette's famous imperative "Look . . . look . . ." [Colette's last words before her death, according to her husband, Maurice Goudeket, in *Close to Colette* (New York: Farrar, Straus and Cudahy, 1957), 244] is a call to readers to look more objectively at the world about them, to shed their prejudices and their preconceived ideas in an effort to see that world as it really is. Colette's own considerable descriptive powers were so firmly rooted in long-standing habits of observation that Thierry Maulnier wrote: "Colette never supposes, she sees, she hears and she notices, implacably."[1] His is a judgment almost universally shared by critics, who agree that she was, in fact, a writer who took no detail for granted.

Many of Colette's readers discover with surprise, therefore, that she dabbled in the occult. Her fascination with the material world and her insistence on the importance of the senses in evaluating terrestrial phenomena might seem to preclude the idea that she could be seriously interested in such activity. That is not the case. Colette gives the senses the chief role to play in interpreting the world only because most of the time she is dealing with material phenomena, which must be sensually perceived. But her basic canon of objectivity holds true for every kind of experience. In the twenty or so volumes of fiction, essays, and correspondence that she left to posterity, references to the occult reveal that Colette had direct contact with certain occult practices and that, although she was far from being credulous, she at no time dismissed occult phenomena as nonsense.

Her ventures into this domain were, however, both haphazard and intermittent. Her first important encounter with it took place early in the century, when she accompanied a friend to visit a Russian psychic "Saphira." The friend, a lesbian, was told that she would soon run off with a young man. This event, which none but the psychic foresaw,

Colette: The Woman the Writer, eds. Mari McCarty and Erica Eisinger. University Park and London: Pennsylvania State University Press, 1981, 54–65, © 1981 by the Pennsylvania State University. Reproduced by permission of the publisher.

proved to be true. Over the years, Colette visited other psychics, of various kinds. Two women, "the sleeping woman of Caulaincourt Street" and Elise, "the woman with the candle," demonstrated, she says, a "not very believable (but verified) infallibility" (*L'Etoile vesper*, XIII: 271)[2] to read the past and the future of their clients; while a third, whom she calls simply "Mme B . . ." and who "saw" the spirits of Colette's father and brother (*Sido*, VII: 216–19), gave her pause to reflect by mentioning certain facts known only to Colette herself. These visits were few in number, but Colette mentions them time and again in her essays.[3] She finds them fascinating, because they are incomprehensible. Looking back, some thirty years later, on her initial experiences, she writes: "Who will give me the key to Saphira? How does one distinguish, among all the hodge-podge of tinsel, banality, Slavic origins, kabbalistic names, make-up, huge rings and fitted frock coats, the extent to which he possessed real lucidity and powers of sorcery, to use the word that satisfies me the most?" (*L'Etoile vesper*, XIII: 269–270). That showmanship, and even quackery, often play a role in such practices, she readily admits, but her observations left her persuaded that there is sometimes an authentic gift involved. An essay of 1922 sets out her position on the whole subject: "Do I believe, then, in this candle that burns and drips tears of stearin, in the images of the future and the past its disagreeable-smelling fumes form and dissipate? Not exactly. Yes and no . . . Let's get this clear. Pierre Faget and his colleagues in magic . . . they only make me shrug my shoulders. Reading coffee grounds is childish. Playing with yarrow sticks is gross superstition. But the woman with the candle . . ." (*Prisons et paradis*, VII: 396).[4] Colette's view remained unchanged until her death. She held that, although one must not be blindly superstitious, anything may be possible in this world: personal experience is the only real test.

This is precisely the position taken by the narrator of "La Lune de pluie" when confronted with the enigma of Délia Essendier, sister of Rosita Barberet. In this *nouvelle*, published in 1940 and the only one of Colette's fictional works in which the occult is a major theme, the narrator is presented with a whole series of riddles. Why is Rosita so secretive about Délia? Why has she been crying? How can "thinking" make Délia so tired? What does Délia do with the scissors? Though the narrator is reluctant to abandon her original idea that Délia is pining for her estranged husband, these and other considerations lead her to say: "Since I had come to know Délia Essendier, it . . . seemed to me that more than ever I needed to know [things] by myself, and

without consulting anybody else" (p. 385). None of the explanations
she can think of seems to stand. Yet she is completely unprepared for
Rosita's disclosure that Délia is practicing black magic, that the young
woman is attempting to "convoke" Eugène Essendier and thereby
weaken and destroy him.

To believe or not to believe in black magic? That is the question
posed to the reader of "La Lune de pluie." It is never openly presented
as such. Colette has long had the reputation of a writer who weds prose
style to matter. In "La Lune de pluie" she goes farther than that. The
entire work is built upon a network of structural elements—narrative
movement, digressions, symbols and leitmotifs, symmetrical character-
izations and relationship of characters—so carefully arranged that all
serve to decoy the reader into a position where he is obliged to pose
this ultimate question to himself, and even to answer it in a certain
way.

The tale (for such it may be called) gives the impression of being
constructed upon very informal lines. The narrative seems rambling.
Passages on what is ostensibly the subject—"the Barberet story" (p.
374)—are interrupted by reminiscences and discussions of apparently
irrelevant topics. Close examination reveals, however, that there is not
one narrative movement but two, and that the digressions have important functions of their own.

The narrator begins by relating how, on her first visit to her new
typist Rosita Barberet, she discovered that Rosita was living in an
apartment in which she herself had once spent many unhappy hours
brooding on the unfaithfulness of her (now ex-) husband. As she recognizes one familiar object after another—the window catch, a panel of
old wallpaper, the ceiling rosette, the floor plan, the sound of a door,
the slope of the front steps—she is left in no doubt but that the house
was previously her own. What renders the situation even more strange
is that it is because of a man from B . . . , whose accent recalls that
of her former husband, "that other man from B . . ." (p. 367), that
she has visited the house once more. At her next visit, she learns that
the apartment is shared by Rosita's sister Délia, who, estranged from
her husband, spends most of her time in the room the narrator calls
"*my* room." The coincidence becomes too much to resist. She pene-
trated into the room, sees the young woman on the divan, and believes
she has found in her what she later calls "my young self that I would
never be again, that I never stopped disowning yet regretting" (p.
378). Thus is born the narrator's fascination for Délia Essendier.

The double narrative movement arises out of the narrator's decision to keep secret her discovery of the "coincidence." Colette establishes the duality in the opening scene. There, she presents, in carefully alternated passages, the banal conversation and gestures of Rosita and the narrator, as well as the secret small discoveries that the latter is simultaneously making. For example:

> I lifted the muslin curtain with my forehead and placed my hand on the window catch. Immediately, I experienced the slight, rather pleasant giddiness that accompanies dreams of falling and flying . . . For I was holding in my hand that singular window catch, that little cast-iron mermaid whose form my palm had not forgotten, after so many years [. . .]

> Not having put her glasses on, Mlle Barberet noticed nothing . . . [. . .] a few square inches of wallpaper remained bare: I could distinguish its roses whose color had nearly vanished, its purple convulvus fading to grey and . . . I could see again all that I had once left behind [. . .]

> this view is pretty . . .

> Most of all, it's bright for an upstairs storey. Let me arrange your papers, Madame [. . .]. (p. 361)

And during all the rest of the *nouvelle* the narrator continues, through an alternating inner-outer movement of past description and monologue, to relate what is, in effect, two separate series of events: one, external, centering on the activities of Délia and Rosita; another, internal, centering on the narrator's own reactions and thoughts. Each furnishes the reader with a series of mysteries, strange events, and questions, which are one by one cleared up or answered in the course of the story, but only as they give way in turn to new mysteries, events, and questions.

Actually, the story has begun with an emphasis on strangeness, for the narrator's interest in Délia has been engendered by her discovery of the coincidence of the lodging. It is nourished, however, by concerns that are narcissistic (and not altruistic, as her readiness to accede to Rosita's request that she "talk to" Délia might suggest). This explains why she is so slow to understand that there is something sinister about Délia's behavior. She is given a whole series of clues, dating even from before the discovery that she has once lived in the apartment. Rosita seems to lie about the length of time she has lived there (p. 360); she does not want to discuss her sister at all (p. 368); she is vague about the nature of Délia's "sickness" (p. 371); she says that Délia has an *idée fixe* (p. 377). As for Délia herself, she claims that her "work" is extremely fatiguing, though she seems to do nothing but lie about all day; she says also that it is good for her to touch pointed objects (p. 392); "I'm looking after him," she says, ironically, of her "boyfriend" standing in the street (p. 394). But so caught up is the narrator by the coincidence of the lodging, that for a long time she fails to realize that the picture she has painted of Délia's psychology has its counterpart only in her own memory.

The reader soon ceases to marvel at the "coincidence." Instead, one's attention is drawn first to the clues, that is, to the many small mysteries in the behavior of the two sisters, and secondly to the narrator's changing attitudes. More than once the latter is tempted to wash her hands of the sisters, but each time something occurs to change her mind. Early in the story, she experiences a moment of aversion on learning that Délia is unhappily married, for, she says, she does not care for "other people's conjugal difficulties" (p. 372); then, her first sight of the "rain-moon"—a halo of refracted light on the wall—and the news that Délia is actually living in her old room reawaken her interest (pp. 372–373). A sinister movement takes place when she first suspects Rosita of jealousy, because, she admits, she does not like jealousy either; but again the movement is checked, this time by another mystery—when, reluctantly, she knocks once more at the sister's door, Délia's prostrate form bars her way (pp. 380–382).

It is only after this visit, about halfway through the story, that the narrator herself analyzes the situation. Her awareness of her own emotional attachment in which, however, affection plays no part, now becomes equal to the reader's understanding of it. She says, "Yet I did not like Délia Essendier, and the cherished companion whom I sought, was it not my former self, its pathetic form stuck between the walls of this wretched lodging like a petal between two pages?" (p. 388). She understands that she has *wanted* the coincidence to be significant. Now, she sees, as well, that the sisters present a mystery far more challenging than the strangeness of the original event. And so, as has always been her habit, she seeks enlightenment in her own experience. But no amount of reflection sheds light on the enigma of Délia's behavior. Nor, indeed, does further investigation, for Délia's bizarre replies to her questions furnish more mystery than explanation, and the only conclusion supplied by her observations is that the resemblance she has believed to exist between Délia's situation and her former one has no basis in fact: " 'It's fatigue.' But what kind of fatigue? That caused by an unhealthy life? No unhealthier than mine, and just as healthy as that of other women and girls of Paris. A few days earlier, Délia had touched her forehead and clutched at her temples, saying: 'That's what makes me tired . . . And that . . .' The fixed idea, yes, the absent, the unfaithful Essendier . . . In vain I contemplated that perfect beauty—and, studied feature by feature, Délia's face was flawless—in vain I sought there signs of suffering, signs, that is, of suffering from love" (p. 394). The narrator has finally joined the reader in remarking the oddity of the two sisters' conduct. But the reader's interest in her psychology will continue, for her reaction to Rosita's revelations will be every bit as intriguing as was her reaction to the coincidence of the lodging.

With Rosita's disclosure, the narrator comes into possession of all the facts. The disclosure takes place in two stages—the initial one at the sisters' apartment, and its continuation the next evening at the home of the narrator. The latter remarks that Rosita herself has changed. "In less than two weeks," she says, "my 'old young girl' had become a real old maid" (p. 397). And, even though for her visit to the narrator's she has redonned her usual correct costume, Rosita "seemed to have repudiated forever the two little ringlets on her shoulder. The brim of her hat came down over the mournful snail-shaped bun, symbol of all renouncements" (p. 406). This change is significant: Rosita has given up the struggle to save Eugène, believing him doomed.

The tale is remarkable for the abruptness with which it ends. The day after Rosita's visit, the narrator renounces the two sisters, even though she is still enough attracted to Délia to arrange to meet her "by chance" three more times. Then one final time, she happens to see Délia from afar. Délia is wearing widow's weeds. All the events preceding this last one are reported with commentary, but the last incident is described briefly, cryptically. The abruptness of the ending strikes the reader, for it is extremely effective, dramatically. In the course of the narrative, mystery after mystery has been dispelled or cleared up, but not the final mystery of Eugène's death. And, at intervals during her rambling recital, the narrator has informed the reader of her views on a good many subjects, but on the last and most important subject she is silent. The result is that the reader finishes the story with two questions uppermost in his mind. Has Délia's magic actually been successful? And what is the narrator's opinion on the matter?

On the surface, it appears that the reader is free to judge of these questions for himself. But there is evidence that Colette actually wishes to influence the reader, that she wishes, in fact, to abandon a good part of any skepticism to which he may be prone.

The first corroboration of this idea can be found in the inner narrative movement, which suggests that the narrator is secretly willing to admit of the efficacy of Délia's activities. Very early in the story, she has shown herself to be secretive, by concealing from the sisters—for no very clear reason—her discovery of the "coincidence." Later, she conceals something else from them, something more important: a familiarity with the occult. Immediately after her first visit, long before she expects that any untoward activities are taking place in her former abode, she reminisces on her own visits to psychics. "Among fortunetellers," she says, "those to whom a fleeting gift of second sight is given on our behalf are rare" (p. 366). It is a statement of faith. Further passages mention similar experiences (pp. 374, 402–402). And, indeed, the narrator confesses that even on the subject of black magic she is not uninformed. "Certainly," she says, "on the subject of simple and popular magic, I was not so unknowledgeable as I had wished to appear in Mlle Barberet's eyes" (p. 403). The inner narrative and the digressive passages are thus useful. They serve, in part, as a portrait of the narrator, leading the reader into her mind so that he may be influenced by her attitude whether he wants to be or not. And they also show that she is not the complete skeptic she pretends to be in front of Rosita Barberet.

They do more. They reveal that, despite the impression she gives the reader of confiding everything about herself, it is completely within the narrator's character to withhold important information. And if she does that with Rosita, why not with the reader as well?

The reader at whom this particular deceit is aimed is, of course, the die-hard skeptic, whose attitude is such that he has decided *a priori* that any so-called experience of the occult is so much nonsense. Ordinarily, such a reader might be expected to dismiss the story from his mind once he gets to the end of it, even assuming that he does get to the end. But the narrator has laid down a special trap for him. Throughout the story, she has continually emphasized the fact that all her judgments are based on the observations of empirical data; she has given numerous examples of this type of reasoning.[5] She therefore appeals to the skeptical reader on his own ground of rationality, so that if he accepts the idea that the data she presents on "the Barberet story" is accurate, then he must also accept the conclusion implied. But why does she not state what that conclusion is? Because the conclusion to which the narrator is obliged to come is one at which the rational mind balks. The skeptical reader who identifies with the rational viewpoint repeatedly expressed by the narrator becomes, then, at the end of the story, a skeptic at bay.

Other influences are at work on the more pliable reader. The subject matter of the digressive passages themselves is significant here, for they fall into two main groups. One group deals with what the narrator's past can conjure up of strangeness, that is, with coincidences and contacts with the occult. More than once, in these passages, she concludes that nowhere has she encountered anything quite like the two sisters. For instance: "Thus, I reckoned up everything inexplicable that had more or less become part of my experience thanks to dull-witted intermediaries, vacant creatures whose emptiness reflects fragments of destinies, modest liars and vehement visionaries. None had done me harm, none had frightened me. But those two dissimilar sisters . . ." (p. 409). The second group deals with her current activities—writing, bicycling, dining out, going to the flea market, and entertaining her mother, whose presence, she says, "recalled my life to dignity and to kindness" (p. 396). These two types of passages seem to have little in common; but, in fact, the harmlessness of the *voyantes* and the eminent sanity of the narrator's own activities serve to set the present situation in relief and to point up the reason for her uneasiness: "the Barberet story" is singular because it is of evil.

What disturbs the narrator, then, is not Délia's practice of the occult, but her evil intent. After the renouncement, the latter's attraction lingers on, but the narrator is prudent. Recalling the three "chance" meetings, she says of Délia, "Something unnamable, deep within me, stirred and spoke in her favor. But I did not respond" (p. 415). The truth is that Rosita's disclosure had pushed her to the limits of her credulity, for Rosita has insisted that the practice of black magic is far from rare. "She [Délia] isn't the only one who does it. It's quite common," she says (p. 401). In our neighborhoods there are lots who repeat the name. [. . .] It's well known" (p. 412). The narrator muses on this idea: "Whispers, an ignorant faith, even the habits of a whole neighborhood, were *those* the forces, the magic philters that procure love, decide questions of life and death, and move that haughty mountain: an indifferent heart?" (p. 412). She offers no answer, and the reader is left with the question still open three pages later, when the narrative ends.

The double narrative movement and the digressive passages both support, therefore, the idea that, however much the narrator may *wish* not to take the idea of black magic seriously, her rational mind is tempted to accept it, because even in her own broad experience the case is exceptional. Rosita has believed in it all along, and, since events suggest finally that the latter's opinion on this one case has been well-founded, the implication is that perhaps her remarks on society as a whole repose on something more solid than superstition as well. The idea that, under the apparently humdrum stream of everyday life, there flows a darker, persistent current, which many people cannot or do not choose to recognize is suggested many times by Rosita. "And the confectioner from downstairs, what has she done, then, with her husband?" she asks. "And the dairy-man from number 57, it's a bit strange that he's a widower for the second time, isn't it?" (p. 408). "It's very well-known" (p. 412). Rosita reproaches the narrator for her ignorance: "A person as well-educated as you . . ." (p. 407). And, indeed, in the lives of the two sisters themselves the narrator has seen evidence that people, and events, are not always what they seem.

This idea is central to the deeper significance of "La Lune de pluie": the notion that individuals and society as a whole have often a hidden side which we are sometimes reluctant even to know. Certainly, Délia Essendier is not what she seems when the narrator first meets her; nor, according to Rosita is the little society of the *quartier*, which the narrator has always considered so innocent and picturesque. And Délia and her fellow-practitioners of magic are not even exceptional in this way. Colette suggests, by her portrayal of the other two major characters, that the situation may be universal. The narrator has shown herself to be garrulous or secretive according to the moment. And in Rosita's eyes, her image is that of a "woman alone" (p. 395), that is, of the separated or divorced woman obliged to live, in that first decade of the century, outside respectable society; yet we know, through what the narrator says about herself, that her conduct gives rise to no scandal and that her activities are, in fact, thoroughly wholesome.

As for Rosita she is, oddly enough, the key personage of the three. Colette has distributed the weight of the narrative interest more or less equally on the three women. The plot, or dramatic interest, weighs more heavily on Délia, since both the narrator and Rosita are interested primarily in her. The psychological interest is, of course, borne by the narrator, in her reactions to events both inner and outer. But the import of the tale is concentrated in Rosita. She is quite unlike Délia. As she says, "First of all, there is a certain difference of age between us, and she is dark. Besides, as far as our characters are concerned, we're not at all alike" (p. 373). She is also different from the narrator, in that she is considered respectable where the narrator is not, and in that she harbors ideas completely at variance with those sanctioned by the respectable society of which she is a part, while the narrator displays no such leanings. And, whereas Délia and the narrator have "hidden" sides, Rosita reveals considerable paradox within herself. This "old young girl" whose correctness of dress and manner is the first thing that one notices about her, invites the narrator to watch her step, saying, "My sister is lying on the floor" as if she were saying, "My sister has gone to the post-office" (p. 382). Even her beliefs are unsoundable. "And what about the devil, Rosita?" asks the narrator, attempting to comprehend the other's ideas. And Rosita replies, surprised, "But, Madame, what do you mean? The devil is for imbeciles. The devil, just imagine . . ." (p. 413). In a flash of intuition, the narrator guesses that "it's in Rosita, so colorless and prim, that one must seek the solution to this little puzzle" (p. 395). And, indeed, it is Rosita's character which most accurately reflects the central meaning of the tale: that paradox and strangeness are but the obverse of the commonplace.

The characteral significance is supported, in part, by symbolic names. Actually, the narrator herself is never named. To all appearances, she is one of the many Madame Colettes whose lives resemble their creator's own. But Rosita calls her simply "Madame," so that that assumption is never completely valid and the ambiguity of her identity merely adds to the general atmosphere of secrecy surrounding her. On the other hand, "Rosita" signifies "little rose," and is coupled here with the surname Barberet, a play on the French word *barbare* (Latin *barbarus*; Greek *barbaros*), meaning, in its first sense, an outsider, a foreigner, a stranger, and in its second sense, an uncivilized person. Together the two names are perfectly descriptive of Rosita, who in many respects is an innocent young girl but who places faith in practices banned by the civilization to which she presumably belongs.

Her enigmatic sister is "this Délia who did not want to be called

Adèle" (p. 415). Adèle is a saint's name,[6] but Délia is an epithet of
the goddess Artemis, derived from the name of her birthplace, Delos.
The adoption of the name Délia is therefore symbolic of her intention.
Less innocent than Rosita, she has abandoned altogether the Christian
religion into which she was born, in order to participate in rites that
seek their origin in pagan antiquity. The name Délia is well chosen,
for Artemis is goddess of the hunt and of the moon. It is therefore apt
that she should assign to herself that identity while she "hunts" Eugène
Essendier under the auspices of the "rain-moon."

These names form part of a network of minor symbolic elements
designed to support the main idea and to add to the accumulated
impression of strangeness. The central symbol is the one designated
by the title, the "rain-moon." In the story, the term refers to a halo
of refracted light, by which the sunlight separates into its component
colors as it passes through thick glass and is projected on the wall. It
seems at first to be merely one more of the many things the narrator
recognizes as she confirms the fact the the apartment was once her
own. But, unlike the other objects, it is mentioned again and again,
and takes on additional importance with every repetition. Although
the narrator has once considered it to be a symbol of hope, Rosita says
that her sister is afraid of it, that Délia calls it "an omen" (p. 372).
Later, the narrator asks, "A blind alley haunted by evil plans, was that
what had become of the little apartment where once I had suffered so
innocently, under the guardianship of my rain-moon?" (pp. 403–404).
In folklore, the term used in its original sense signifies something else:
a moon with a diffused halo around it, and the belief is that the "rain-
moon" betokens rain for the morrow.[7] So Délia is right. Just such an
announcement, just such an "omen" it turns out to be, not of love
requited but of death.

A system of number and color symbolism is related to the central
symbol and to the central meaning of the tale. The number three,
which has mystical overtones because of its association with the Trinity
as well as with various unholy mythical trios, recurs often. There are
three women, of whom now one and now another becomes prominent,
depending upon which aspect of the tale is being considered. Three
segments of society are also presented: the wholesome one in which
the narrator moves, the strange but harmless milieu to which the *voyantes* belong, and the sinister world of the two sisters. Three times the
narrator speaks of her experiences of the occult and three times she
arranges to meet a weakened Délia in the street. Symbolically, three

represents the synthesis of duality and unity, so that its use here evokes the idea that room must be made in our concept of reality for the hidden side, for the incomprehensible, because it, too, is part of the whole.

Seven is equally important. "The three is after the seven," observes Rosita, as she rearranges the narrator's pages (p. 362). She offers to retype the last page, since "it will only take seven minutes" (p. 362). As she arrives to confide in the narrator for the last time, the clock strikes seven, and her revelations are delayed only long enough for her to drink "a glass of Lunel wine" (p. 406), which is, she says, "a magic drink" (p. 406). In the language of the occult, the number seven signifies completion, termination, and so in despair Rosita tells the narrator that Eugène is doomed, that "six moons have already passed, the seventh is here, it is the fatal moon, the poor man knows that he has been summoned" (p. 407).[8]

Significantly, the number of colors in the spectrum and so of the "rain-moon" itself is seven, with the seventh color being violet. Mention of this color runs like a refrain throughout the tale, as Rosita asks what color of typed copies she should make: "In violet or in black?" (p. 362). But at the last visit she does not ask. "Like a stranger, Rosita listened and said, 'Very well . . . Fine . . . In black and in violet . . . It will be finished Wednesday' " (p. 398). And events do prove finally that the two colors signify the same thing, for when the seventh and fatal moon is past Délia wears "a dress whose black turns to violet in the sunlight" (p. 415). The seventh color, like the seventh moon, is death.[9]

"La Lune de pluie" is not a particularly profound work, although Colette is a far more profound writer than she is currently given credit for. But in any case, this tale certainly provides ample evidence that she is a superb craftsman. What seems to be a rambling but simple narrative is actually a tightly constructed maze of significant detail, ordered in such a way as to lead the reader down one or more paths of the author's choosing. Even in her use of digression Colette achieves considerable economy, for she ensures that at one and the same time these apparently superfluous passages dramatize the exterior action, offer the reader insight into the narrator's psychology, and provide the skeptic with food for thought.

Many of these passages also add to the immense accumulation of suggestive matter that Colette amasses to back up the main idea. References to coincidences, mysteries, presentiments, experiences with the occult, symbolic names, numbers and colors, and, of course, the ever-recurring "rain-moon": the sheer weight of these is impressive. Events, we are shown, are not necessarily what they seem, nor are people. Every phenomenon has two aspects, the seen and the unseen, and, in that, it resembles the room wherein Délia weaves her spell, "dark on one side, bright on the other" (p. 363). What we consider to be true depends, like the color of Délia's dress, on our perspective.

So suggests Colette in "La Lune de pluie," where the narrator consciously chooses to rely on her rational mind, on her experience, on *herself*, but in the end can only suspect.

Is Colette, finally, asking the readers of "La Lune de pluie" to believe in the occult? Not necessarily, for her intention is always to tell a good tale. But many times in her works, she expresses the thought that man is afraid of anything which upsets his serenity, his sense of being in control. Any occult phenomenon will disturb him in that way. Of her own contacts with the occult, Colette wrote: "I believe that during my lifetime I have not consulted more than four or five persons gifted with second sight. But it gives me pleasure to recognize that their various gifts had the potential to upset our human view of events" (*L'Etoile vesper*, XIII: 268). The structure of "La Lune de pluie" is designed to do the same thing.

Notes

1. *Introduction à Colette* (Paris: La Palme, 1954), p. 58.

2. Unless otherwise stated, all references to Colette's works are to the fifteen-volume *Oeuvres complètes* (Paris: Flammarion, 1948–1950). References to works other than "La Lune de pluie," which is in Volume XI, will give both volume and page numbers. Translations are mine.

3. The most important passages dealing with the occult are, in addition to "La Lune de pluie," the following: *Aventures quotidiennes*, VI: 428–31; *Sido*, VII: 216–19; *Prisons et paradis*, VIII: 394–96; *L'Etoile vesper*, XIII: 264–273; *Journal intermittent*, XIV: 260–261.

4. Pierre Faget was a country sorcerer whose arrest and trial caused a minor sensation in France during the winter of 1921–22.

5. See, for example, p. 359, where the narrator discusses the differences in the wear of cuffs and sleeves between scribes and typists; and pp. 384–85, where she remarks on how the movements of certain animals betray their species, and how certain gestures and tics reveal the innermost thoughts of people.

6. The Benedictine abbess, Saint Adela, daughter of Dagobert II, c. 675–734.

7. In a letter to Lucie Saglio, tentatively dated by researchers as mid-September, 1940, Colette wrote: "You know, it's the moon that has a rainbow halo around it and that announces bad weather" (*Lettres à ses pairs* [Paris: Flammarion, 1973], p. 135).

8. According to J. E. Cirlot's *A Dictionary of Symbols* (trans. Jack Sage [New York: Philosophical Library, 1962], p. 223), seven is "symbolic of perfect order, a complete period or cycle." *The Encyclopedia Americana* (Canadian ed., 1950, Vol. 24) gives this explanation: "Various reasons have been given for the peculiar regard had for this number, such as that seven is a symbol of completeness, being compounded of three and four, perfect numbers, they being representable in space by the triangle and the square."

9. Color symbolism is more variable than number symbolism. However, Cirlot says that a superficial classification will have the "cold, 'retreating' colors" ("blue, indigo, violet and, by extension, black") corresponding to "processes of dissimulation, passivity and debilitation" (p. 50). The novel suggests a movement from violet to black in the progressive debilitation of Eugène that will end in his death. This idea is consistent with the more obvious symbolism of violet in the tale, for there violet derives most of its symbolism from its relationship to the number seven, being the seventh and last color of the spectrum. Beyond it lies (in nonscientific terms) the void (i.e., blackness). As an echo of seven, therefore, violet acquires the meaning of something ended to completed, and in "La Lune de pluie" that something is Eugène's life. In this way, black—a universal symbol of death—is but the extension of violet, or, in other terms, Eugène's potential death realized.

Mari McCarty*

Women are other in a world in which the structures of society, meaning, and language are defined and controlled by men. "On the boundary" of the male world, women can only overcome their Otherness by becoming consciously marginal, by reveling in marginality. Mere "equality" with men within the phallic constructs would mean an acceptance of patriarchal space; but by entering the boundary zone voluntarily, women can cast off Otherness. In doing so, women become aware that this "boundary" is in fact infinitely expanding space.[1]

Many of Colette's characters are "on the fringe" of society, part of the aptly-named "demimonde," such as courtisans, actresses, and homosexuals. Other characters, because they are not defined by their attachment to a male, are also "on the boundary": the divorced woman, the widowed woman, any woman not basking in the reflected glory of a man. In this fringe world, Colette is showing us a refuge from phallic constructs. Establishment critics who praised her "matchless style" did not see the new dimension of Colette's gynocentric optic. Her literary success, even as she de-valorized androcentric space, is revelatory of one important characteristic of the boundary zone: it is invisible to those who have not entered it. People in the new space are of course physically present in the same old world, yet are emotionally, psychologically, and linguistically unfettered by patriarchal convention.

But how to reach this new space? As any traveler entering unfamiliar territory, we can benefit from the presence of a guide, a mentor.[2] In Colette's time, not many women had made that voyage. The women who were consciously marginal were subjects of scandal: *The Pure and the Impure*, Colette's groundbreaking study of the fringes of sexuality, documents her sometimes vain attempt to create new space. But Colette herself did not adopt sexual deviance as her route to liberation. Instead, writing itself became her way to create a written self, a "Colette" who wrote herself into existence.

Women's Studies 8 (1981): 367–374. Copyright Gordon and Breach Science Publishers, Inc. Reproduced by permission of the publisher.

144

In this enterprise, Sido is her guide, her "model." We cannot take Sido to mean Colette's flesh and blood mother, but rather Colette's *idea* and *reconstruction* of her mother in the text. After creating herself, Colette created her own mentor. In *La Naissance du jour* (translated as *Break of Day*, but literally "the birth of the day"), Sido transcends her earthly status to become a seer, a goddess in touch with cosmic forces. *La Naissance du jour* is Colette's definitive assumption of her own space. While patriarchal critics see in it a renunciation (of love for a man), it is in reality a vital reaffirmation of the new possibilities outside the male domain. With herself (and "model" Sido) as mentor, she will achieve a new understanding, she will give birth to herself "on the boundary." At the end of the book the cramped confines of patriarchal space are behind her, while before her lies the vast, limitless scope of female potential.

Colette finds her identity with Sido in the mirror, which reveals an older Colette "little by little taking on her likeness."[3] Reminded of Sido by her own reflection, Colette creates a second self to serve as confidante and observer of her own actions: "I write that without laughing, and, raising my head, I look at myself, without laughing, in the inclined mirror; then I turn to my writing again." The detachment, the distance necessary for impartial comment on one's actions is gained through the mirror's mundane yet almost magical feat of splitting the self into two "entities," which thereafter can query and compliment each other.[4] The mirror is a portal to that new space, and the mirror image is one's guide and role-model.

Many of Colette's characters use mirrors at crucial moments when self-knowledge can lead to positive actions.[5] A true feeling can be verified, a false one uncovered by the contact between the self and its image. Armed with the certainty gained through self-scrutiny, the characters can act and thus take the first step to cast off Otherness and to enter the new space.

The Vagabond Renée Néré's famous "painted mentor," her reflection, is located "in that mysterious reflected room"—the other space which at first seems unreachable. Her fear that there may be no face under her makeup represents a glimpse of her non-person status in patriarchal space. Near the end of the book, Renée will decide against the phallic confines of marriage at the moment when she gazes out on the reflective sea, a vista which expands ever outward. Renée's fate at the end of *The Shackle*, sequel to *The Vagabond*, is an ironic reversal of this moment. She again sits of the edge of the sea, but this time she is "moored in place," prevented from entering its limitless possibilities. Colette herself expressed displeasure at the ending of the book, but professed to be unable to change it. *The Shackle* shows that all attempts to reach the new space are not fortuitous, and that, once having arrived, one must be constantly on guard against unwitting return to male confines.

All of Colette's work can be seen as an exodus from patriarchal space. Claudine's *Retreat From Love* is not a withdrawal in deference to her husband's memory, but a refusal of the androcentric community. Claudine's friend Annie leaves her husband to embark on a frightening but exhilarating voyage of discovery. *Duo*'s Alice returns to her sister's flat after Michel's death to find the *toutounier*, a refuge from the male world and a representation of the positive non-phallic values of childhood. (Colette, too, remembered her childhood as an "earthly paradise" of gynocentric space). In *Chéri*, Léa builds her mirrored spaces around men; in *The Last of Chéri*, she lives in a new space free from men. At the end of *The Other One*, Fannie and Jane have just begun their escape from male shallowness by cultivating their "inner reserves, which man had not dared to affront."

One short story, "The Tender Shoot" ("Le Tendron"), is revelatory of Colette's view of female space.[6] While "tendron" can refer to a tender shoot of a plant, it also means a very young nubile girl who is often the object of desire by an older man. The *Petit Robert* dictionary provides an old aphorism to illustrate its common usage: "Il lui faut des tendrons" ("He must have young girls"). This story will trace the fascination of the aging Lothario Albin for young Louisette, an attraction which the aphorism seems to codify as once having been fairly accepted, if not widespread. Colette allows Albin to tell the tale in his own words, but within her own narrative framework. She herself, as narrator, introduces Albin Chevariat to the reader. Albin himself is unaware of the reader; he is simply recounting his story to his friend Colette. Once he begins the body of his tale, always within quotation marks (conversational dashes in the French version), Colette does not interrupt him. She does, however, react to his story with an occasional raised eyebrow of interjection which we perceive through Albin's response to it.

Albin's fascination for a girl who has "gone beyond certain limits" takes place when he is visiting friends in an exclusive country estate whose definite boundaries are ill tended and beginning to crumble. Albin professes his sense of direction to be unerring ("I never do get off my track, you know"), but one day, when "outside the domain," he sees a dwelling shrouded in mist, surrounded by an overgrown garden. Just outside the garden he finds a modern-day Eve, Louisette, a young girl without artifice who wears a homemade necklace of berries. Later, Albin will offer her a store-bought necklace "whose beads were exactly the same bright pink as the 'square-cap' berries"—this she refuses, preferring the natural to the manufactured.

The magical garden contains a spring (*source* in French, indicating source of ever-flowing water and perhaps source of life as well) from which Albin wishes to drink, but Louisette refuses through fear of her mother. She does, however, lead Albin down "the sheltered path at the end of the wood, the whole length of the low, half-collapsed wall" which separates the garden from the conventional scenery around it. Although Albin would like to visit the mystical spring, he cannot do so without "crossing the barrier," so Louisette brings him a drink. Once back at the domain of his friends, Albin finds "a definite charm in playing bridge on a shady terrace, in reading the illustrated papers with the cool six o'clock wind ruffling their pages." These "civilized" pursuits are reassuring reminders that he is in control of his male world.

As the days go on, however, and his fascination for Louisette deepens, he marvels that she responds "so naturally, so eagerly" to his kisses: "I believe that the sensuality of any grown-up woman who behaved like Louisette would have revolted me," Albin forgives a child like Louisette for "having gone beyond certain limits" of sensual propriety, but is nevertheless disgruntled and faintly scandalized that she never expresses any gratitude or devotion to him: "she treated sensual pleasure as a lawful right." From a different "domain" than Albin, Louisette is also attuned to different stimuli beyond his capacity: "She listened to me certainly, but she was also listening to other sounds I did not hear and now and then would sign to me, sometimes rather rudely, to be quiet." He is also baffled when she continues to refuse his gifts: "She tore the ring off her finger and brutally flung it back to me. 'I've already commanded you (she said commanded) not to give me anything.' When I had sheepishly taken back my humble jewel, she made sure that the little cardboard box, the tissue paper and the blue tinsel ribbon were not still lying about on our chair of rocks and lichen. Odd, wasn't it??" Of course, it is not odd at all. Louisette does not want the unspoken charm of her garden soiled by his artificial accoutrements. It is as if she senses the danger inherent in accepting something that is not of her world. A Persephone who refuses the

147

pomegranate offered by Albin / Pluto, she will be able to remain with her mother / Demeter.

Although enjoying Albin's kisses, Louisette has thus far refused him entrance into the garden itself (and to her body), curtailing their meetings to "the spot where the garden wall overhung the path and gave it deepest shelter"—that is, the boundary zone itself. But a sudden rainstorm one night causes Louisette to take Albin by the hand and guide him into her domain: "I realized, from the denser darkness, that I had crossed a threshold, the threshold of Louisette's chateau.' " Once in that female space, Albin finds himself without his normal male defense: "my spirit of aggression was severely checked by this unfamiliar haven and the total darkness." Louisette reacts quite differently, feeling "warm and relaxed" in her home space. Suddenly, a light appears: "there is a great difference between electric light and any other kind. It was a flame of a lamp, beyond all possibility of doubt, that was coming toward us." Electricity, invention of a phallic industrial society, has no place in this female zone. Rather a natural "flame" (not "fire," with its more destructive connotations) warms and protects. Louisette's mother, the bearer of the flame, is a striking figure with mythic proportions. Like Sido, Louisette's mother rises every morning before dawn, and her gaze "imperiously insisted on seeing everything." (Sido's eyes, too, are all-seeing, and her imperative "regarde!" leads Colette to imagine her in tune with all worldly and cosmic elements.) Louisette immediately screams for help: "Mamma!"[7] Louisette's flirtation with a man from outside the walls of her female domain is immediately forgotten, and she allies herself solidly with her mother, who berates and ridicules Albin. When Louisette offers to join her mother in chasing him out of the house, Albin suddenly flees: "Any set-to between men, even war, is less alarming to us men, less alarming to our nerves, than the fury of a woman." Reaching that "narrow path that skirted the outer wall," he forces himself to slow down until he reaches a breach in the wall. There he is suddenly inspired by belated rage "to assault the breach and the two hussies": "No doubt they too suddenly recovered their reason and remembered that they were females, and I was a male, for, after hesitating, they fled and disappeared into the neglected garden behind some pyramid fruit trees and a feathery clump of asparagus." Albin's posturings notwithstanding, his gesture of bravado has not sent them scurrying back to their cottage in fright. On the contrary, the women are returning to their own territory not out of fear, but from relief at again finding their space (the paradisaical garden) once more inviolate. Having gone beyond Demeter, Louisette's mother has actively prevented her daughter from being abducted by the male, and, indeed, has sent the male away forever (Albin admits to having lost his taste for young girls after that episode). It is interesting that "Green Sealing-wax," the story which follows "The Tender Shoot" in the collection,[8] begins with an account of Sido's journey to rescue the young Colette from a lecherous man who gazed at her "like the meditative Demon on the edge of Notre-Dame" as she played in a garden. Like Louisette's mother, Sido was successful in her mission.

The mission of these mothers is not the repressive condemnation of desire in young girls. Both mothers / mentors are intervening not to keep their daughters forever virgin, but to prevent them from becoming the victim in a sexual power relationship. Indeed, it can be argued that Louisette brought Albin into the house for the very purpose of being discovered by her mother. Louisette's motivation may have been subconscious, but she must have sensed the inherent inequality in the relationship. The "tender shoot" must be nurtured and cared for in the garden, an allegorical embodiment of female space in which diffused and abundant sexuality is a positive force. If Albin had been an appropriate (equal) partner for Louisette, the couple would have made love in the garden, in a natural setting (as do the young lovers in *The Ripening Seed*), with the mother's blessing—and with Colette's as well. But Albin is an aging roué without real love for Louisette, a patriarchal power figure who will do nothing but corrupt her native sensuality; this makes him a demon who must be exorcized.

By serving as the narrator, and a character as well in "The Tender Shoot," Colette has exercised dominion over the story much as Louisette's mother reigns over her female domain. Colette's environment is the page on which she writes, and in this story, as in many others, she has retained control of her own space. It is no accident that "Colette" appears as narrator and / or character in many of her works. In "The Tender Shoot," Albin's patriarchal assumptions do not go unchallenged, for Colette's understated yet constant presence does not really leave him the last word. The ending quotation marks are visible reminders that Albin is only a guest on the page, and that Colette herself, as mentor, has discovered her power to tap into ever-expanding, non-limiting space.

Notes

1. I am indebted to Mary Daly's discussion of patriarchal space. See Mary Daly, "Theology After the Demise of God the Father," *Women and Religion*, ed. J. Plaskow and J. Arnold (Missoula, Montana: Scholars Press, 1974), pp. 3–17.

2. In the Odyssey, Mentor was a friend of Telemachus. When the goddess Athena wished to protect Telemachus, she assumed the guise of his friend, mentor, and thus remained close to him throughout his travels. Fénélon's play *Télémaque* (1799) popularized the mentor character, and his name entered the language meaning friend, helpmate. But through Athena, its origin remains rooted in the tradition of *female* helpmates. See Edward Barthell, Jr., *Gods and Goddesses of Ancient Greece* (Coral Gables, Florida: University of Miami Press, 1971).

3. Colette, *Break of Day*, trans. Enid Mcleod (New York: Farrar, Straus, and Giroux, 1961), p. 6.

4. The need for dispassionate advice in behavior is satisfied in Colette by mirrors, whereas in Doris Lessing's *Children of Violence*, Martha Quest speaks of "this detached observer, felt perhaps as a clear-lit space situated just behind the forehead." See Lessing, *Martha Quest, Children of Violence* (New York: New American Library, 1970), p. 8.

5. Elsewhere I have tied mirrors to the conscious self-presentation of the stage. See Mari McCarty, "Colette: Theatrical Aspects of the Novel," Diss. University of Wisconsin-Madison, 1977, Chapter 5.

6. Colette, "The Tender Shoot," *The Tender Shoot*, trans. Antonia White (New York: Farrar, Straus, and Giroux, 1958).

7. This cry of "Mamma" also exorcizes the demons surrounding the boy in *L'enfant et les sortilèges*, Colette's opera libretto.

8. "Green Sealing-wax" also follows "The Tender Shoot" in the original French version, which includes both stories within the collection titled *Le Képi*.

Jacob Stockinger*

Popular revival and critical revisions have at last untamed Colette. Each new reading of her major works—*The Vagabond*, *Chéri* and *The Last of Chéri*, *Break of Day*, *The Pure and the Impure*—confirms her release from the old stereotypes of the woman writer as a socially safe observer of nature, domestic life, and love. Freed from the biases of her own time, Colette has survived to become a key commentator on the women's issues that confront us today.

The better part of Colette's literary reputation rests on her novels, where many of her most direct and even daring responses to feminist questions can be found. Yet as we have increasingly learned, the greatness of Colette can also be seen in her smaller works, and she must clearly rank among the master of the short story in this century. Her short fictions promise to be, in fact, one of the most fertile grounds of current research into Colette.

"The Patriarch," which appears in the collection *Bella Vista* (1937) is a case in point. That the story has so far escaped the attention of Colette's critics is unfortunate, for it provides in miniature a summary introduction to our new understanding of Colette. Moreover, the text may even supplement our insights into this pioneering writer by bringing to light the purpose behind Colette's taste for sexual scandal and transgression and by making manifest certain ideological implications of her work. On the surface the text bears all the hallmarks of Colette. It is not a short story in the strictest sense, and lacks the single focal point and narrative economy that make the stories in *The Hidden Woman* so exceptional.[1] Rather it is an associative narrative, similar to the information and episodic tales in *My Mother's House*, *Sido*, *My Apprenticeships*, and *The Blue Lantern*. The story also seems typical in its reliance on autobiographical material. Sido, Achille, the scenes of country life, the descriptions of flora and fauna, the narrative "I"—all are familiar to the reader of Colette. And although the terms themselves are never

Women's Studies 8 (1981):359–366. Copyright © Gordon Breach Science Publishers, Inc. Reproduced by permission of the publisher.

used, the tale turns on "purity" and "impurity," those imprecise concepts that provide a constant in Colette's ethical and esthetic visions from the early Claudine novels to the ambitious *The Pure and the Impure* where the ambiguities of such moralist terminology generate an entire system of narration, characters, events, and images.

As the narrative line of "The Patriarch" meanders, however, it reveals some quiet but disquieting surprises. It soon becomes evident that this is more than just another example of vintage Colette, that the story should compel our interest for special reasons.

The opening of the story, like so many of Colette's expositions, is a simple premise of recollection: "Between the ages of sixteen and twenty-five, Achille, my half-brother by blood—but wholly and entirely my brother by affection, choice and likeness—was extremely handsome. Little by little, he became less so as a result of leading the hard life of a country doctor in the old days; a life which lacked all comfort and repose."[2]

Since family affections and dramas so often form the core of Colette's writings, there appears to be nothing unexpected about the passage. It is, at least on first reading, simply an homage to Achille, a portrait of what seems an ideal sibling relationship. So strong is Colette's identification with her brother that she projects her feelings onto the natural world, describing the harmony that exists between him and his grey mare who accompanies him on his rounds, listening to his words during medical procedures, and recognizing the classical music he hums to himself.

Affinity between brother and sister runs deep because of their mutual attachment to nature and the person who sealed that bond: "Happily, his professional curiosity never left him. Neither did that other curiosity which both of us inherited from our mother." What makes Achille an influential role model, and also one of the most positive male figures in Colette, is his blending of strength and sensitivity to both the human and natural worlds. Not only does the young Colette energetically help him in his daily practice, she aspires to be like him: "I was fifteen or sixteen; the age of great devotions, of vocations. I wanted to become a woman doctor."

Of course Colette never did study medicine. But she did become a writer, and we might recall certain figures—Rabelais, Chekhov, Joyce, Céline, William Carlos Williams—who underscore the historical links between the two disciplines. A doctor's interest in diagnosis and pathology is comparable to a writer's attention to detail and denomination.

The observation is particularly pertinent to Colette, for although stereotypes of women writers credit them with an intuitive sense of natural detail, Colette goes beyond the stereotypes by bringing into texts such as this one the kind of technical competence and medical exactitude—split lips, deep cuts, sutures, amputations—that the social mythology holds squeamish women to find repulsive rather than engaging.

More than a record of Colette's adolescent aspirations, medicine turns out to be the transitional topic of the story. It provides Colette with a pretext for discussing what really interests her: a pathology of country life where rustic myths give way to hard rural realities. The young Achille, she notes, "was surprised when he first came up against the peaceful immorality of country life, of desire which is born and satisfied in the depths of the ripe grass or between the warm flanks of sleeping cattle. Paris and the Latin Quarter had not prepared him for so much amorous knowledge, secrecy and variety."

It is not just the correction of Achille's preconceptions about the country that Colette wants to record; she also wants to revise the misconceptions of readers in an urban age which naively entertains notions about the innocence of a country life it no longer knows firsthand. By destroying the equations of city = impurity and country = purity, Colette is undertaking a demystification of the provinces in the realist and naturalist traditions of Balzac, Flaubert, DeMaupassant, and Zola. She wants to violate taboos, to speak about such unspeakables as the accepted practice of rural abortion and "the women who knew about herbs."

She does this, moreover, through the main characters of the story. The next anecdote concerns a young woman, "the Hardon girl," who is a virgin but who claims to be pregnant and insists on a gynecological examination from Achille. Having planned her moves and made her advances, her seduction is successful. This farm maiden exhibits neither ignorance nor guilt, but, responsible for her own defloration, leaves Achilles's office "victorious, her head held high, her basket on one arm and her woolen shawl knotted once more over her breasts."

But the brother's participation is not just a surrender, for he continues to "consult" with her in the fields. "From these almost silent encounters, a very beautiful child was born. And I admit," adds Colette, "That I should be glad to see, even now, what his face is like." Once again, Colette faces with enthusiasm the kind of events that women, according to patriarchal values, should condemn. Typically she offers no reproaches, no accusations aimed at the unwed mother, the consenting brother, or the fatherless child. Instead she summons the image of Sido, always amorally curious, who confides to her daughter her approval of the beautiful and independent-minded mother and admits her almost irresistible desire to take the child, against the proud mother's wishes, into her own home.

Viewed from the perspective of doctor-patient relations, of peer models for young women, of male standards of parenting which stigmatize bastards, the incident should be scandalous. Not for Colette, however, who remarks: "However, everything in our neighborhood was not so simple as this warm idyll, cradled on its bed of pine-needles, and these silent lovers who took no notice of the autumn mists or a little rain, for the grey mare lent them her blanket." The incident between Achille and the Hardon girl proves them to be, at least to Colette's cool eyes and empathetic allegiances, at peace with themselves and nature. Wrongdoing lies with imposed mythologies and moralities, not with these country lovers.

But lest we think that Colette is ready to sanction all forms of sexual behavior as natural, she contrasts this comparatively "pure" incident, however impure our social code might call it, with one that is for her genuinely impure: "There is another episode of which I have a vivid and less touching memory. We used to refer to it as 'The Monsieur Binard story.' "

The anecdote concerns Achille who is summoned by Monsieur Binard to deliver his frail daughter of fourteen and a half of "a remarkably fine and well-made boy." Binard, the patriarch of the story's title, is a completely unsympathetic character. He is gruff with the doctor, indifferent to his daughter, and unadmiring of the child. When Achille suggests that the girl was lucky to have survived this delivery and asks if Binard knows the boy who impregnated her, it becomes obvious that Binard is the father of his daughter's son. And from his remarks, we glean that Binard, whose wife has died and who has no sons, has had incestuous relations with his three other daughters. His power and privilege as a patriarch are total.

Achille leaves the scene, where a certain normality is lent to this rural situation by the health of the in-bred baby and the celebration of the sisters, without comment. But as always, there is Sido as a reference point and observer: "Sido, my mother, did not like this story which she often turned over in her mind. Sometimes she spoke violently about Monsieur Binard, calling him bitterly 'the corrupt widower,' sometimes she let herself go off into commentaries for which afterwards she would blush.''

With that introduction, Colette gives us an example. Sido begins her remarks by expressing a certain admiration tinged with fondness: "Their house is very well kept. The child of the youngest one has eyelashes as long as *that*. I saw her the other day, she was suckling her baby on the doorstep, it was enchanting.''

For Sido and Colette alike, beauty is the primary appeal.

But Sido suddenly catches herself and checks her remarks: "Whatever am I saying? It was abominable, of course, when one knows the facts." Her first impulse is to accept things, and only then to judge them. Tolerance is a telling trait of this mother-daughter conversation in a tale about patriarchy. Offering a matriarchal lesson that her daughter learned well, Sido reduces condemnation to an afterthought which can only lead to silence: "She went off into a dream, impatiently untwisting the entangled steel chain and black cord from which hung her two pairs of spectacles.

After all, she began again, the ancient patriarchs . . .

But she suddenly became aware that I was only fifteen and a half and she went no further.''

It is, of course, an artificially unresolved ending. It is too late for silence to have meaning since Sido has already imparted to her daughter, who is a year older than the Binard girl, the pertinent facts and the correct priority of values.

For the reader, the ending is rich in suggestions for interpreting the story. With Sido's final and unfinished words, the inevitable question lingers: What about the modern patriarchs? And by way of answering that questions we can formulate some of the features which define purity and impurity for Colette and can make sense of the seemingly unrelated anecdotes in the story.

What clearly distinguishes two forms of illegitimacy from each other, the Achille-Hardon girl affair from the Binard incest, making the first one pure and the second impure, is the loss of female equality. What patriarchy, ancient or modern, takes away from women is the power to act, to initiate and to consent; what it imposes on them is domination and subjugation. Colette, like Sido, remains ideologically reluctant and will not belabor the point, let alone develop and articulate it polemically. Though unstated, her stand is not absent; it is communicated through the structure of the story, not the words of the narrator. Contrary to traditional critical notions, Colette was not wholly apolitical simply because she did not forcefully identify herself and her work with the women's movement of her time. As this story proves, she was aware of the women's condition and did protest its injustices—but in her own, largely literary way.

To arrive at sociopolitical conclusions, however implicit, through tales of illicit sex and incest seems a curiously irregular route. But if we return to the opening of the story, we see the care Colette takes to prepare her narrative progress. Her closeness to Achille announces the incest motif, and her fortuitous choice of words to describe her feelings for him—"affection, choice and likeness"—pinpoints the very qualities that redeem some forms of illegitimacy and condemn others. It also stresses the features that allow women in love, familial or romantic, to remain free.

Similarly, the mother-daughter coupling of Colette and Sido is not a gratuitous remembrance but sets off the father-daughter relationship of Binard's by contrasting matriarchal nurturing with patriarchal violence, sharing with exploitation. Colette's structuring of a text is digressive only in appearance. On closer and more suggestive readings, it is almost always found to be rigorous and creative, ordered and purposeful.

This short text is, then, typical of Colette in many ways. It reveals her preoccupation with a narrative vision that is, by prescriptive social standards, amoral in its stance toward humans, animals, and plants. It also illustrates Colette's interest in all forms of desire and the idiosyncratic values that allowed her to condemn the normal and normalize the aberrant. The story is a fine example of the conscientiousness with which, as we now recognize, Colette crafted her writings beyond the purely anecdotal or confessional methods her early critics imputed to her. In addition, it emphasizes the degree to which the mother-daughter relationship constitutes an axis of Colette's entire corpus. Finally, "The Patriarch" helps us to discern the social critic in Colette. Though hardly a militantly feminist statement about sexual politics, it nonetheless forces us to rethink and revise the mythologies, categorizations, and moral codes we bring to bear on human affairs. In style and substance, the story is a timely and undeservedly obscure reminder of why Colette is, perhaps more than ever, a contemporary.

Notes

1. Selections from *La Femme cachée* ("The Hidden Women") appear in Colette's *The Other Woman* New York: New American Library, 1975.

2. Colette, "The Patriarch," in the *The Rainy Moon and Other Stories*, translated by Antonia White (Penguin Books, 1975), pp. 126–132. All references to this work are to this edition. An American edition of the same work and same translation is published by Farrar, Straus & Giroux under the title *The Tender Shoot and Other Stories*. The French edition is called "Le Sieur Binard" and can be found in Volume XI of Colette's *Oeuvres complètes* (Paris: Flammarion, 1950).

Lynne Huffer*

The final chapters of *My Mother's House*, "The Sempstress" and "The Hollow Nut," reproduce the mother-daughter split that was mediated and reconciled in "The Abduction." The "I," having returned to her own mother through maternal abduction-seduction in "The Abduction," again confronts the conflict between separation and symbiosis as the mother of Bel-Gazou. Sido's fear of her daughter's abduction in "The Abduction" is paralleled by the daughter-turned-mother's fear of Bel-Gazou's sexual awakening in "The Sempstress." Significantly, the act of sewing foreshadows Bel-Gazou's sexual curiosity and inevitable abandonment of the maternal domain: Bel-Gazou's silence signifies a mental chasm that divides the mother from the daughter. The narrator confesses her maternal fear: "She [Bel-Gazou] is silent, she—why not write down the word that frightens me—she is thinking. . . . [S]he is thinking, as well I know. She thinks rapidly when she is listening, with a well-bred pretense of discretion, to remarks imprudently exchanged above her head. But it would seem that with this needle-play she has discovered the perfect means of descending, stitch by stitch, point by point, along a road of risks and temptations. Silence . . ."[1] The act of sewing represents the rite of passage through which Bel-Gazou will eventually, like the "I," leave her mother for male-oriented sexuality. At the same time, because sewing is also associated with the image of Sido in "The Little One," "The Sempstress" indirectly suggests a symbolic return to the mother. Through the temporal blurring produced by the narrative structure, the trope of female sewing signifies, simultaneously, connection (Sido) and separation (Bel-Gazou).

Similarly, the shift in narrative voice—the "I"-as-child is now "I"-as-mother—recalls the literary function of maternity: the inevitable return to the mother, a dissolution of identities, and the destabilizing displacement of the authority of speech. In these final chapters, the

*ANOTHER COLETTE: THE QUESTION OF GENDERED WRITING by Lynne Huffer, Copyright © 1992 by the University of Michigan, 26–29; 107–115. Reproduced by permission of the publisher.

158

structure of the book closes in upon itself, as the constellation of mother / Sido and daughter / "I" is transformed to include the dual role of the "I" as daughter and mother. If the sewing theme of "The Sempstress" recalls Sido within the circle of light in "The Little One," "The Hollow Nut" functions as a miniature counterpart to the "house" that forms the unifying element of the book. And just as Sido appears throughout *My Mother's House* as a figure of the infinite expansions of the creative self, so Bel-Gazou closes the book with the promise of further acts of artistic production.

Both Sido and Bel-Gazou ultimately serve to affirm the creativity of the "I"-as-writer, for it is only through them that she is able to speak as both mother and daughter. Although "The Sempstress" establishes the certainty of a mental, and eventual physical, separation between the mother and daughter, the prospect of this separation is attenuated by the retrospective knowledge that the process is cyclical, that leaving the mother will bring about an inevitable return to the maternal matrix. By representing three forms of maternity in the figures of Sido, the "I" and, in the future beyond the book, Bel-Gazou, the narrative becomes not the story of mothers as individuals, but rather of mother as a figure or paradigm that inscribes the relationship of writing daughter to a literary heritage. This literary relationship undeniably involves, like the sexual one, a movement toward men and masculinist institutions, but this movement toward the *hetero* is counteracted and corrected by maternal (en)gendering. Hence it is only maternally that the "I" is able to speak as text and, consequently, inscribe through writing the modalities of the artistic self.

This inscription of maternal creativity becomes explicit in the final lines of the book, where Bel-Gazou, holding a hollow nut to her ear, declares euphorically, "I can see it! I can see the song! It's as thin as a hair, as thin as a blade of grass!" (MH, 141). Here Bel-Gazou, as a product of maternal engendering, becomes a figure of the visionary artist who synesthetically possesses "the superiority of her sense that can taste a scent on her tongue, feel a color and see—'thin as a hair, thin as a blade of grass'—the line of an imaginary song . . ."[2] Just as the daughter in "The Little One" is able to envision never-ending circles of light radiating from Sido's bethimbled hand, so Bel-Gazou is able to "see" the song that radiates from the hollow but fecund space of an empty nut. Similarly, just as the "I" in "The Abduction" was able to expand her vision to a limitless present, so through Bel-Gazou the limits of past and future dissolve in the ellipses of an imaginary song. *Through* mother and daughter, *as* mother and daughter—in the textual space between Sido and Bel-Gazou—the "I" both speaks and is spoken.

Travels through a Tapestry: Writing Colette
Ariadne's Thread

Long before Colette adopts sewing as a metaphor for her own act of creative production, she introduces the image in connection with Sido and questions of gendered destinies. In a section of *My Mother's House* entitled "The Little One," sewing is framed precisely in relation to a favorite image of what little boys might want to become—a sailor. In a game of "Qu'est-ce qu'on sera" [What shall we be when we're grown up?], the Little One proclaims her own *misplaced* predilection for oceanic voyage as an image of her future aspirations: "I? Oh, I shall be a sailor!" (MH, 23). She aspires to this dream "because she sometimes dreamed of being a boy, and wearing trousers and a blue beret. The sea, of which Minet-Chéri knows nothing, the ship breasting a wave, the golden island and the gleaming fruit, all that only surged up much later, to serve as a background to the blue blouse and the cap with the pompom" (MH, 23–24).

Evoking the clichés of tourism—exotic islands, luminous fruits, the ship, and the open sea—the passage constructs a typical image of a boy's destiny by drawing on masculine mythology of oceanic adventure. However, the semes of exoticism, although potent, are not the motivating force behind the little girl's aspiration to become a sailor. For her, gender is a disguise, an external construct or dream of cross-dressing, where being a boy means wearing a "blue blouse" and a "cap with a pompom."

This dream of the conscious construction of a gendered destiny—a form of self-construction as future fiction—provides a context for the focus of the chapter, which is the figure of Sido sewing. Immediately following the Sido passage, the Little One questions her vision of masculinity and sailing: "Travel? Adventure? . . . Such words have neither force nor value. They evoke only the printed page, the coloured picture" (MH, 24). Because the Little One is "a child who twice a year, at the periods of the great spring and winter provisioning, leaves the confines of her district, and drives in a victoria to her county town"

(MH, 24), her previous ideas of Baudelarian escape seem flat, artificial, and, most important, incompatible with the limits imposed by the provincial setting that defines her culturally imposed destiny as a girl. Realizing that her notions are based only on banal images—"the printed page, the coloured picture"—the Little One decides that even a simple dream of "being a boy" is beyond her reach, and renounces sailing in favor of sewing. The narrative focus shifts from the garden where the Little One was playing to the interior of the house, where a red flame of light is momentarily eclipsed by a hand: "A hand has passed in front of the flame, a hand wearing a shining thimble" (MH, 24). This image of Sido's bethimbled hand marks a recognition of femininity and sewing as the vehicles for aesthetic transformation.

> At the mere sight of this hand, the Little One starts to her feet, pale, gentle now, trembling slightly as a child must who for the first time ceases to be the happy little vampire that unconsciously drains the maternal heart; trembling slightly at the conscious realization that this hand and this flame, and the bent, anxious head beside the lamp, are the centre and the secret birthplace whence radiate in ripples ever less perceptible, in circles ever more and more remote from the essential light and its vibrations, the warm sitting-room with its flora of cut branches and its fauna of peaceful creatures; the echoing house, dry, warm and crackling as a newly-baked loaf; the garden, the village. . . . beyond these all is danger, all is loneliness. (MH, 24–25)

The narrator here reveals sewing as model of transcendence by, paradoxically, narrowly focusing onto two objects, the hand and the lamp, that symbolize the maternal presence. Through a restriction of vision that encompasses a microcosmic view of the domestic circle, the narrative opens out onto greater and greater circles in a vision of outward projection that rivals the earlier masculine mythology of oceanic adventure. This expansion is explicitly gendered: it is the mother's sewing, within a narrowly circumscribed, domestic space, that allows the transformation to occur. Leaving the garden to return to the house, the little "sailor" once again asks herself: "Adventure? Travels?" (MH, 25). No, she is content, proud to be "a child of her village, hostile alike to colonist and barbarian, one of those whose universe is bounded by the limits of a field, by the entrance of a shop, by the circle of light spreading beneath a lamp and crossed at intervals by a well-loved hand drawing thread wearing a silver thimble" (MH, 25).

The scene of oceanic adventure is eclipsed in this evocation of an image of a maternally inscribed domestic space. That transformation pivots on shifting constructions of gender: the dream of cross-dressing becomes the dream of domestic bliss, "the sailor" becomes once again "a child" who leaves the unfamiliar space of home. Yet despite the evident celebration of female creativity and maternal love in this shift away from the dream of becoming a boy, the notions of limits, circumscription and domesticity pose the question of the implications of a gendered destiny defined by the borders that separate public and private. In her vision of Sido as a symbol of aesthetic transformation through a traditionally female and domestic art, has the Little One eradicated her public desire to be a boy? The juxtaposition of two stereotypical images of male and female destiny—sailing and sewing—suggests that the final focus on Sido as symbol should not obfuscate the cultural context within which it is placed. If Sido is Ariadne ("drawing a thread"), where is Theseus?[3] Does her thread bind or release her? Will she and her daughter remain safely and happily in the concentric labyrinth of domestic bliss, or will one (or both) of them desire an escape toward the outside, beyond a masturbatory, private space? Toward what gendered destiny does Sido's "well-loved" finger—figuratively—point?

Philomène / Philomela

If Sido's labyrinth, at least initially, provides her daughter with an image of a triumphant domestic art, that utopian maternal figure soon becomes a web that confines other daughters in decidedly dystopian traps. While "The Little One" ends with a celebration of sewing as a vehicle of aesthetic renewal and expansion, "The Sempstress" stages another mother-daughter encounter that is significantly less celebratory. In this chapter of *My Mother's House*, Colette, a responsible mother, reluctantly encourages her daughter to learn to sew. Bel-Gazou, like all dutiful daughters, willingly takes up needle and thread, but her submission to this traditional women's pastime provokes only maternal fear and discomfort: "I shall write the truth: I don't much like my daughter's sewing" (MH, 136, translation modified). Colette continues

> [T]he hand armed with the steel dart moves back and forth. . . .
> Nothing will stop the unchecked little explorer. At what moment

must I utter the "Halt!" that will brutally arrest her in full flight? Oh, for those young embroiderers of bygone days, sitting on a hard little stool in the shelter of their mother's ample skirts! Maternal authority kept them there for years and years, never rising except to change the skein of silk, or to elope with a stranger. . . . Philomène de Wateville and her canvas on which she embroidered the loss and the despair of Albert Savarus . . .

"What are you thinking about, Bel-Gazou?"

"Nothing, mother. I'm counting my stitches."

Silence. The needle pierces the material. A coarse trail of chain-stitch follows very unevenly in its wake. Silence. (MH, 137, translation modified)

In this exploration of another mother-daughter connection through sewing, the dangers of passivity, domesticity, and silence are exposed. Projected through the grid of a literary model, Balzac's *Albert Savarus* (1842), Bel-Gazou's silence marks the virile, even militaristic underside of an ostensibly private, feminine art ("the hand *armed* with the steel dart," "the little *explorer*"). In Balzac's tale, Philomène de Wateville plots the undoing of the man she desires while embroidering her father's slippers. The severity of this feminine plotting is signaled by a subtle but significant overstepping of the bounds of domestic propriety: "[Philomène], my little one, what then are you thinking about, you're overstepping the pattern, said the baroness to her daughter who was making tapestry slippers for the baron."[4] The danger of going beyond the limits—"overstepping the pattern"—is confirmed by the story's conclusion, where Philomène indirectly precipitates her father's death and causes the tragic rupture between Albert and his lover. Balzac's message seems to be that stifling, rigidly conforming education of girls can, because of the emptiness and the idleness of a life filled only with sewing, lead to tragic consequences. Rather than harnessing her ambition into productive activities, Philomène's frustrated desire is channeled into the paternal slippers, symbols of the restrictive domesticity in which women are imprisoned. Further, the umbilical connection between mother and daughter, within this context, reveals, not the bonding of Sido and the Little One, but rather the divisions that separate mother from daughter, and the extent to which women can be complicitous in women's oppression. Far from spinning a web of transformation, Philomène signs her *father's* name (the paternal slippers), acquiring from her mother the skills that will ensure their mutual entrapment.

As the story of a young bourgeoise in provincial France, Philomène's tale offers a vision of a girl's destiny that differs little from that of the Little One in the earlier evocation of maternal sewing. However, the Balzacian intertext in "The Sempstress," complicates the utopian view of the mother presented in "The Little One," revealing the dangers and traps of a return to sewing and the domestic sphere. In "The Sempstress" the opposition between sailing and sewing established in "The Little One" is skewed by the image of Bel-Gazou who becomes, through sewing, an "unchecked little explorer" (MH, 137), embarking on a voyage of her own that rejects the dangers of passivity and domesticity represented by "those embroiderers of bygone days" (MH, 137). Through the movements of sewing, Bel-Gazou descends "stitch by stitch, point by point, along a road of risks and temptations" (MH, 137), and reveals the hidden underside of domestic "bliss"; her "voyage in" risks the dangers of seduction and male sexuality.[5] Because daughters suffocate beneath maternal skirts while stitching together a system, however slippery, that upholds paternal authority, their only escape is to flee "with a stranger" (MH, 137). It is this need to escape the patriarchal construction of a restrictive, gender-specific domain that underlies the danger of femininity and sewing.

The two scenes that frame *My Mother's House* present two opposing views of femininity, exposing the particular tensions and contradictions that characterize women's roles in a late-nineteenth- and early-twentieth-century bourgeois society. As a figure of silence, sewing "speaks" the feminine textile form by recounting women's stories of both desire and oppression, and can be read as a metaphor for the woman writer's ambivalent relation to her own literary production. As a symbol of maternal transcendance in "The Little One," sewing becomes a celebration of the specificity of women's cultural work, an art form that reveals, albeit silently, a feminine aesthetic. On the other hand, "The Sempstress" discloses the dangers of a retrospective "flight" that accompanies sewing; further, by highlighting maternal complicity in paternal oppression, "The Sempstress" dramatizes the gulf that separates mother from daughter within the shared domestic space. When Colette echoes Balzac's baronness in her question to Bel-Gazou: "What are you thinking about, Bel-Gazou?," she is met only with an uncomfortable chasm of silence.

Whether celebratory of a specifically feminine production or the sign of the patriarchal oppression of women, the aesthetics of sewing is upheld by an aesthetics of silence. Like Philomène de Watteville's namesake, Philomela, the figure of Bel-Gazou frames an aesthetic form whose content is, paradoxically, an inability to speak. Her silence both marks the potential powerlessness resulting from sexual violation and, at the same time, speaks her creativity, just as Philomela, who is raped and then silenced by Tereus, weaves a tapestry to narrate the crime that rendered her speechless. In that sense, Philomela's literal silence becomes the means of her access to metaphorical speech. The connection between Bel-Gazou and Philomela is fortuitous but not arbitrary, for the Ovidian myth provides a figure for the contradictions of female creativity already explored in *The Pure and the Impure* (1941), particularly as represented by Sarah Posonby, "who says nothing, and embroiders."[6] Having woven her tapestry, Philomela returns to society to join her sister, Tereus' wife; together they avenge the crime, and both are later transformed into birds. In some versions of the story, Philomela becomes a nightingale, known for the beauty of her song; the myth thus completes the metamorphosis through which violence is confronted and transfigured to produce speech in another form.

Philomela haunts Colette's narrative through her onomastic connection to Philomène de Watteville. In her violation and revenge, as well as in her final triumph as a nightingale, Philomela discloses the necessity of disguise—of speaking otherwise—that marks women's efforts at creativity.[7] Although Philomela does function as a symbol of liberation in her final metamorphosis, she also serves as a reminder that women *only* speak "without a tongue" of their own, as it were, through mimicry or discursive cross-dressing. Female discursive agency remains caught, then, between the powerlessness of an aesthetics of silence and the inauthenticity of an aesthetics of disguise.

The two models of sewing explored here touch only indirectly upon Colette herself, for the figure of sewing is displaced onto the maternal and filial models. This displacement away from the self of a metaphor for a specifically feminine art may mark Colette's particular attempt to avoid being implicated in that general tradition. Although as past and future facets of the present writing self, Sido and Bel-Gazou represent two possible models (archetype and copy) of gendered literary production—a utopian *écriture féminine* that speaks the specificity of women's subjectivity, or a contradictory and dangerous writing as violation and silence—Colette herself does not sew. In fact, during these middle years of her creative output—the 1920s and 1930s—Colette is much more likely to adopt the masculine topos of sailing as a metaphor for the construction of the self in writing.

Notes

1. *Colette, My Mother's House and Sido*, trans. U. V. Troubridge and E. McLeod (New York: Farrar, Straus, and Giroux, 1953), 136–37. Translation modified. Hereafter cited as MH.

2. Colette, *La Maison de Claudine* in *Oeuvres complètes* 6 (Paris: Flammarion, 1973): 150. Translation mine. Hereafter cited as MC.

3. Ariadne, having fallen in love with the adventurer Theseus, helped him to escape the Labyrinth after killing the Minotaur by giving him a thread to follow out of the maze. After taking Ariadne with him to the island of Naxos, Theseus abandoned Ariadne for Phaedra, her sister.

4. Balzac, Honoré de, *La Comédie humaine* I (Paris: Gallimard, 1977): 983. Translation mine.

5. I borrow the term "voyage in" from Elizabeth Abel, Marianne Hirsch, and Elizabeth Langland, eds., *The Voyage In: Fictions of Female Development* (Hanover, N.H.: University Press of New England, 1983).

6. Colette, *The Pure and the Impure*, trans. Herma Briffault (New York: Farrar, Straus, and Giroux, 1966), 126.

7. The nightingale is an important image in Colette's oeuvre, especially in *The Tendrils of the Vine* (1908) and *The Pure and the Impure*. The myth of Philomela is, perhaps, an important intertext of these works as well.

Chronology

1873   Sidonie-Gabrielle Colette born in Saint-Sauveur-en-Pui-
saye, Burgundy, on 28 January. Daughter of Jules-Joseph
Colette and Adèle-Eugénie-Sidonie Landoy ("Sido").
She has a half brother, Achille (born 1863), a half sister,
Juliette (born 1860), and an older brother, Léopold (born
1868).

1890   Family moves to Châtillon-Coligny, the home of Achille,
following the sale of her birthplace at public auction.

1893   Marries Henry Gauthier-Villars ("Willy") on 15 May.
Moves to the rue Jacob, in Paris. During this year, is
introduced into Parisian literary and musical salons, where
she meets many well-known writers and artists of the
Belle Epoque.

1894   Following a long illness suffered the year before, travels
with Willy to Saint-Sauveur. Begins writing her first book,
Claudine at School.

1900–1903   Publication of the four Claudine novels: *Claudine at School*
(1900), *Claudine In Paris* (1901), *Claudine Married* (1902),
and *Claudine and Annie* (1903), all signed by Willy.

1904   *Minne*, signed by Willy. *Dialogues de bêtes* (*Creature Conversations*), signed by Colette Willy, a signature she retains
until 1923.

1905   Death of father on 17 September. Begins studying mime
with Georges Wague. Legal separation from Willy filed.

1906   Begins to tour as a mime performer, which she continues to do until 1913. Death by suicide of her half sister,
Juliette. Initiates liaison with the ex-Marquise de Belbeuf
("Missy"), which she maintains over a period of about
five years.

1907   *Retreat from Love.*

1908   *Les Vrilles de la vigne.*

1909   Willy sells the rights to the Claudine novels.

1910   Final divorce from Willy granted on 21 June. Begins publishing articles and stories in *Le Matin* and meets Henry de Jouvenel, editor-in-chief.

1912   Death of Sido on 25 September. Marries Jouvenel on 19 December.

1913   *Music-Hall Sidelights.* Birth of daughter, Colette de Jouvenel ("Bel Gazou") on 3 July. Death of her half brother, Achille on 31 December.

1916   *La Paix chez les bêtes* (*Creature Comfort*), first work published under her name alone.

1919   Appointed literary editor of *Le Matin.*

1920   *Chéri.* Named chevalier of the Légion d'Honneur.

1922   *My Mother's House.*

1923   *The Ripening Seed.* Première of stage version of *The Vagabond.* Separates from Jouvenel in December.

1924   *The Other Woman.* Divorce from Jouvenel.

1925   Meets Maurice Goudeket in April.

1926   Purchase of summer home in Provence, La Treille Muscate.

1927   Moves to 9, rue de Beaujolais in Paris, where she lives until 1930.

1928   *Break of Day.*

1929   *Sido.*

1932   *Paradis terrestres. Prisons et paradis. Ces plaisirs,* reedited in 1941 as *The Pure and the Impure.*

1935   Elected to the Académie royale de langue et de littérature françaises de Belgique. Marries Maurice Goudeket on 3 April. In June, sails with Goudeket to New York on the maiden voyage of the *Normandie.*

1936   *My Apprenticeships.* Acceptance speech at the Académie royale de Belgique. Becomes commander of the Légion d'honneur.

1937   *Bella-Vista.*

1938   Moves to second floor at 9, rue de Beaujolais (overlooking the gardens of the Palais royale) where she remains until her death. Visit to Fez, Morocco, for *Paris-Soir* to cover a murder trial.

1940   *Chance Acquaintances*. Death of her brother, Léopold, on 7 March. Leaves Paris during the Occupation to stay with her daughter in the Corrèze district on 12 June. Returns to Paris on 11 September.

1941   *Looking Backwards*. Goudeket arrested by the Germans on 12 December.

1942   Goudeket released on 6 February.

1943   *The Képi. Flore et Pomone*. Begins to suffer greatly from arthritis of the hip.

1944   *Gigi et autres nouvelles*.

1945   *Belles saisons*. Elected to the Académie Goncourt.

1946   *The Evening Star*. Travels to Geneva for treatment of arthritis, where she returns in 1947.

1951   Première on Broadway of *Gigi*, starring Audrey Hepburn.

1953   Named grand officier of the Légion d'Honneur.

1954   On 3 August, dies at her apartment. Following a secular funeral, she is buried in Père Lachaise cemetery on 7 August.

Bibliography

Primary Works

Short Fiction

Bella-Vista. Paris: Ferenczi et fils, 1937. ("Bella-Vista," "Gribiche," "The Rendezvous," "The Patriarch" included *The Tender Shoot and Other Stories.* Translated by Antonia White. New York: Farrar, Straus, and Giroux, 1958.)

Chambre d'hôtel. Paris: A. Fayard, 1940. ("Chance Acquaintances" included in *Julie de Carneilhan and Chance Acquaintances.* Translated by Patrick Leigh Fermor. London: Secker and Warburg, 1952. "The Rainy Moon" included in *The Tender Shoot and Other Stories.*)

L'envers du music-hall. Paris: Flammarion, 1913. ("The Halt," "Arrival and Rehearsal," "A Bad Morning," "The Circus Horse," "The Workroom," "Matinée," "The Starveling," "Love," "The Hard Worker," "After Midnight," " 'Lola,' " "Moments of Stress," "Journey's End," " 'The Strike, Oh Lord, the Strike!,' " "Bastienne's Child," "The Accompanist," "The Cashier," "Nostalgia," "Clever Dogs," "The Child Prodigy," "The Misfit," " 'La Fenice,' " " 'Gitanette' " included in *Music-Hall Sidelights.* Translated by Anne-Marie Callimachi. In *Mitsou and Music-Hall Sidelights.* New York: Farrar, Straus, and Giroux, 1957.)

La Femme cachée. Paris: Flammarion, 1924. ("The Hidden Woman," "The Dawn," "One Evening," "The Hand," "A Dead End," "The Fox," "The Judge," "The Omelette," "The Other Wife," "Monsieur Maurice," "The Burglar," "The Advice," "The Murderer," "The Portrait," "The Landscape," "The Half-Crazy," "Secrets," " 'Châ,' " "The Bracelet," "The Find," "Mirror Games," "Habit," "The Victim" included in *The Collected Stories of Colette.* Edited by Robert Phelps. New York: Farrar, Straus, and Giroux, 1983.)

La fleur de l'âge. Paris: Editions Le Fleuron, 1949. ("Florie," "In the Flower of Age," "The Rivals," "The Respite," "April" included in *The Collected Stories of Colette.*)

Gigi et autres nouvelles. Lausanne, La Guilde du Livre, 1944. Includes "Flore et Pomone" ("Flora and Pomona"). ("The Sick Child" and "The Photographer's Missus" included in *The Tender Shoot and Other Stories.*)

Le Képi. Paris: A. Fayard, 1943. (*The Tender Shoot and Other Stories.* Includes

170

"The Kepi," "Armande," "Green Sealing Wax," "The Tender Shoot.")

La Maison de Claudine. Paris: J. Ferenczi et fils, 1922. ("Where are the Children?," "The Savage," "Jealousy," "The Little One," "The Abduction," "The Priest on the Wall," "My Mother and the Books," "Propaganda," "Father and Madame Bruneau," "My Mother and the Animals" "Epitaphs," " 'My Father's Daughter,' " "The Wedding," "My Sister and the Long Hair," "Maternity," " 'The Rage of Paris,' " "The Little Bouilloux Girl," "Toutouque," "The Spahi's Cloak," "The Friend," "The Friend," "Ybanez Is Dead," "My Mother and the Curé," "My Mother and Morals," "Laughter," "My Mother and Illness," "My Mother and the Forbidden Fruit," "Bygone Spring," "The Sempstress," "The Hollow Nut" included in *My Mother's House*. Translated by Uno Vicenzo Troubridge and Enid McLeod. In *"My Mother's House" and "Sido."* London: Penguin Edition, 1966.)

Paysages et portraits. Paris: Flammarion, 1958. ("A Letter," "The Sémiramis Bar," "If I Had a Daughter . . . ," "Rites," "Newly Shorn," "Grape Harvest," "In the Boudoir," "Alix's Refusal" included in *The Collected Stories of Colette*.)

Les Vrilles de la vigne. Paris: Editions de la vie parisienne, 1908. ("Morning Glories," "What Must We Look Like," "The Cure," "Sleepless Nights," "Gray Days," "The Last Fire," "The Tendrils of the Vine" included in *The Collected Stories of Colette*.)

Unless otherwise specified, English translations are cited from *The Collected Stories of Colette*. Edited by Robert Phelps. New York: Farrar, Straus, and Giroux, 1983.

Works by Colette

The definitive edition of Colette's complete works is currently in progress. The first three volumes, covering works published through 1939, have already been published as *Oeuvres*. Edited by Claude Pichois. vols. I, II, III. Paris: Editions de la Pléiade, 1984–1991.

Au concert. Edited by Alain Galliari. Paris: Le Castor Astral, 1992.

Aventures quotidiennes. Paris: Flammarion, 1924. (In *Journal for Myself: Selfish Memories*. Translated David Le Vay. New York: Bobbs-Merrill, 1972.)

Belles saisons. Paris: Editions de la Galerie Charpentier, 1945.

Le Blé en herbe. Paris: Flammarion, 1923. (*The Ripening Seed*. Translated by Roger Senhouse and Herma Briffault. New York: Farrar, Straus and Giroux, 1978.)

Broderie ancienne. Monaco: Editions du Rocer, 1944.

Cahiers de Colette. Paris: Les Amis de Colette, 1935–36.

Ces Plaisirs. Paris: J. Ferenczi et fils, 1932. Retitled in 1941 as *Le Pur et l'impur*.

Bibliography

(*The Pure and the Impure*. Translated by Herma Briffault. New York: Farrar, Straus and Giroux, 1979.)

La Chambre éclairée. Paris: Edouard Joseph, 1920.

Chats. Paris: Jacques Nam, 1936.

Chats de Colette. Paris: Albin Michel, 1949.

La Chatte. Paris: Grasset, 1933. (*The Cat*. Translated by Antonia White. In *Seven by Colette*. New York: Farrar, Straus and Cudahy, 1955.)

Chéri. Paris: A. Fayard, 1920. (*Chéri* in *Chéri and The Last of Chéri*. Translated by Roger Senhouse. Baltimore: Penguin, 1974.)

Chéri, comédie en quatre actes, par Colette et Léopold Marchand. Paris: Librairie Théâtrale, 1922.

Claudine à l'école. Paris: Ollendorff, 1900. (*Claudine at School*. In *The Complete Claudine*. Translated by Antonia White. New York: Farrar, Straus and Giroux, 1976.)

Claudine à Paris: Ollendorff, 1901. (*Claudine in Paris*. In *The Complete Claudine*.)

Claudine en ménage. Paris: Mercure de France, 1902. (*Claudine Married*. In *The Complete Claudine*.)

Claudine s'en va. Paris: Ollendorff, 1903. (*Claudine and Annie*. In *The Complete Claudine*.)

Claudine et les contes de fées. Paris: Pour les amis du docteur Lucien Graux, 1937.

Contes des mille et un matins. Paris: Flammarion, 1970. (*The Thousand and One Mornings*. Translated by Margaret Crosland and David Le Vay. New York: Bobbs-Merrill, 1973.)

Dans la foule. Paris: Georges Crès et Cie., 1918.

De la patte à l'aile. Paris: Editions Corrêa, 1943.

De ma fenêtre. Paris: Aux Armes de France, 1942. (In *Looking Backwards*. Translated by David Le Vay. Bloomington: Indiana University Press, 1975.)

Dialogues de bêtes. Paris: Mercure de France, 1904. (*Creature Conversatons*. In *Creatures Great and Small*. Translated by Enid McLeod. New York: Farrar, Straus and Giroux, 1978.)

Douze dialogues de bêtes. Paris: Mercure de France, 1930. (*Creature Conversatons*. In *Creatures Great and Small*.)

Duo. Paris: J. Ferenczi et fils, 1934. (*Duo*. In *Duo and Le Toutounier*. Translated by Margaret Crosland. New York: Dell, 1974.)

Les Egarements de Minne. Paris: Ollendorff, 1905.

Les Enfants dans les ruines. Paris: Editions de la Maison du Livre, 1917.

L'Enfant et les sortilèges. Paris: Durand et Cie., 1925. (*The Boy and the Magic*. Translated by Christopher Fry. New York: Putnam, 1965.)

En Pays connu. Paris: Manuel Bruker, 1949. (Selections in *Places*. Translated by David Le Vay and Margaret Crosland. New York: Bobbs-Merrill, 1971.)

L'Entrave. Paris: Librairie des Lettres, 1913. (*The Shackle*. Translated by Antonia White. New York: Farrar, Straus and Giroux, 1978.)

L'Etoile Vesper. Geneva: Editions du Milieu du Monde, 1946. (*The Evening Star.* Translated by David Le Vay. London: Peter Owen, 1973.)

Le Fanal bleu. Paris: J. Ferenczi et fils, 1949. (*The Blue Lantern.* Translated by Roger Senhouse. New York: Farrar, Straus and Giroux, 1963.)

La Fin de Chéri. Paris: Flammarion, 1926. (*The Last of Chéri.* In *Chéri* and *The Last of Chéri.* Translated by Roger Senhouse. Baltimore: Penguin, 1974.)

Gigi. Adaptation pour la scène par Colette et Anita Loos. Paris: France Illustration, 1954.

Les Heures longues. Paris: A. Fayard, 1917.

Histoires pour Bel-Gazou. Paris: Stock, 1930.

L'Ingénue libertine. Paris: Ollendorff, 1909. (*The Innocent Libertine.* Translated by Antonia White. New York: Farrar, Straus and Giroux, 1978.)

Journal à rebours. Paris: A. Fayard, 1941. (*Looking Backwards.* Translated by David Le Vay. Bloomington: Indiana University Press, 1975.)

Journal intermittent. Paris: Le Fleuron, 1949. (Selections in *Places.*)

Julie de Carneilhan. Paris: A. Fayard, 1941. (*Julie de Carneilhan.* In *Julie de Carneilhan* and *Chance Acquaintances.* Translated by Patrick Leigh Fermor. London: Secker and Warburg, 1952.)

La Jumelle noire. Paris: J. Ferenczi et fils, 1934–38.

Mes Apprentissages. Paris: Ferenczi et fils, 1936. (*My Apprenticeships.* Translated by Helen Beauclerk. New York: Farrar, Straus and Giroux, 1978.)

Minne. Paris: Ollendorff, 1904.

Mitsou ou comment l'esprit vient aux filles. Paris: A. Fayard, 1919. (*Mitsou.* Translated by Raymond Postgate. In *"Mitsou" and "Music Hall Sidelights."* New York: Farrar, Straus and Giroux, 1957.)

La Naissance du jour. Paris: Flammarion, 1928. (*Break of Day.* Translated by Enid McLeod. New York: Farrar, Straus, and Giroux, 1979.)

Nudité. Paris: Editions de la Mappemonde, 1943.

La Paix chez les bêtes. Paris: Georges Crès et Cie., 1916. (*Creature Comfort.* In *Creatures Great and Small.*)

Paradis terrestres. Lausanne: Gonin et Cie., 1932.

Pour un herbier. Lausanne: Mermod, 1948.

Prisons et paradis. Paris: J. Ferenczi et fils, 1932. (Selections in *Places.*)

Quatre saisons. Paris: Philippe Ortiz, 1925. (In *Journey for Myself: Selfish Memories.* Translated by David Le Vay. New York: Bobbs-Merrill, 1972.)

Renée Vivien. Abbeville: Imprimerie F. Paillart, 1928.

La Retraite sentimentale. Paris: Mercure de France, 1907. (*The Retreat from Love.* Translated by Margaret Crosland. New York: Harcourt, Brace, Jovanovich, 1980.)

Rêverie de nouvel an. Paris: Stock, 1923.

La Seconde. Paris: J. Ferenczi et fils, 1929. (*The Other One.* Translated by Elizabeth Tait and Roger Senhouse. New York: Farrar, Straus and Giroux, 1960.)

Bibliography

Sept dialogues de bêtes. Paris: Mercure de France, 1905. (*Creature Conversations.* In *Creatures Great and Small.*)
Splendeurs des papillons. Paris: Plon, 1937.
Le Toutounier. Paris: J. Ferenczi et fils, 1939. (*Le Toutounier.* In *"Duo" and "Le Toutounier."*)
La Treille muscate. Paris: Aimé Jourde, 1932.
Trois . . . six . . . neuf. Paris: Editions Corrêa, 1944. (Selections in *Places.*)
La Vagabonde. Paris: Ollendorff, 1911. (*The Vagabond.* Translated by Enid McLeod. New York: Farrar, Straus and Giroux, 1955.)
La Vagabonde, comédie en quatre actes, par Colette et Léopold Marchand. Paris: Imprimerie de L'Illustration A. Chatenet, 1923.
Le Voyage égoïste. Paris: Editions d'Art Edouard Pelletan, 1922. (Selections in *Journey for Myself: Selfish Memories.*)

Secondary Works

Biographies

Beaumont, Germaine and Parinaud, André. *Colette.* Les ecrivains de Toujours, Paris: Seuil, 1951.
Belles Saisons: A Colette Scrapbook. Edited by Robert Phelps. New York: Farrar, Straus and Giroux, 1978.
Colette. *Earthly Paradise: An Autobiography.* Edited by Robert Phelps. Translated by Herma Briffault, Derek Coltman and others. New York: Farrar, Straus, and Giroux, 1966.
Crosland, Margaret. *Colette: The Difficulty of Loving.* New York: Dell, 1973.
Goudeket, Maurice. *Près de Colette.* Paris: Flammarion, 1956. Translated as *Close to Colette.* New York: Farrar, Straus, and Cudahy, 1957.
Lottman, Herbert. *Colette: A Life.* Boston: Little, Brown and Co., 1991.
Richardson, Joanna. *Colette.* New York: Franklin Watts, 1984.
Sarde, Michèle. *Colette, Free and Fettered.* Translated by Richard Miller. New York: William Morrow and Co., 1962.

Correspondence

Lettres à Hélène Picard. Paris: Flammarion, 1958.
Lettres à Marguerite Moreno. Paris: Flammarion, 1959.
Lettres de la vagabonde. Paris: Flammarion, 1961.
Lettres au petit corsaire. Paris: Flammarion, 1963.
Lettres à ses pairs. Paris: Flammarion, 1973.
Letters from Colette. Translated by Robert Phelps. New York: Farrar, Straus and

Giroux, 1980. Excerpts from the preceding collections are to be found in this translation.

Criticism: Books

Abel, Elizabeth, Mariane Hirsch and Elizabeth Langland, eds. *The Voyage In: Fictions of Female Development.* Hanover, N.H.: University Press of New England, 1983.

Aycock, Wendell M., ed. *The Teller and the Tale: Aspects of the Short Story.* Lubbock, Texas: Texas Tech Press, 1982.

Bal, Mieke. *Complexité d'un roman populaire.* Paris: La Pensée universelle, 1981.

Beauvoir, Simone de. *Le Deuxième sexe.* 2 vols. Paris: Gallimard, 1949.

Benstock, Shari. *Feminist Issues in Literary Scholarship.* Bloomington: Indiana University Press, 1987.

Biolley-Godino, Marcelle. *L'Homme-objet chez Colette.* Paris: Klincksieck, 1972.

Butler, Judith. *Gender Trouble: Feminism and the Subversion of Identity.* New York: Routledge, 1990.

Catalogue of the Colette Exhibition, Bibliothèque Nationale, 1973.

Chambers, Ross. *Story and Situation.* Minneapolis: University of Minnesota Press, 1984.

Courtivron, Isabelle de and Elaine Marks, eds. *New French Feminisms.* New York: Schocken, 1981.

Davidson, Cathy N. and E. M. Broner. *The Lost Tradition: Mothers and Daughters in Literature.* New York: Ungar, 1980.

Dubrow, Heather. *Genre.* London and New York: Methuen, 1982.

Eisinger, Erica and Mari McCarty, eds. "Charting Colette." Special issue of *Women's Studies* 8, no. 3 (1981).

———. *Colette: The Woman, The Writer.* University Park and London: Pennsylvania State University Press, 1981.

Evans, Martha Noel. *Masks of Tradition: Women and the Politics of Writing in Twentieth Century France.* Ithaca and London: Cornell University Press, 1987.

Flieger, Jerry Aline. *Colette and the Fantom Subject of Autobiography.* Ithaca: Cornell University Press, 1992.

Freud, Sigmund. *The Complete Psychological Works of Sigmund Freud.* Edited by James Strachey. London: The Hogarth Press, 1955.

Gilbert, Sandra and Susan Gubar. *The Madwoman in the Attic: The Woman Writer and the Nineteenth Century Imagination.* New Haven: Yale University Press, 1979.

Giry, Jacqueline. *Colette et l'art du discours intérieur.* La Pensée universelle, 1980.

Harris, Elaine. *L'Approfondissement de la sensualité dans l'oeuvre de Colette.* Paris: Nizet, 1976.

Holmes, Diana. *Colette.* New York: Saint Martin's Press, 1991.
Huffer, Lynne. *Another Colette.* Ann Arbor: The University of Michigan Press, 1992.
Jouve, Nicole Ward. *Colette.* Bloomington: Indiana University Press, 1987.
Kofman, Sarah. *L'énigme de la femme: la femme dans les textes de Freud.* Paris: Galilée, 1980.
Lanning, Gerald. *The Short Story Today: A Kenyon Review Symposium.* Kent, Ohio, 1970.
Leitch, Thomas M. *What Stories Are: Narrative Theory and Interpretation.* University Park and London: Pennsylvania State University Press, 1986.
Lohafer, Susan and Jo Ellyn Clarey. *Short Story Theory at a Crossroads.* Baton Rouge and London: Louisiana State University Press, 1989.
Marks, Elaine. *Colette.* New Brunswick: Rutgers University Press, 1960.
McClave, Heather, ed. *Women Writers of the Short Story.* Englewood, New Jersey: Prentice-Hall, Inc., 1980.
Miller, Nancy K. *Subject to Change: Reading Feminist Writing.* New York: Columbia University Press, 1988.
Moi, Toril. *Sexual/Textual Politics: Feminist Literary Theory.* London: Routledge, 1985.
O'Connor, Frank. *The Lonely Voice: A Study of the Short Story.* World Publishing Company, 1962.
Pratt, Mary Louise. *Toward a Speech Act Theory of Literary Discourse.* Bloomington and London: Indiana University Press, 1977.
Raaphorst-Rousseau, Madeleine. *Colette, sa vie, son art.* Paris: Nizet, 1964.
Reid, Ian. *The Short Story.* London and New York: Methuen, 1977.
Resch, Yannick. *Corps féminin, corps textuel.* Paris: Klincksieck, 1973.
Stanton, Domna and Jeanine Plottel, eds. *The Female Autograph.* New York: New York Literary Forum, 1984.
Shaw, Valerie. *The Short Story: A Critical Introduction.* New York: Longman, 1983.
Stewart, Joan Hinde. *Colette.* Boston: Twayne Publishers, 1983.

Criticism: Articles

Abel, Elizabeth. "(E)merging Identities: The Dynamic of Female Friendship in Contemporary Fiction by Women." *Signs* (Spring 1981): 413–35.
Berg, Elizabeth L. "The Third Woman." *Diacritics* 12 (Summer 1982): 11–20.
Burgess, Anthony. "Anthony Burgess on the Short Story." *Journal of the Short Story in English* 2 (1984):31–47.
Chonez, Claudine. "Hier, aujourd'hui, demain." *La Table ronde* 99 (March 1956): 60–64.
Courtivron, Isabelle de. "Weak Men and Fatal Women: The Sand Image." *Homosexualities and French Literature.* Ed. Elaine Marks and George Stambolian. Ithaca: Cornell University Press, 1979, 210–27.

Cortázar, Julio. "Some Aspects of the Short Story." *Review of Contemporary Fiction* 3 (Fall 1983): 24–33.

Dehon, Claire. "La dame du photographe: sa structure, son sens." *Revue du pacifique* 4 (Spring 1978): 59–67.

Deltel, Danielle. "Le scandale soufflé: le paradoxe dans l'écriture de Colette." In *Colette, nouvelles approches critiques*. Actes du colloque de Sarrebruck (June 22–23, 1984). Paris: Nizet, 1986, 151–65.

Feral, Josette. "Antigone or the Irony of the Tribe," *Diacritics* (September 1978): 2–14.

Gillespie, Gerald. "Novella, Nouvelle, Novelle, Short Novel?: A Review of Terms." *Neophilologus* 51 (July 1967): 225–30.

Gullason, Thomas H. "The Short Story: An Underrated Art." *Studies in Short Fiction* 2 (Fall 1964): 13–31.

Jay, Martin. "In the Empire of the Gaze: Foucault and the Denigration of Vision in Twentieth Century Thought." In *Foucault, A Critical Reader*. Ed. David Couzens Hoy. (New York: Basel Blackwell, 1986, 175–204.

Jones, Ann Rosalind. "Writing the Body, Towards an Understanding of 'L'écriture féminine.' " In *Feminist Criticism: Essays on Women, Literature, and Theory*, ed. Elaine Showalter, 361–77. New York: Pantheon, 1985.

Kahn, Coppélia. "The Hand that Rocks the Cradle: Recent Gender Theories and Their Implications." *The (M)other Tongue: Essays in Feminist Psychoanalytic Interpretations*. Ed. Shirley Nelson Garner, Claire Kahane, and Madelon Sprengnether. Ithaca: Cornell University Press, 1985, 72–88.

Keller, Evelyn Fox and Christine R. Grontkowski. "The Mind's Eye." In *Discovering Reality: Feminist Perspectives on Epistemology, Metaphysics, Methodology, and Philosophy of Science*. Ed. Sandra Harding and Merrill B. Hintikka. Dordrecht, Holland: D. Reidel, 1983, 207–24.

Miller, Nancy K. "Emphasis Added: Plots and Plausibilities in Women's Fiction." *PMLA* 96 (January 1981): 36–48.

Mitchell, Valory and Ravenna Helson. "Object Relations and Social Interaction in Short Stories." *Poetics* 17 (October 1988): 367–84.

Olson, Gary M., Robert L. Mack and Susan A. Duffy. "Cognitive Aspects of Genre." *Poetics* 10 (June 1981): 283–315.

Pratt, Mary Louise. "The Short Story: The Long and the Short of It." *Poetics* 10 (June 1981): 175–94.

"Questions à Julia Kristéva." *Revue des sciences humaines* 168 (1977): 495–507.

Resch, Yannick. "Colette ou le plaisir-texte." In *Colette: nouvelles approches critiques*. Actes du colloque de Sarrebruck (June 22–23, 1986). Paris: Nizet, 1986, 167–74.

Rivière, Joan. "Womanliness as Masquerade." In *Formations of Fantasy*. Ed. Victor Burgin, James Donald, and Cora Kaplan. London and New York: Methuen, 1986, 35–44.

Rohrberger, Mary and Dan E. Burns. "Short Fiction and the Numinous Realm:

Bibliography

Another Attempt at Definition." *Modern Fiction Studies* 28 (Spring 1982): 5–12.

Ryan, Marie-Laure. "On the Why, What and How of Generic Taxonomy." *Poetics* 10 (June 1981): 111–12.

Schor, Naomi. "Eugénie Grandet: Mirrors and Melancholia." In *The (M)other Tongue: Essays in Feminist Psychoanalytic Interpretations*. Ed. Shirley Nelson Garner, Claire Kahane, and Madelon Sprengnether. Ithaca and London: Cornell University Press, 1985, 217–37.

Showalter, Elaine. "Feminist Criticism in the Wilderness," *Critical Inquiry* (Winter 1981): 179–205.

Stewart, Joan Hinde. "Colette's Gynaceum: Regression and Renewal." *French Review* 53 (April 1980): 662–69.

Strand, Dana. "Colette's 'La Cire verte': Breaking the Law." *Modern Language Studies* 21 (Winter 1991): 37–44.

———. "The 'Third Woman' in Colette's 'Chance Acquaintances.' " *Studies in Short Fiction* 29 (Fall 1992): 499–508.

Index

179

Index

The Author

Dana Strand, who received an A.B. from Vassar College, holds a master's degree from Cornell University and both a master's and Ph.D. in French Literature and Language from Vanderbilt University. Currently an Associate Professor of Romance Languages at Carleton College, in Northfield, Minnesota, where she teaches courses in comparative literature, twentieth-century French literature, and French film, she has published a number of articles on modern French writers, including two on the short stories of Colette.

The Editor

General Editor Gordon Weaver earned his B.A. in English at the University of Wisconsin-Milwaukee in 1961; his M.A. in English at the University of Illinois, where he studied as a Woodrow Wilson Fellow, in 1962; and his Ph.D. in English and creative writing at the University of Denver in 1970. He is author of several novels, including *Count a Lonely Cadence, Give Him a Stone, Circling Byzantium*, and most recently *The Eight Corners of the World* (1988). Many of his numerous short stories are collected in *The Entombed Man of Thule, Such Waltzing Was Not Easy, Getting Serious, Morality Play, A World Quite Round*, and *Men Who Would Be Good* (1991). Recognition of his fiction includes the St. Lawrence Award for Fiction (1973), two National Endowment for the Arts Fellowships (1974, 1989), and the O. Henry First Prize (1979). He edited *The American Short Story, 1945–1980: A Critical History*, and is currently editor of *Cimarron Review*. He is professor of English at Oklahoma State University. Married, and the father of three daughters, he lives in Stillwater, Oklahoma.